PAGANISM SURVIVING IN CHRISTIANITY

BY

ABRAM HERBERT LEWIS, D.D.

AUTHOR OF "BIBLICAL TEACHINGS CONCERNING THE SABBATH AND THE SUNDAY,"
"A CRITICAL HISTORY OF THE SABBATH AND THE SUNDAY IN THE
CHRISTIAN CHURCH," "A CRITICAL HISTORY OF SUNDAY
LEGISLATION FROM 321 TO 1888, A.D.," ETC.

———

G. P. PUTNAM'S SONS

NEW YORK   LONDON
27 WEST TWENTY-THIRD STREET   24 BEDFORD STREET, STRAND

The Knickerbocker Press

1892

TO

GEORGE H. BABCOCK

CO-WORKER IN HISTORIC RESEARCH AND FRIEND
THROUGH MANY YEARS, THIS VOLUME
IS RESPECTFULLY DEDICATED

THE AUTHOR

PREFACE.

———

HE who judges the first century by the nineteenth will fall into countless errors. He who thinks that the Christianity of the fourth century was identical with that of the New-Testament period, will go widely astray. He who does not look carefully into the history of religions before the time of Christ, and into the pagan influences which surrounded infant Christianity, cannot understand its subsequent history. He who cannot rise above denominational limitations and credal restrictions cannot become a successful student of early Church history, nor of present tendencies, nor of future developments. History is a series of results, not a medley of happenings. It is the story of the struggle between right and wrong; the record of God's dealing with men. The " historic argument " is invaluable, because history preserves God's verdicts concerning human choices and actions. Events and epochs, transitions and culminations, are the organized causes and effects which create the never-ceasing movement, and the organic unity called history. Hence we learn that ideas and principles, like apples, have their time for development and ripening ; that the stains of sin, the weakness of error, and the influence of truth commingle and perdure through the centuries ; that good and evil, sin and righteousness, persist, or are eliminated, in proportion as men heed God's voice, and listen to His verdicts.

The scientific study of history reveals the norm by which ideas, creeds, movements, and methods are to be tested. Such a standard, when contrasted with the speculations of philosophy, is granite, compared with sand. God's universal law, enunciated by Christ, is : " By their fruits ye shall know them."

The efforts of partisans to manipulate early history in the interest of special views and narrow conceptions, have been a fruitful source of error. Equally dangerous has been the assumption that the Christianity of the third, fourth, and fifth centuries was identical with that of the New Testament, or was a fair representative of it. The constant development of new facts shows that at the point where the average student takes up the history of Western Christianity, it was already fundamentally corrupted by pagan theories and practices. Its unfolding, from that time to the present, must be studied in the light of this fact. The rise, development, present status, and future history of Roman Catholicism and Protestantism, cannot be justly considered, apart from this fact. The fundamental principles, and the underlying philosophy of these divisions of Christendom originated in the paganizing of early Christianity. This fact makes the re-study of the beginnings of Christianity of supreme importance. The pagan systems which ante-dated Christ, exercised a controlling influence on the development of the first five centuries of Western Christianity, and hence, of all subsequent times. This field has been too nearly " an unknown land," to the average student, and therefore correct answers have been wanting to many questions which arise, when we leave Semitic soil, and consider Christianity in its relation to Greek and Roman thought. " Early Christianity " cannot be understood except in the light of these powerful, pre-Christian currents of influence ; and present history cannot be separated from them.

This book presents a suggestive rather than an exhaustive treatment of these influences, and of their effect on historic Christianity. The author has aimed to make a volume which busy men may read, rather than one whose bulk would relegate it to the comparative silence of library shelves. The following pages treat four practical points in Christianity, without attempting to enter the field of speculative theology, leaving that to a future time, or to the pen of another—viz. : The influence of pagan thought upon the Bible, and its interpretation ; upon the organized Church, through the pagan water-worship cult ; upon the practices and spiritual life of the Church by substituting pagan holidayism for Christian Sabbathism, through the sun-worship cult ; and upon the spiritual life and subsequent character of the Church, by the union of Church and State, and the subjugation of Christianity to the civil power, according to the pagan model. Facts do not cease to be facts, though denied and ignored. They do not withdraw from the field of history, though men grow restive under their condemnation. I have dealt mainly with facts, giving but brief space to " conclusions." I have written for those who are thoughtful and earnest ; who are anxious to know what the past has been, that they may the better understand the duties of the present and the unfolding issues of the future. Such will not read the following pages with languid interest nor careless eyes.

The issues involved are larger than denominational lines, or the boundaries of creeds. They are of special interest to Protestants, since they involve not only the reasons for the revolt against Roman Catholicism, but the future relations of these divisions of Christendom, to each other, and to the Bible. The supreme source of authority in religion is directly at issue in the questions here treated. That is a definite and living question which cannot be waived aside. At this threshold, the author extends the welcome which each searcher after facts and fundamental truths gives to fellow investigators.

ABRAM HERBERT LEWIS.

Room 100, Bible House,
    New York City, May, 1892.

CONTENTS.

CHAPTER XII.

CHAPTER XIII.

CHAPTER XIV.

PAGANISM IN CHRISTIANITY.

CHAPTER I.

REMAINS OF PAGANISM IN CHRISTIANITY.

Preliminary Survey—An Imaginary Past—Issue between Protestantism and Romanism—General Testimony Relative to Pagan Elements in Christianity, from Dyer, Lord, Tiele, Baronius, Polydore Virgil, Fauchet, Mussard, De Choul, Wiseman, Middleton, Max Müller, Priestley, Thebaud, Hardwick, Maitland, Seymore, Renan, Killen, Farrar, Merivale, Westropp and Wake, and Lechler.

A PRELIMINARY survey is the more necessary lest the general reader fail to grant the facts of history a competent hearing and a just consideration. Unconsciously men think of the earliest Christianity as being like that which they profess. They measure the early centuries by their own. Their Church, its doctrines, forms, creeds and customs, stands as the representative of all Christianity. It seems like a "rude awakening" to ask men to believe that there is a "pagan residuum" in their faith, or in the customs of their fathers. The average Christian must pass through a broadening process, before he can justly consider such a question.   Unhappily, there are too many who are unwilling to undergo such an enlargement of their religious and historical horizon as will make them competent to consider those facts which every earnest student of history must face.   But the Christian who believes in the immortality of truth, and in the certainty of its triumph, will welcome all facts, even though they may modify the creed he has hitherto accepted.

A writer in the *Edinburgh Review and Critical Journal,* commenting on the revised volumes of Bishop Lightfoot on *Ignatius* and *Polycarp,* speaking of the tendency to judge the early centuries by our own, thus vitiating our conclusions, says :

"The danger of such inquiries lies in the difficulty of resisting the temptation to frame pictures of an imaginary past ; and the passion for transferring to the past the peculiarities of later times may be best corrected by keeping in view the total unlikeness of the first, second, or third centuries to anything which now exists in any part of the world."

Protestants in the United States are poorly prepared to consider so great a question as that which this book passes under review, because they have not carefully considered the facts touching their relations to Roman Catholicism.   The Anglo-Romish controversy, in England, in the earlier part of the present century made the question of paganism in Christianity prominent for a time.   But the discussion was so strongly partisan and contro-versial that it could not produce the best results. Truth was much obscured by the determined effort of Protestant writers to show that the pagan re-siduum was all in the Catholic Church ; whereas the facts show that there could have been no Roman Catholic Church had not paganism first prepared the way for its development by corrupting the earliest Christianity. The facts show, with equal vividness, that Protestantism has retained much of paganism, by inheritance. Protestantism, theo-retically, means the entire elimination of the pagan residuum ; practically, that work is but fairly begun. It must be pushed, or the inevitable backward drift, the historical "undertow" will re-Romanize the Protestant movement. The expectations and purposes of Roman Catholicism all point towards such a result.

This chapter will make a general survey of the field, as it is seen by men of different schools, that the reader may be the better prepared for a more specific treatment of the subject.

DYER says :

"The first Roman converts to Christianity appear to have had very inadequate ideas of the sublime purity of the gospel, and to have entertained a strange medley of pagan idolatry and Christian truth. The emperor Alexander Severus, who had imbibed from his mother,

Mammæa, a singular regard for the Christian religion, is said to have placed in his domestic chapel the images of Abraham, of Orpheus, of Apollonius, and of Christ, as the four chief sages who had instructed mankind in the methods of adoring the Supreme Deity. Constantine himself, the first Christian emperor, was deeply imbued with the superstitions of paganism; he had been Pontifex Maximus, and it was only a little while before his death that he was formally received by baptism into the Christian Church. He was particularly devoted to Apollo, and he attempted to conciliate his pagan and his Christian subjects by the respect which he appeared to entertain for both. An edict enjoining the solemn observance of Sunday was balanced in the same year [1] by another directing that when the palace or any other public building should be struck by lightning, the haruspices should be regularly consulted." [2]

In a similar strain Professor LORD speaks yet more strongly:

" But the church was not only impregnated with the errors of pagan philosophy, but it adopted many of the ceremonials of Oriental worship, which were both minute and magnificent. If anything marked the primitive church it was the simplicity of worship, and the absence of ceremonies and festivals and gorgeous rites. The churches became in the fourth century as imposing as the old temples of idolatry. The festivals became authoritative; at first they were few in number and voluntary. It was supposed that when Christianity super-

[1] It was the next day.
[2] *History of Rome*, by Thomas H. Dyer, LL.D., p. 295, New York and London, 1877.

seded Judaism, the obligation to observe the ceremonies of the Mosaic law was abrogated. Neither the apostles nor evangelists imposed the yoke of servitude, but left Easter and every other feast to be honored by the gratitude of the recipients of grace. The change in opinion, in the fourth century, called out the severe animadversion of the historian Socrates, but it was useless to stem the current of the age. Festivals became frequent and imposing. The people clung to them because they obtained a cessation from labor, and obtained excitement. The ancient rubrics mention only those of the Passion, of Easter, of Whitsuntide, Christmas, and the descent of the Holy Spirit. But there followed the celebration of the death of Stephen, the memorial of St. John, the commemoration of the slaughter of the Innocents, the feasts of Epiphany, the feast of Purification, and others, until the Catholic Church had some celebration for some saint and martyr for every day in the year. They contributed to create a craving for outward religion, which appealed to the sense and the sensibilities rather than the heart. They led to innumerable quarrels and controversies about unimportant points, especially in relation to the celebration of Easter. They produced a delusive persuasion respecting pilgrimages, the sign of the cross, and the sanctifying effects of the sacraments. Veneration for martyrs ripened into the introduction of images—a future source of popular idolatry. Christianity was emblazoned in pompous ceremonies. The veneration of saints approximated to their deification, and superstition exalted the mother of our Lord into an object of absolute worship. Communion tables became imposing altars typical of Jewish sacrifices, and the relics of martyrs were preserved as sacred amulets. . . .

" When Christianity itself was in such need of reform, when Christians could scarcely be distinguished from pagans in love of display, and in egotistical ends, how could it reform the world? When it was a pageant, a ritualism, an arm of the state, a vain philosophy, a superstition, a formula, how could it save if ever so dominant? The corruptions of the Church in the fourth century are as well authenticated as the purity and moral elevation of Christianity in the second century. Isaac Taylor has presented a most mournful view of the state of Christian society when the religion of the cross had become the religion of the state, and the corruptions kept pace with the outward triumph of the faith, especially when the pagans had yielded to the supremacy of the cross." [1]

Many of the corrupting elements which entered into early Christianity came from the Orient, by way of Greece and Rome. TIELE speaks of the influx of these in the following words:

" The Greek deities were followed by the Asiatic, such as the Great Mother of the gods, whose image, consisting of an unhewn stone, was brought at the expense of the state from Pessinus to Rome. On the whole, it was not the best and loftiest features of the foreign religions that were adopted, but rather their low and sensual elements, and these too in their most corrupt form. An accidental accusation brought to light in the year 186 B.C. a secret worship of Bacchus which was accompanied by

[1] *The Old Roman World*, by John Lord, LL.D., chap. xiii., p. 558 ff., New York, 1873.

all kinds of abominations, and had already made its way among thousands. . . .

"The eyes of the multitude were always turned toward the East, from which deliverance was expected to come forth, and secret rites brought from there to Rome were sure of a number of devotees. But they were only bastard children, or at any rate the late misshapen offspring of the lofty religions which once flourished in the East, an un-Persian Mithra worship, an un-Egyptian Serapis worship, an Isis worship which only flattered the senses and was eagerly pursued by the fine ladies, to say nothing of more loathsome practices. And yet even these aberrations were the expression of a real and deep-seated need of the human mind, which could find no satisfaction in the state religion. Men longed for a God whom they could worship, heart and soul, and with this God they longed to be reconciled. Their own deities they had outgrown, and they listened eagerly therefore to the priests of Serapis and of Mithra, who each proclaimed their God as the sole-existing, the almighty, and the all-good, and they felt especially attracted by the earnestness and strictness of the latter *cultus*. And in order to be secure of the eradication of all guilt, men lay down in a pit where the blood of the sacrificial animal flowed all over them, in the conviction that they would then arise entirely new-born."[1]

Many Roman Catholic writers, with an honesty which all classes might well emulate, openly recog-

[1] *Outlines of the History of Religions,* by Prof. C. P. Tiele, translated from the Dutch by J. E. Carpenter, pp. 242, 244. London and Boston, 1877.

nize the paganizing of the Church, which took place before the organization of the papacy.

BARONIUS says:

" It was permitted the Church to transfer to pious uses those ceremonies which the pagans had wickedly applied in a superstitious worship, after having purified them by consecration; so that, to the greater contumely of the devil, all might honor Christ with those rites which he intended for his own worship. Thus the pagan festivals, laden with superstition, were changed into the praise-worthy festivals of the martyrs; and the idolatrous temples were changed to sacred churches, as Theodoret shows."[1]

POLYDORE VIRGIL says:

" The Church has borrowed many customs from the religion of the Romans and other pagans, but it has meliorated them and applied them to a better use."[2]

FAUCHET says:

" The bishops of this kingdom employ all means to gain men to Christ, converting to their use some pagan cere-monies, as well as they did the stones of their temples to the building of churches."[3]

PIERRE MUSSARD says:

[1] *Epitome Annalium Cardinalis Baronii, a Spondano.* In Dues Partes. P. 79, Lugduni, 1686.
[2] *De Inventore Rerum*, lib. v., cap. i., Venetus, 1490.
[3] *Antiquities of France*, lib. 2, cap. i.

" William de Choul,[1] counsellor to the king and bailiff of the mountains, composed, an age ago, a treatise of the religion of the ancient Romans, wherein he shows an entire conformity between old Rome and new. On the point of religion he closes with these words[2]: ' If we consider carefully,' says he, ' we shall see that many institutions in our religion have been borrowed and transferred from Egyptian and Pagan ceremonies, such as tunics and surplices, priestly ornaments for the head, bowing at the altar, the solemnity at mass, music in churches, prayers, supplications, processions, litanies, and many other things. These our priests make use of in our mysteries, and refer them to one only God, Jesus Christ, which the ignorance of the heathen, their false religion, and foolish presumption perverted to their false gods, and to dead men deified.' "[3]

During the Tractarian controversy in England, John Poynder wrote *Popery in Alliance with Heathenism*, to show that Roman Catholicism is essentially pagan. Cardinal Nicholas Wiseman, then a professor in the University at Rome, replied under the title: *Letters to John Poynder, Esq., upon his Work Entitled "Popery in Alliance with Heathenism,"* London, 1836.

In Letter Second, WISEMAN says :

---

[1] *Faux Visage de l'Antiquité.*

[2] Which are to be found in the edition printed with the king's privilege, at Lyons, by William Rouille, anno 1556.

[3] *Conformity between Ancient and Modern Ceremonies*, Leyden, 1677, pp. 4, 5.

For the original, see *Veterum Romanorum Religio*, Guilielmo du Choul, Amstelædami, 1685, p. 216.

" I will, for a moment, grant you the full extent of your assumptions and premises ; I will concede that all the facts you have brought forward are true, and all the parallels you have established between our rites and those of paganism, correct ; and I will join issue with you on your conclusions, trying them by clearly applicable tests. . . . The first person who argued as you have done was Julian the Apostate, who said that the Christians had borrowed their religion from the heathens. This proves at once that even then the resemblance existed, of which you complain as idolatrous.   So that it is not the offspring of modern corruption, but an inheritance of the ancient church.   It proves that the alliance between Christianity and heathenism existed three hundred years after Christ, and that consequently so far popery and ancient Christianity are identical.   The Manichees also are accused by St. Augustine, writing against Faustus, of having made the same charge."

As Paul said in 68AD "all those in Asia have turned away from me" — they would not have truth. (2 Tim 1:15)

Dr. Wiseman enumerates many items of resemblance which Poynder does not, and retorts by showing that the English Church yet retains the paganism which it inherited from papacy.   He emphasizes the pagan characteristics which appear in the building, adornment, and services of St. Paul's Cathedral, London, claiming that if a Roman pagan were to be resurrected and brought to St. Paul's he would recognize the likeness to his ancient faith on every hand.   Dr. Wiseman's testimony is of great value, since, as a defender of Romanism, he also defends the policy which corrupted early Christianity in the West, by conforming it to the popular paganism in order to secure a nominal conversion of the pagans.

CONYERS MIDDLETON, whose *Letter from Rome* forms one of the standard authorities concerning the paganism of the early Church, says :

"Aringhus, in his account of *Subterraneous Rome,* acknowledges this conformity between the pagan and popish rites, and defends the admission of the ceremonies of heathenism into the service of the Church, by the authority of their wisest popes and governors, who found it necessary, he says, in the conversion of the Gentiles, to dissemble and wink at many things, and yield to the times ; and not to use force against customs which the people were so obstinately fond of ; nor to think of extirpating at once everything that had the appearance of profane ; but to supersede in some measure the obligation of the sacred laws, till these converts, convinced by degrees, and informed of the whole truth by the suggestions of the Holy Spirit, should be content to submit in earnest to the yoke of Christ." [1]

Further important testimony is found in the following. Writing of the first three centuries after Christ, MAX MÜLLER says :

" That age was characterized far more than all before it, by a spirit of religious syncretism, an eager thirst for com-

[1] *Middleton's Works,* vol. iii., pp. 117, 118, London, 1752. See also Aringhus, *Rom. Subter.,* tom. 1, lib. i., c. 21.

promise. To mould together thoughts which differed fundamentally, to grasp, if possible, the common elements pervading all the multifarious religions of the world, was deemed the proper business of philosophy, both in the East and West. It was a period, one has lately said, of mystic incubation, when India and Egypt, Babylonia and Greece, were sitting together and gossiping like crazy old women, chattering with toothless gums and silly brains about the dreams and joys of their youth, yet unable to recall one single thought or feeling with that vigor which once gave it light and truth.

" It was a period of religious and metaphysical delirium, when everything became everything, when Maya and Sophia, Mithra and Christ, Viraf and Isaiah, Belus, Zarvan, and Kronos were mixed up in one jumbled system of inane speculation, from which at last the East was delivered by the positive doctrines of Mohammed, the West by the pure Christianity of the Teutonic nations." [1]

Dr. JOSEPH PRIESTLEY says :

" The causes of the corruptions were almost wholly contained in the established opinions of the heathen world, and especially the philosophical part of it ; so that when those heathens embraced Christianity, they mixed their former tenets and prejudices with it. . . . The abuse of the *positive institutions* of Christianity, monstrous as they were, naturally arose from the opinions of the purifying and sanctifying virtue of rites and

---

[1] *Last Results of Persian Research*, in *Outlines of the Philosophy of History*, by C. C. J. Bunsen, chap. 3, sec. 1, part 1, of First Part, London, 1854.

ceremonies, which was the very basis of all the worship of the heathens." [1]

THEBAUD says :

" Therefore this same 'high civilization,' as it is called, in the midst of which Christianity was preached, was a real danger to the inward life of the new disciple of Christ.

" How could it be otherwise, when it is a fact, now known to all, that, even at the beginning of the fifth century, Rome was almost entirely pagan, at least outwardly and among her highest classes; so that the poet Claudian, in addressing Honorius at the beginning of his sixth consulship, pointed out to him the site of the Capitol, still crowned with the temple of Jove, surrounded by numerous pagan edifices, supporting in air an army of gods; and all around, temples, chapels, statues without number; in fact, the whole Roman and Greek mythology, standing in the city of the catacombs and of the pope.

" The public calendars, preserved to this day, continued to note the pagan festivals, side by side with the feasts of the Saviour and his apostles. Within the city and beyond, throughout Italy and the most remote provinces, idols and their altars were still surrounded by the thronging populace, prostrate at their feet." [2]

HARDWICK describes the tendency to reproduce pagan theories and customs in the early Church as follows :

[1] *History of the Corruption of Christianity*, vol. ii., pp. 441, 442, Birmingham, 1782.

[2] *The Irish Race in the Past and the Present*, by Rev. Aug. Thebaud, S. J., p. 63, New York, 1876.

" Or take again the swarm of heresies that soon invaded almost every province of the early Church. Abandoning, as they did, the more essential of the supernatural truths of revelation, they were virtually and in effect revivals of paganism, and family likenesses may accordingly be traced among the older speculations current in the schools of heathen philosophy. In discussing, for example, the nature of the divine Son-ship, Sabellius and his party taught a doctrine very similar to that already noticed in the Trimurrti of India; while Docetism, starting from a notion that the spiritual and the material cannot permanently co-exist, had merely reproduced the Hindu doctrine of Avataras. The inward correspondence in the texture of ideas had issued in a similar deprivation of revealed truth. Or if, penetrating below the surface, we investigate the elementary thoughts and feelings that hereafter found utterance in monastic institutions of the Church, we find that on one side those ideas are alien from the spirit of primitive Christianity, and on the other that they had long been familiar in the East, before they were appropriated or unconsciously reproduced among one class of Christians in Syria and Egypt. India was the real birthplace of monasticism, its cradle being in the haunts of earnest *yogins*, and self-torturing devotees, who were convinced that evil is inherent not in man only, but in all the various forms of matter, and accordingly withdrew as far as possible from contact with the outer world. At first, indeed, the Christian hermit, like the earliest of his Hindu prototypes, had dwelt alone on the outskirts of his native town, supporting himself by manual labor, and devoting all the surplus of his earnings to religious purposes.

"But during the fourth century of the present era many such hermits began to flock together in the forest, or the wilderness, where regular confraternities were organized upon a model more or less derived from the Egyptian Therapeutæ, and the old Essenes of Palestine; the members in their dress and habits most of all resembling those of the religious orders who still swarm in Thibet and Ceylon."[1]

MAITLAND bears important testimony touching many points in which Christianity was paganized. He sums up the general results in the following concerning the worship of martyrs:

"The degrees of worship and adoration, since defined with fatal precision by the Romish Church, were not then fixed; and the heathen, even less willing than the Christian laity to enter into refinements on the subject, saw no distinction between one form and another. The consequences were disastrous in the extreme; the charge of idolatry, mutually urged by the contending parties, lost the force, or rather was effectively employed by the pagans, after it had become powerless in Christian hands. Thus it was that, although the pure doctrines of our faith speedily displaced the profligate polytheism of the empire, the after conflict was long doubtful, being maintained by a religion enfeebled by admixture with foreign elements, against one that had profited by adversity, and had not scrupled to borrow largely from its rival. We read in fable of the struggle between the man and the

[1] *Christ and Other Masters*, by Charles Hardwick, M.A., part 2, p. 183, Cambridge, 1857.

serpent, in which at length the combatants become transformed into the shapes of each other. In the last contest between paganism and Christianity we find the sophist contending for the unity of God, and accusing the Christian of undisguised polytheism; and on the other side the Christian insisting on the tutelary powers of glorified mortals, and the omniscience of departed spirits." [1]

Similar testimony is borne by SEYMORE, who says :

" The apostasy of the Church of Rome will be more apparent when we reflect that the character of the mediation which Romanism ascribes to its saints is precisely the same as that which heathenism ascribes to its demi-gods. It was believed among the heathen that when a man became illustrious for his deeds, his conquests, his inventions, or aught else that distinguished him as a benefactor of mankind, he could be canonized and enrolled among inferior deities. He thus became a mediator whose sympathies with his fellow-men on the one hand, and whose merits with the gods on the other fitted him for the mediatorial office of bearing the prayers and wants of mortals to the presence of the gods. The heathen philosophers, Hesiod, Plato, and Apuleius, all thus speak of those persons. The last named philosopher says: ' They are intermediate intelligences, by whom our prayers and wants pass unto the gods. They are mediators between the inhabitants of the earth and the inhabitants of heaven, carrying thither our prayers, and drawing down

[1] *The Church in the Catacombs*, etc., by Chas. Maitland, M.D., p. 306, London, 1846.

their blessings. They bear back and forwards prayers for us, and supplies for them ; or they are those that explain between both parties, and who carry our adorations.' This was the creed of heathenism, and in nothing but the name does it differ from the corresponding creed of Romanism. When the Church of Rome finds members of her communion whom she regards as signally pious, or illustrious for supposed miraculous powers, she holds that they be canonized and enrolled among her saints ; that they can mediate between God and man ; that they have sufficient favor or influence with God to obtain compliance with our prayers, and therefore they are fitting objects to whom our confessions, invocations, and prayers may be offered ; or, as she expresses it in her creed, 'that the saints reigning with Christ are to be honored and invoked, and that they offer prayers to God for us.' The principle of heathen Romanism, and the principle of Christian Romanism are one and the same, the only difference is in the details of the names. And the origin of the practice is demonstrative of this ; for when it was found, after the establishment of Christianity in the times of Constantine, when the great object of the court was to promote uniformity of religion, that many of the heathen would outwardly conform to Christianity if allowed to retain in private their worship of their guardian or tutelar divinities, they were so allowed, merely on changing the names of Jupiter to Peter, or Juno to Mary, still worshipping their old divinities under new names, and even retaining old images that were baptized with Christian names. This is apparent in the writings of those times, and was thought a measure of wisdom, a stroke of profound policy, as tending to produce a uniformity of religion among the unthinking masses. The invocations of Juno have been transferred to Mary; the prayers to Mercury have been transferred to Paul. We see not how the substitution of the names of Damian or Cosmo, for those of Mercury or Apollo, or how the substitution of the names of Lucy or Cecelia, for those of Minerva or Diana, can alter the idolatrous character of the practice. In some instances they have not even changed the names, and Romulus and Remus are still worshipped in Italy, under the more modern names of St. Romulo and St. Remugio. The simple people believe them to have been two holy bishops. I have myself witnessed this near Florence, and even Bacchus is not without his votaries, under the ecclesiastical name of St. Bacco. The principle and practice of papal Rome are identical with the principle and practice of pagan Rome. Every argument to justify one may be equally urged to justify or extenuate the other. And if the principle and practice of pagan Rome are to be pronounced as idolatrous, I see not why the very same principle and practice in papal Rome should not be pronounced as idolatrous likewise." [1]

In the light of all the facts Mr. Seymore cannot fasten the pagan residuum upon Romanism alone. The controlling trend into paganism was established before the papacy was developed; and if new forms of expression appeared afterward, they were but the fruitage of earlier tendencies.

Renan, speaking of the relation between the religious *cultus* of the Orient and early Christianity, says :

[1] *Evenings with the Romanists*, pp. 221–223, London, 1854.

"This is the explanation of the singular attraction which about the beginning of the Christian era drew the population of the ancient world to the religions of the East. These religions had something deeper in them than those of Greece and Rome ; they addressed themselves more fully to the religious sentiment. Almost all of them stood in some relation to the condition of the soul in another life, and it was believed that they held the warrant of immortality. Hence the favor in which the Thracian and Sabasian mysteries, the *thiasi*, and confraternities of all kinds, were held. It was not so chilly in these little circles, where men pressed closely together, as in the great icy world of that day. Little religions like the worship of Psyche, whose sole object was consolation for human mortality, had a momentary prevalence. The beautiful Egyptian worship, which hid a real emptiness beneath a great splendor of ritual, counted devotees in every part of the empire. Isis and Serapis had altars even in the ends of the world. A visitor to the ruins of Pompeii might be tempted to believe that the principal worship which obtained there was that of Isis. These little Egyptian temples had their assiduous worshippers, among whom were many of the same class as the friends of Catullus and Tibullus. There was a morning service ; a kind of mass, celebrated by a priest, shorn and beardless. There were sprinklings of holy water ; possibly benediction in the evening. All this occupied, amused, soothed. What could any one want more ?

"But it was above all the Mithraic[1] worship which, in the second and third centuries, attained an extraordinary prevalence. I sometimes permit myself to say that, if Christianity had not carried the day, Mithraicism would

[1] Eastern sun-worship.

have become the religion of the world.   It had its mysterious meetings, its chapels, which bore a strong resemblance to little churches.   It forged a very lasting bond of brotherhood between its initiates ; it had a Eucharist, a supper so like the Christian mysteries that good Justin Martyr the Apologist can find only one explanation of the apparent identity, namely, that Satan, in order to deceive the human race, determined to imitate the Christian ceremonies, and so stole them.   A Mithraic sepulchre in the Roman catacombs is as edifying, and presents as elevated a mysticism, as the Christian tombs." [1]

Describing the earliest Christianity, KILLEN bears valuable testimony to the fact that the features of paganism which became prominent at a later period were wholly wanting in the earliest Christianity.   He shows that the Church was Judaistic in forms and practice.

These are his words :

" A Roman citizen, when present for the first time at the worship of the Church, might have remarked how profoundly it differed from the ritual of paganism. The services in the great heathen temples were but an imposing scenic exhibition.   The holy water for lustration, the statues of the gods with wax tapers burning before them, the officials robed in white surplices, and the incense floating in clouds and diffusing perfume all around, could only regale the sense or light up the imagination.   No stated time was devoted to instruct the assembly ; and the liturgy— often in a dead language—as it was mumbled over by the

---

[1] *Influence of Rome on Christianity*, Hibbert Lectures for 1880, p. 33 ff.

priest, merely added to the superstition and the mysticism. But the worship of the Church was, in the highest sense, a 'reasonable service.' It had no parade, no images, no fragrant odors; for the first hundred years it was commonly celebrated in private houses or the open fields; and yet it addressed itself so impressively to the understanding and the heart that the congregations of the faithful frequently presented scenes incomparably more spirit-stirring and sublime than anything ever witnessed in the high places of Greek or Roman idolatry.

.   .   .   .

" No individual or church court is warranted to tamper with symbolic ordinances of divine appointment; for as they are the typical embodiment of great truths, any change essentially vitiates their testimony. But their early administrators overlooking this grave objection, soon ceased to respect the integrity of baptism and the Lord's Supper. In the third century a number of frivolous and superstitious ceremonies—such as exorcism, unction, the making of the sign of the cross on the forehead, and the kiss of peace—were already tacked to baptism; so that the beautiful significance of the primitive observance could not be well seen under these strange trappings. Before the middle of the second century the wine of the Eucharist was mixed with water; fifty years afterwards the communicants participated standing; and at length the elements themselves were treated with awful reverence. The more deeply to impress the imagination, baptism and the Eucharist began to be surrounded with the secrecy of the heathen mysteries, and none save those who had received the ordinances were suffered to be present at their dispensation. The ministers of the Church sadly compromised their religion when they thus imitated the meretricious decorations of the pagan worship. As might have been expected, the symbols so disfigured were misunderstood and misrepresented. Baptism was called regeneration, and the Eucharist was designated a sacrifice. Thus a door was opened for the admission of a whole crowd of dangerous errors." [1]

The tendency to religious syncretism, during the early centuries, was a prolific source of corruption to New Testament Christianity. Speaking of the results of this tendency, and of the composite character of the religious *cultus* at Alexandria, in the time of Hadrian (117–138 A.D.). Canon FARRAR says :

"There was no city in the empire in which a graver task was assigned to the great scholars and teachers of Christianity than the city of Alexandria. It was the centre of the most energetic intellectual vitality ; and there, like the seething of the grapes in the vine cluster, the speculations of men of every religion and every nationality exercised a reciprocal influence on each other.

"A single letter of Hadrian presented by Vopiscus will show the confusion of thought and intermixture of religions which prevailed in that cosmopolitan city, and the aspect presented by its religious syncretism to a cool and cynical observer. 'Those who worship Serapis,' he says in a letter to a friend, 'are Christians, and those who call themselves Bishops of Christ are votaries of Serapis.

[1] *The Old Catholic Church*, etc., W. D. Killen, D.D., pp. 44–6, Edinburgh, 1871.

There is no ruler of a synagogue there, no Samaritan, no presbyter of the Christians, who is not an astrologer, who is not a soothsayer, who is not a gymnast. The patriarch of the Jews himself when he comes to Egypt is forced by one party to worship Serapis, by the other Christ. They have but one God who is no God; him Christians, him Jews, him all races worship alike.' To the disdainful and sceptical mind of the emperor, who deified his own unhappy minion, Christianity, gnosticism, Judaism, paganism were all forms of one universal charlatanry and sham."[1]

In writing of Leo the Great (440–461) founder of the papacy, Dean MERIVALE gives a graphic picture of the state of Christianity at that time. Space is here taken for a copious extract that the weight of Merivale's name and words may add force to the facts. He says :

"It will be admitted, I trust, without entering upon disquisitions which would be inappropriate to this occasion, that the corruptions of Christian faith against which our own national Church and many others rose indignantly at the Reformation had for the most part struck their foundations deep in the course of the fifth century; that though they had sprung up even from an earlier period, and though they developed more in some directions, and assumed more fixity in the darker times that followed, yet the working of the true Christian leaven among the masses was never more faint, the approximation of Christian usage to the manners and customs of paganism never really closer, than in the age of which we are now speak-

[1] *Lives of the Fathers*, vol. i., pp. 350–1, Edinburgh, 1889.

ing. We have before us many significant examples of the facility with which the most intelligent of the pagans accepted the outward rite of Christian baptism, and made a nominal profession of the faith, while they retained and openly practised, without rebuke, without remark, with the indulgence even of genuine believers, the rites and usages of the paganism they pretended to have abjured. We find abundant records of the fact that personages high in office, such as consuls and other magistrates, while administering the laws by which the old idolatries were proscribed, actually performed pagan rites, and even erected public statues to pagan divinities. Still more did men, high in the respect of their fellow-Christians, allow themselves to cherish sentiments utterly at variance with the definitions of the Church. Take the instance of the illustrious Bishop Synesius. Was he a Christian, was he a pagan ; who shall say ? He was famous in the schools of Alexandria as a man of letters, a teacher of the ancient philosophies, an admirer of the pagan Hypatia. The Christian people of Ptolemais, enchanted with his talents, demanded him for their bishop. He protests not indeed that he is an unbeliever—but that his life and habits are not suitable to so high an office. He has a wife whom he cannot abandon, as the manners of the age might require of him ; whom he will not consort with secretly, as the manners of the age would, it seems, allow. ' But further I cannot believe,' he adds, ' that the human soul has been breathed into flesh and blood ; I will not teach that this everlasting world of matter is destined to annihilation ; the resurrection, as taught by the Church, seems to me a doubtful and questionable doctrine. I am a philosopher, and cannot preach to the people popularly.' In short, he maintains to all appearance that if he is a believer in Jesus Christ, he is a follower of Plato ; and such doubtless were many others. The people leave him his wife and his opinions, and insist that he shall be their bishop. He retains his family ties, his philosophy, his Platonism, his rationalism, and accepts the government of the Church notwithstanding. Again we ask, was Synesius a Christian or a pagan ? The instance of such a bishop, one probably among many, is especially significant ; but the same question arises with regard to other men of eminence of the period. Was Boëthius, a century later, the imitator of Cicero, Christian or pagan ? Was Simplicius, the commentator on Plato ? Was Ausonius, the playful poet and amiable friend of the Bishop Paulinus, who celebrates Christ in one poem, and scatters his allusions to pagan mythology indiscriminately in many others ? We know that Libanius, the intimate friend and correspondent of Basil, was a pagan of the pagans ; but he did not on that account forfeit the confidence of a sainted father of the Christian Church. So indifferent as Christians seem to have been at this period to their own creed, so indifferent to the creed of their friends and associates, we cannot wonder if it has left us few or but slight traces of a vital belief in the principles of divine redemption.

" We must make, indeed, large allowance for the intellectual trials of an age of transition when it was not given to every one to see his way between the demands urged upon an intelligent faith by the traditions of a brilliant past on the one hand, and the intimations of an obscure and not a cheerful future on the other. We hardly realize, perhaps, the pride with which the schools of Athens and Alexandria still regarded their thousand years of academic renown, while the Christian Church was slowly building up the recent theological systems on which its own foundations were to be secured for the ages to follow. We need not complain of Leo, and other Christian doctors, if they shrank, as I think they did, from rushing again into polemics with the remnant of the philosophers, whose day, they might think, was sure to close at no distant date. But the real corruption of the age was shown in the unstinted adoption of pagan usages in the ceremonial of the Christian Church, with all the baneful effects they could not fail to produce on the spiritual training of the people. There are not wanting, indeed, passages in the popular teachings of St. Leo, in which he beats the air with angry denunciations of auguries, and sortilege, and magic, stigmatizes idolatry as the worship of demons, and the devil as the father of pagan lies. But neither Leo, nor, I think, the contemporary doctors of the Church, seem to have had an adequate sense of the process by which the whole essence of paganism was throughout their age constantly percolating the ritual of the Church and the hearts of the Christian multitude. It is not to these that we can look for a warning that the fasts prescribed by the Church had their parallel in the abstinence imposed by certain pagan creeds, and required to be guarded and explained to the people in their true Christian significance; that the monachism they extolled so warmly, and which spread so rapidly, was in its origin a purely pagan institution, common to the religions of India, Thibet, and Syria, with much, no doubt, to excuse its extravagance in the hapless condition of human life at the period, but with little or nothing to justify it in the charters of our Christian belief; that the canonizing of saints and martyrs, the honors paid them, and the trust reposed in them, were simply a revival of the old pagan mythologies; that the multiplication of formal ceremonies, with processions and lights and incense and vestments, with images and pictures and votive offerings, was a mere pagan appeal to the senses, such as can never fail to enervate man's moral fibre; that, in short, the general aspect of Christian devotion, as it met the eye of the observer, was a faint and rather frivolous imitation of the old pagan ritual, the object of which, from first to last, was not to instruct, or elevate man's nature, but simply to charm away the ills of life by adorning and beautifying his present existence." [1]

Witness also the following from WESTROPP and WAKE:

" In popular customs, and even in religious institutions, these things are as plainly perceived to-day as when Adonis and Astarte were the Gods of the former world. The sanctities, the powers, the symbols, and even the utensils of the ancient faith have been assumed, if not usurped or legitimately inherited, by its successors. The two holies of the Gnostics and Neo-Platonists, Sophia and Eirene—Wisdom and Peace—were adopted as saints in the calendar of Constantinople. Dionysius, the god of the mysteries, reappears as St. Denys in France, St. Liberius, St. Eleutherius, and St. Bacchus; there is also a St. Mithra; and even Satan, prince of shadows, is revered as St. Satur and St. Swithin. Their relics are in

---

[1] *Four Lectures on Some Epochs of Early Church History*, by Charles Merivale, D.D., Dean of Ely, pp. 149–155, New York, Randolph; no date.

keeping. The holy virgin Astræa or Astarte, whose return was announced by Virgil in the days of Augustus, as
introducing a new golden age, now under her old designa-
tion of Blessed Virgin and Queen of Heaven, receives
homage as ' the one whose sole divinity the whole orb of
the earth venerates.' The Mother and Child, the latter
adorned with the nimbus or aureole of the ancient sun-
gods, are now the objects of veneration as much as were
Ceres and Bacchus, or Isis and Horus, in the mysteries.
Nuns abounded alike in Christian and Buddhist countries,
as they did formerly in Isis-worshipping Egypt; and if
their maidenhood is not sacrificed at the shrine of Baal-
Peor, or any of his cognate divinities, yet it is done in a
figure; they are all ' brides of the Saviour.' *Galli* sing
in the churches, and consecrated women are as numerous
as of old. The priestly vestments are like those formerly
used in the worship of Saturn and Cybele; the Phrygian
cap, the pallium, the stole, and the alb. The whole
Pantheon has been exhausted, from the Indus, Euphrates,
and the Nile, to supply symbolic adornment for the
apostles' successors. Hercules holds the distaff of Om-
phale. The Lily has superseded the Lotus, and celibacy
is exalted above the first recorded mandate of God to
mankind.

.　　.　　.　　.　　.　　.　　.

"It is true, doubtless, that there is not a fast or festival,
procession or sacrament, social custom or religious symbol,
that did not come ' bodily ' from the previous paganism.
But the pope did not import them on his own account;
they had already been transferred into the ecclesiastical
structure, and he only accepted and perhaps took advantage of the fact. Many of those who protest because of

these corruptions are prone to imitate them more or less, displaying an engrafting from the same stock." [1]

A late German writer of note and authority, LECHLER, thus states the relative influence of paganism and Judaism on early Christianity :

" Putting together all that has been said, we get the impression that, in respect to the Gentile Christians in the second half of the Apostolic age, heathenism was the vastly predominant power that partly from without threatened the Church, and partly from within prepared the most hazardous disputes. It was an anti-Christian *gnosis* proceeding from heathen ideas ; frequently also a moral error stained with heathen licentiousness, that became dangerous to souls. On the other hand, according to all the documents of that later apostolic time that we possess, Judaism, broken as a political power, was no longer a dangerous opponent of the Church of Christ as a spiritual power ; the time in which Judaizing errorists possessed a powerful influence over spirits was visibly passed." [2]

With such a preview, made up from writers of such authority and ability, the fact of the existence of an immense amount of pagan residuum in Christianity is placed beyond question. The reader may be surprised ; may shrink from such facts. But shrinking from facts, or denying them, does

[1] *Ancient Symbol Worship*, Westropp and Wake, pp. 94, 96, New York, 1874.

[2] *Apostolic and Post-Apostolic Times*, G. V. Lechler, D.D., pp. 262, 263.

not remove or destroy them.   Facts are immortal. He who will take the trouble to follow through the successive chapters will see by what means, and in what ways, Christianity was corrupted, and whence came the pagan residuum that yet remains.   Suggestions in outline will also be found, as to how the remaining residuum can be removed.

CHAPTER II.

PAGAN METHODS OF INTERPRETING THE SCRIPTURES.

Contrast between the Christianity of the New Testament and That of the Later Centuries—Gnosticism and Allegorical Interpretation—Testimony of Harnack and Bauer Concerning the "Hellenization of Christianity"—Hatch on "Pagan Exegesis"—The "Fathers" as Allegorists; Justin, Clement of Alexandria, Barnabas, and Others—Examples: "The Red Heifer a Type of Christ"; "Spiritual Circumcision"; "Scriptural Significance of Foods"; "The Cross in the Old Testament"; "Why Are There One Hundred and Fifty Psalms?" "The Phœnix a Type of the Resurrection"; "Gnostic Exposition of the Decalogue"; "Types of Christ"; Various Examples from Augustine.

THE student of history cannot fail to note the wide difference between the Christianity of the New Testament period and that of the fourth century. The religion which Christ taught was a direct outgrowth of Judaism. His mission was "not to destroy but to fulfil." This He did by giving a higher conception and a broader view of all which Judaism had held hitherto. He gave a new meaning to the fatherhood of God. He explained and enforced the moral precepts of the Old Testament, developing their deeper spiritual sense, and giving them a new application to the inner life of men. He enlarged Judaism without destroying it. He clarified and intensified the ten commandments. He discarded the outward formalities of the Jews, and "reached the heart of things" by His interpretation of the ancient Scriptures, by His new precepts, and by His example. He developed Christianity within the Jewish Church, making it the efflorescence of all that was best in the ancient dispensation.

Christ presented love for God, for truth, and for man, as the mainspring of action in all religious living. Under His teachings Christianity arose as a new life, springing from the law of God, written in the hearts of men. New Testament Christianity was a life born of love, and finding expression in loving obedience. It was a system of right living, as in the divine presence, and by the help of the divine Spirit. Men were drawn to each other and to Christ by the power of this love. Such was Christianity at its birth.

The earliest Christian congregations were communities for holy living, upon the ground of a mutual faith in Christ. They expected still greater revelations of Him, and through Him, in the near future. The facts connected with His life and the memory of His teachings formed the soil in which Christianity had its earliest roots. A common hope and the struggle for holy living according to the law of God bound these communities together.

They were made up of Jews alone, or of Jews and those Gentiles who had been converts to Judaism. Beyond this common hope there was no settled doctrine, no formal ecclesiastical organization. There were no written scriptures except the Old Testament. As the history of Christianity progressed, its enlarging spirit brought about a conflict with the narrower phases of Judaism, and hence more or less antagonism towards certain Judaistic interpretations of the Old Testament.

The Christianity of the third and fourth centuries presents the strongest possible contrast when placed alongside of that which existed during the New Testament period. The Sermon on the Mount was the promulgation of a new law of conduct. " The Nicene Creed is a statement partly of historical facts, and partly of dogmatic inferences."[1] Some adequate reason must be found for this difference. How did this change in the central character of Christianity come to pass ? By what influences was it transformed from a system of right living to a system of metaphysical belief ; to right thinking rather than right doing ? The answer is suggested by the fact that this change in character is contemporaneous with the transferring of Christianity from Semitic to Greek influence. Thus we are brought to face the fact

[1] *Cf.* Hibbert Lectures for 1888, by Edwin Hatch, D.D., Lecture i.

3

that the religion of a given people at a given time bears certain definite relations to the mental attitude of that time. Religion is a part of common life which cannot be separated from its surroundings. While we may consider religious problems as distinct from other questions, they can never be understood except as a part of the complex life with which they are interwoven.

We therefore must commence by inquiring after the characteristics of the pagan world into which the infant Christianity passed when the stream of its history left the soil of Palestine and entered the field of Greek and Roman influences.

Gnosticism.

Long before the time of Christ the Oriental religions had developed a system of philosophy in which were the seeds of that which in later times was known as gnosticism. This claimed to hold within itself " the knowledge of God and of man, of the being and the providence of the former, and of the creation and destiny of the latter."[1] In its journey westward this system had mingled with Jewish thought and given rise to the Kabbalists or Jewish Gnostics. In the Oriental religions all external phenomena expressed a hidden meaning.

[1] See *The Gnostics and Their Remains*, by C. W. King, M.A. p. 5, London, 1887.

Applying this doctrine to the Scriptures, the Jewish Gnostics taught that a hidden meaning was to be found in all laws, ceremonies, and rituals. They invented the theory that a secret tradition had been handed down from the time of Moses; the interpretation of the Jewish Scriptures had been greatly perverted in this way. Gnosticism said: " Nothing is what it seems to be; everything tangible is the symbol of something invisible. By this means the history of the Old Testament was sublimated into a history of the emancipation of reason from sense.[1] This application of the allegorical method of interpretation to the Old Testament enabled pagan philosophers to draw from it whatever fancies they chose. This method also favored a tendency among the early Christians to interpret the Old Testament so as to find upon every leaf of the book some reference to Christ and the Christian religion. Thus gnosticism had prepared the way for the obliteration of the concrete positiveness of the Old Testament, and destroyed its authority in a great degree.

The entire Grecian world was thoroughly permeated as to its literature and philosophy with the spirit and practice of gnosticism. It formed the bridge between Judaism on its intellectual side, and the Oriental, Grecian, and Egyptian cults. When

[1] See Harnack, *Dogmengeschichte*, vol. i., chap. 4.

the infant Christianity came in contact with Greek thought, gnostic influences and tendencies assailed it on every hand. Thus, through a gnostic element already within the Jewish Church, and the cultured, powerful gnostic influences in the pagan world, nascent Christianity was like the traveller from Jerusalem to Jericho who fell among thieves. The intellectual unrest of the age favored the process of corruption which went rapidly forward.

Biblical Exegesis.

Whatever touches the Bible and its interpretation touches Christianity at a vital point. The fundamental difference between the pagan gnosticism and Christianity lay in the fact that Christianity was a revealed religion, finding its beginning and end in the divine love and life unfolded in Christ Jesus as the Jewish Messiah. On the contrary, gnosticism found its source in human reasoning, human philosophy, and speculations.

Dr. SCHAFF describes its influence when he says:

" It exaggerates the Pauline view of the distinction of Christianity from Judaism, sunders Christianity from its historical basis, resolves the real humanity of the Saviour into a doketistic illusion, and perverts the freedom of the Gospel into Antinomian licentiousness. The author or first representative of this baptized heathenism, according to the uniform testimony of Christian antiquity, is Simon Magus, who unquestionably adulterated Christianity with pagan ideas and practices, and gave himself out, in pantheistic style, for an emanation of God. Plain traces of [of the existence of] this error appear in the later epistles of Paul to the Colossians, to Timothy, and to Titus, the second epistle of Peter, and the first two epistles of John, the epistle of Jude, and the messages of the Apocalypse to the seven churches." [1]

This rapid survey of the field shows us that gnostic influences represent what Professor HARNACK calls " *The acute vulgarization of Christianity, or its Hellenization.*" We are therefore prepared to accept his testimony relative to the influence of the Gnostics as formulators of Christian doctrine. The following are his words :

" Under this view the Gnostics should be given their place in the history of dogmas as has not been done hitherto. They are simply the theologians of the first century ; they were the first to transform Christianity into a system of doctrines. They were the first to elaborate tradition systematically ; they undertook to prove Christianity to be the absolute religion, and by it to hunt down all other religions, including Judaism ; but to them the absolute religion, so far as its content was concerned, was identical with the results of religious philosophy, for which a revelation was to be sought as a foundation. Thus they became Christians who tried by quick measures to win Christianity for the Hellenic culture, and the Hellenic culture for Christianity. To this end they would

[1] *Church History*, vol. i., p. 566, N. Y., 1882.

surrender the Old Testament that they might make it more easy to establish the union between the two powers, and to gain the possibility of proclaiming the absoluteness of Christianity.

.　　　.　　　.　　　.　　　.　　　.　　　.

"We may also consider the majority of the gnostic efforts as efforts to transform Christianity into a theosophy, or, so to say, into a system of revealed metaphysics, with a complete disregard for the Jewish Old Testament foundation, on which it originated, and by the use of the Pauline ideas. We can also compare later writers, such as Barnabas and Ignatius, with the so-called Gnostics, by which the latter will be seen to possess a well formulated theory, and the former to be in possession of fragments which bear a remarkable likeness to said theory." [1]

BAUER, a careful student of gnosticism, gives a description of its mission and methods which shows how it was prepared to exert such a controlling influence on the history of early Christianity, and how destructive that influence was in the matter of biblical interpretation. He says :

" *Gnosis* and allegory are essentially allied conceptions ; and this affords us a very marked indication of the path which will really lead us to the origin of gnosticism ; for we shall find that allegory plays an important part in most of its systems, especially in those which exhibit its original form.

" It is well known that allegory is the soul of the Alexandrian religious philosophy. Nothing else, indeed, can

----

[1] *Dogmengeschichte*, vol. i., chap. 4.

enable us to understand the rise of the latter, so closely is allegory interwoven with its very nature. Allegory is in general the mediator between philosophy and the religion which rests upon positive tradition. Wherever it is seen on a large scale, we notice that philosophical views have arisen side by side with, and independently of, the existing religion ; and that the need has arisen to bring the ideas and doctrines of philosophy into harmony with the contents of the religious belief. In such circumstances, allegory appears in the character of mediator. It brings about the desired conformity by simply interpreting the belief in the sense of the philosophy. Religious ideas and narratives are thus clothed with a figurative sense, which is entirely different from their literal meaning. It was thus that allegory arose before the Christian time among the Greeks. The desire was felt first by Plato, and afterward still more strongly by the Stoics, to turn the myths of the popular religion to account on behalf of their philosophical ideas, and so to bridge over the gulf between the philosophical and the popular mind ; and with this view they struck out the path of allegory, of allegorical interpretation of the myths. It is well known what extensive use the Stoics made of allegory when they wished to trace their own ideas of the philosophy of nature in the gods of popular belief, and the narratives concerning them.

" But in Alexandria, this mode of interpretation assumed still greater importance. Here it had to solve the weighty problem, how the new ideas that had forced their way into the mind and consciousness of the Jew, were to be reconciled with his belief in the authority of his sacred religious books. Allegory alone made it possible to him, on the one hand, to admire the philosophy of the Greeks, and in particular of Plato, and to make its ideas his own; and, on the other, to reverence the Scripture of the Old Testament as the one source of divinely revealed truth. The sacred books needed but to be explained allegorically, and then all that was wished for, even the boldest speculative ideas of the Greek mind, could be found in the books themselves. How widely this method was practised in Alexandria, may be judged from the writings of Philo, in which we see the most extensive use made of allegorical interpretation, and find the contents of the Old Testament blended intimately with everything that the systems of Greek philosophy could offer. But it would be quite erroneous to think that it was nothing but caprice and the unchecked play of fancy, that called forth this allegorical explanation of the Scriptures, which came to exercise such influence. For to the Alexandrian Jew, at the stage of scriptural development which he had now reached, with his consciousness divided between his ancestral Hebraism and modern Hellenism, this allegorizing was a necessary form of consciousness; and so little did he dream that the artificial link by which he bound together such diverse elements was a thing he had himself created, that all the truth which he accepted in the systems of Greek philosophy seemed to him to be nothing but an emanation from the Old Testament revelation.

" Now the gnostic systems also, for the most part, make very free use of the allegorical method of interpretation; and this is enough to apprise us that we must regard them under the same aspect as the Alexandrian religious philosophy. As far as we are acquainted with the writings of the Gnostics, we see them to have been full of allegorical interpretations, not indeed referring, as with Philo, to the books of the Old Testament (for their attitude toward the Old Testament was entirely different from his); but to those of the New, which were for the Gnostics what the books of the Old Testament were for Philo.

"In order to give their own ideas a Christian stamp, they applied the allegorical method, as much as possible, to the persons and events of the Gospel history, and especially to the numbers that occur in it. Thus for the Valentinians the number thirty in the New Testament, especially in the life of Jesus, was made to signify the number of their æons; the lost wandering sheep was for them their Achamoth; and even the utterances of Jesus, which contain a perfectly simple religious truth, received from them a sense referring to the doctrines of their system.

"The lately discovered *Philosophoumena* of the pseudo-Origen who undertook the task of refuting all the heresies show us even more clearly than before what an extensive use the Gnostics made of allegory.

"They applied it not merely to the books of the Old and New Testaments, but even the products of Greek literature, for instance, to the Homeric poems; their whole mode of view was entirely allegorical.

"The whole field of ancient mythology, astronomy, and physics, was laid under contribution to support their views. They thought that the ideas that were the highest objects of their thought and knowledge were to be found expressed everywhere." [1]

[1] Bauer, *Church Hist.*, vol. i., p. 191, London, 1878.

HATCH offers important testimony as to the pagan elements in early exegesis, in these words:

" The earliest methods of Christian exegesis were continuations of the methods which were common at the time to both Greek and Græco-Judæan writers. They were employed on the same subject-matter. Just as the Greek philosophers had found their philosophy in Homer, so Christian writers found in him Christian theology. When he represents Odysseus as saying,[1] 'The rule of many is not good; let there be one ruler,' he means to indicate that there should be but one God ; and his whole poem is designed to show the mischief that comes of having many gods.[2] When he tells us that Hephæstus represented on the shield of Achilles 'the earth, the heaven, the sea, the sun that rests not, and the moon full-orbed,'[3] he is teaching the divine order of creation which he learned in Egypt from the books of Moses.[4] So Clement of Alexandria interprets the withdrawal of Oceanus and Tethys from each other to mean the separation of land and sea.[5] And he holds that Homer when he makes Apollo ask Achilles, 'Why fruitlessly pursue him, a god,' meant to show that the divinity cannot be apprehended by the bodily powers."[6]

" Some of the philosophical schools which hung upon the skirts of Christianity mingled such interpretations of

---

[1] Hom., *Il.*, ii., 204.

[2] *Ps. Justin.* (probably Apollonius, see Dräseke, in the *Jahrb. f. protestant Theologie*, 1885, p. 144), chap. xvii.

[3] Hom., *Il.*, xviii., 483.

[4] *Ps. Justin.*, chap. xxviii.

[5] Hom., *Il.*, xiv., 206 ; also Clem. Alex., *Stroma.*, v., 14.

[6] *Il.*, xxii., 8 ; Clem. Alex., *Stroma.*, v., 14.

Greek mythology with similar interpretations of the Old Testament. For example, the writer to whom the name Simon Magus is given, is said to have 'interpreted in whatever way he wished both the writings of Moses and also those of the Greek poets'[1]; and the Ophite writer, Justin, evolves an elaborate cosmogony from a story of Herakles narrated in Herodotus,[2] combined with the story of the Garden of Eden.[3] . . .

"A large part of such interpretation was inherited. The coincidences of mystical interpretation between Philo and the *Epistle of Barnabas* show that such interpretation were becoming the common property of Jews and Judæo-Christians. But the method was soon applied to new data. Exegesis became apologetic. Whereas Philo and his school had dealt mainly with the Pentateuch, the early Christian writers came to deal mainly with the prophets and poetical books; and whereas Philo was mainly concerned to show that the writings of Moses contained Greek philosophy, the Christian writers endeavored to show that the writings of the Hebrew preachers and poets contained Christianity; and whereas Philo had been content to speak of the writers of the Old Testament, as Dio Chrysostom spoke of the Greek poets, as having been stirred by a divine enthusiasm, the Christian writers soon came to construct an elaborate theory that the poets and preachers were but as the flutes through which the breath of God flowed in divine music into the soul."[4]

[1] Hippol., *Philosophoumena*, vi., 14.
[2] Herod., iv., 8–10.
[3] Hippol., v., 21.
[4] Hibbert Lectures for 1888, Lecture iii., pp. 69, 70, 72.

The Fathers as Allegorists.

Beginning with Justin, the leaders of thought in the Church, from the middle of the second century, were men who had been brought up as pagan philosophers, or educated under pagan influence. It was therefore unavoidable that this corrupting system of exegesis should be applied to the books of the New Testament. This was done by the Gnostics, according to their theory that the true meaning of all writings was hidden. Christ's life presented many difficulties to the philosophers. To explain its seeming contradiction, they resolved the mission of Christ into a series of superhuman movements, and the New Testament into a sort of hieroglyphic record of those movements. Instance : Simeon, taking the young Christ in his arms in the temple,

"was a type of the Demiurge, who, on the arrival of the Saviour, learned his own change of place, and gave thanks to Bythus. They also assert that by Anna, who is spoken of in the Gospel as a prophetess, and who, after living seven years with her husband, passed all the rest of her life in widowhood until she saw the Saviour, and recognized Him, and spoke of Him to all, was most plainly indicated Achamoth, who, having for a little while looked upon the Saviour with his associates, and dwelling all the rest of the time in the intermediate place, waited for Him till He should come again and restore her to her proper consort. Her name, too, was indicated by the Saviour when he said, 'Yet wisdom is justified by her children.' This, too, was done by Paul in these words, 'But we speak wisdom among them that are perfect.' They declare also that Paul has referred to the conjunctions within the Pleroma, showing them forth by means of one; for, when writing of the conjugal union in this life, he expressed himself thus: 'This is a great mystery, but I speak concerning Christ and the Church.'"[1]

Another instance is found in the interpretation which they made of the raising of Jairus' daughter·

"They maintain further, that that girl of twelve years old, the daughter of the ruler of the synagogue, whom the Lord approached and raised from the dead, was a type of Achamoth, to whom their Christ, by extending himself, imparted shape, and whom he led anew to the perception of that light which had forsaken her. And that the Saviour appeared to her when she lay outside of the Pleroma as a kind of abortion, they affirm Paul to have declared in his *Epistle to the Corinthians* (in these words): 'And last of all, He appeared to me also, as to one born out of due time.' Again, the coming of the Saviour with His attendants, to Achamoth is declared in like manner by him in the same epistle, when he says: 'A woman ought to have a veil upon her head, because of the angels.' Now that Achamoth, when the Saviour came to her, drew a veil over herself through modesty, Moses rendered manifest when he put a veil upon his face. Then,

[1] Irenæus, *Against Heresies*, book i., chap. viii.

also, they say that the passions which she endured were indicated by the Lord upon the cross. Thus, when He said, 'My God, my God, why hast thou forsaken me?' he simply showed that Sophia was deserted by the light, and was restrained by Horos from making any advance forward. Her anguish again was indicated when He said, 'My soul is exceeding sorrowful, even unto death'; her fear by the words, 'Father, if it be possible, let this cup pass from me'; and her perplexity, too, when He said, 'And what I shall say, I know not.' "[1]

This Method Opposed by Some.

Some of the early Fathers, those who were least tinctured with Greek thought, especially Tertullian, opposed this method at the first. He declared that it was one of the arts of Satan, against which Christians must wrestle. But the system was too deep-seated in all the prevailing currents of influence to be displaced. Even while Tertullian was opposing it, it was tightening its grasp upon the Christian communities; a grasp which is by no means yet removed. Starting first at Alexandria and strengthened by the union of Greek philosophy and Hebrew theology, it gathered force like an increasing tide, and overwhelmed all other forms of exegesis. A pertinent example is found in Clement of Alexandria, in a philippic against the Sophists:

[1] Irenæus, *Against Heresies*, book i., chap. viii.

" Look to the tongue and to the words of the glozing man,
  But you look on no work that has been done ;
  But each one of you walks in the steps of a fox,
  And in all of you is an empty mind."

CLEMENT of Alexandria comments on this as follows :

"This, I think, is signified by the utterance of the Saviour, 'The foxes have holes, but the Son of man hath not where to lay his head.' For on the believer alone, who is separated entirely from the rest, who by the Scripture are called wild beasts, rests the head of the universe, the kind and gentle Word, 'Who taketh the wise in their own craftiness. For the Lord knoweth the thoughts of the wise, that they are vain'; the Scripture calling those the wise ($\sigma o\phi o\upsilon s$) who are skilled in words and arts, sophists ($\sigma o\phi\iota\sigma\tau a s$)." [1]

In another place the story of the feeding of the multitude by Christ is explained in these words :

" And the Lord fed the multitude of those that reclined on the grass opposite to Tiberias with the two fishes and the five barley loaves, indicating the preparatory training of the Greeks and Jews previous to the divine grain, which is the food cultivated by the law. For barley is sooner ripe for the harvest than wheat; and the fishes signified the Hellenic philosophy that was produced and moved in the midst of the Gentile billow, given, as they were, for copious food to those lying on the ground, increasing no more, like the fragments of the loaves, but

---

[1] *Stroma.* book i., chap. iii.

having partaken of the Lord's blessing, had breathed into them the resurrection of God-head through the power of the Word. But if you are curious, understand one of the fishes to mean the curriculum of study, and the other the philosophy which supervenes. The gatherings point out the word of the Lord." [1]

Christianity, according to the New Testament, could not be developed under such exegesis. These pagano-Christian leaders had still greater love for the allegorical method because it enabled them to "explain away" the difficulties which they found in considering Christianity—as they conceived of it—to be the product of the old Testament. From the first they had identified the God of the Old Testament with the Demiurge, the creator of the world and of matter, in which was only evil. They claimed that Jehovah could not make a revelation for all time, nor one worthy of their confidence. Hatch, speaking of the Old Testament, says :

"An important section of the Christian world rejected its authority altogether; it was the work, not of God, but of His rival, the god of this world ; the contrast between the Old Testament and the New was part of the larger contrast between matter and spirit, darkness and light, evil and good. This was the contention of Marcion, whose influence upon the Christian world was far larger than is commonly supposed." [2]

[1] *Strom.*, bk. vi., ch. xi.
[2] *Influence of Greek Thought*, etc., p. 77.

Further Examples.

Still further examples of the fanciful perversions of the Scriptures, by the Fathers, are presented in order that the reader may be left without a doubt as to the ruinous effects which the pagan allegorizing methods produced upon the infant Church.

The Epistle of Barnabas, falsely attributed to the companion of Paul, is a notable example of unmeaning allegories which totally pervert the Scriptures. Take the following examples:

"THE RED HEIFER A TYPE OF CHRIST.[1]

" Now what do you suppose this to be a type of, that a command was given to Israel, that men of the greatest wickedness should offer a heifer, and slay and burn it, and that then boys should take the ashes, and put these into vessels, and bind round a stick purple wool along with hyssop, and that thus the boys should sprinkle the people one by one, in order that they might be purified from their sins? Consider how he speaks to you with simplicity. The calf is Jesus; the sinful men offering it are those who led Him to the slaughter. But now the men are no longer guilty, are no longer regarded as sinners. And the boys that sprinkle are those that have proclaimed to us the remission of sins and purification of heart. To these He gave authority to preach the gospel, being twelve in number, corresponding to the twelve tribes of

---

[1] In quotations from the Fathers, words and clauses in brackets are thus printed as " supplied words " in the Ante-Nicene Library of T. & T. Clarke, Edinburgh.

4

Israel. But why are there three boys that sprinkle? To correspond to Abraham, and Isaac, and Jacob, because these were great with God. And why was the wool [placed] upon the wood? Because by wood Jesus holds His kingdom, so that [through the cross] those believing on Him shall live forever. But why was hyssop joined with the wool? Because in His kingdom the days will be evil and polluted in which we shall be saved, [and] because he who suffers in body is cured through the cleansing efficacy of hyssop. And on this account the things which stand thus are clear to us, but obscure to them, because they did not hear the voice of the Lord." [1]

Chapter ix. discusses the spiritual meaning of circumcision. The closing portion of the chapter is as follows:

"Yea, the Egyptians also practise circumcision. Learn then, my children, concerning all things richly, that Abraham, the first who enjoined circumcision, looking forward in spirit to Jesus, practised that rite, having received the mysteries of the three letters. For [the Scripture] saith, 'And Abraham circumcised ten and eight and three hundred men of his household.' What then was the knowledge given to him in this? Learn the eighteen first, and then the three hundred. The ten and the eight are thus denoted—ten by I, and eight by H. You have [the initials of] Jesus, and because the cross was to express the grace [of our redemption] by the letter T, he says also, 'three hundred.' He signifies, therefore, Jesus by two letters, and the cross by one. He knows this, who

----

[1] *Epistle*, ch. viii.

has put within us the engrafted gift of His doctrine. No
one has been admitted by me to a more excellent piece
of knowledge than this, but I know that ye are worthy."[1]

The tenth chapter, which treats of the *Spiritual
Significance of the Precepts of Moses Respecting Different Kinds of Food*, can be quoted only in part ;
portions of it are unfit for the public eye, and yet
these portions, gross as they are, are solemnly set
forth as an exegesis of Scripture. The chapter follows here, except the grosser sentences :

" Now, wherefore did Moses say, ' Thou shalt not eat
the swine, nor the eagle, nor the hawk, nor the raven, nor
any fish which is not possessed of scales ? ' He embraced
three doctrines in his mind [in doing so]. Moreover, the
Lord saith to them in Deuteronomy, ' And I will establish my ordinances among this people.' Is there then
not a command of God that they should not eat [these
things]? There is ; but Moses spoke with a spiritual
reference. For this reason he named the swine, as much
as to say, ' Thou shalt not join thyself to men who resem-
ble swine,' for when they live in pleasure they forget
their Lord ; but when they come to want they acknowledge the Lord. And [in like manner] the swine, when it
has eaten, does not recognize its master ; but when hun-
gry it cries out, and on receiving food is quiet again.
' Neither shalt thou eat,' says he, ' the eagle, nor the hawk,
nor the kite, nor the raven.' ' Thou shalt not join thyself,'
he means, ' to such men as know not how to procure food
for themselves by labor and, sweat, but seize on that of

[1] *Epistle*, ch. ix.

others in their iniquity, and, although wearing an aspect of simplicity, are on the watch to plunder others.' So these birds, while they sit idle, inquire how they may devour the flesh of others, proving themselves pests [to all] by their wickedness. 'And thou shalt not eat,' he says, 'the lamprey, or the polypus, or the cuttle-fish.' He means, 'Thou shalt not join thyself or be like to such men as are ungodly to the end, and are condemned to death.' In like manner as those fishes above accursed, float in the deep, not swimming [on the surface] like the rest, but make their abode in the mud which lies at the bottom. . . .

"Moses then issued three doctrines concerning meats with a spiritual significance; but they received them according to fleshly desire as if he had merely spoken of [literal] meats. David, however, comprehends the knowledge of the three doctrines, and speaks in like manner: 'Blessed is the man who hath not walked in the counsel of the ungodly,' even as the fishes [referred to] go in darkness to the depths [of the sea], 'and hath not stood in the way of sinners,' even as those who profess to fear the Lord, but go astray like swine; 'and hath not sat in the seat of the scorners' even as those birds that lie in wait for prey. Take a full and firm grasp of this spiritual knowledge. But Moses says still further, 'Ye shall eat every animal that is cloven-footed and ruminant.' What does he mean? [The ruminant animal denotes him] who on receiving food recognizes Him that nourishes him, and being satisfied by Him, is visibly made glad. Well spake [Moses] having respect to the commandment. What then does he mean? That we ought to join ourselves to those that fear the Lord, those who meditate in their heart on the commandment which they have received, those who both utter the judgments of the Lord and observe them, those who know that meditation is a work of gladness, and who ruminate upon the word of the Lord. But what means the cloven-footed? That the righteous man also walks in this world, yet looks forward to the holy state [to come]. Behold how well Moses legislated. But how was it possible for them to understand or comprehend these things? We then, rightly understanding his commandments, explain them as the Lord intended. For this purpose He circumcised our ears and our hearts, that we might understand these things." [1]

Chapter xii. is a meaningless discussion of the cross as prefigured in the Old Testament. A part of the chapter will suffice.

" In like manner he points to the cross of Christ in another prophet, who saith, 'And when shall these things be accomplished?' And the Lord saith, 'When a tree shall be bent down, and again arise, and when blood shall flow out of wood.' [2] Here again you have an intimation concerning the cross and Him who should be crucified. Yet again he speaks of this in Moses, when Israel was attacked by strangers. And that He might remind them, when assailed, that it was on account of their sins they were delivered to death, the Spirit speaks to the heart of Moses, that he should make a figure of the cross, and of Him about to suffer thereon; for unless

[1] *Epistle,* chap. x.

[2] This is a real or pretended quotation from some unknown Apochryphal book.

they put their trust in Him they shall be overcome for-ever. Moses, therefore, placed one weapon above another in the midst of the hill, and standing upon it, so as to be higher than all the people, he stretched forth his hands, and thus again Israel acquired the mastery. But when again he let down his hands, they were again destroyed. For what reason? That they might know that they could not be saved unless they put their trust in Him. And in another prophet he declares, 'All day long I have stretched forth my hands to an unbelieving people, and one that gainsays my righteous way.' And again Moses makes a type of Jesus [signifying] that it was necessary for him to suffer, [and also] that He would be the author of life [to others] whom they believed, to have destroyed on the cross when Israel was falling." [1]

Justin Martyr is an eminent example of one who perverted the Scriptures while claiming to explain them. Witness the following from the account of his conversion to Christianity :

"And when I had quoted this, I added, ' Hear then how this man, of whom the Scriptures declare that He will come again in glory after His crucifixion, was sym-bolized both by the tree of life, which was said to have been planted in paradise, and by those events which should happen to all the just.' Moses was sent with a rod to effect the redemption of the people ; and with this in his hands, at the head of the people, he divided the sea. By this he saw the water gushing out of the rock ; and when he cast a tree into the waters of Marah, which

[1] *Epistle*, chap. xii.

were bitter, he made them sweet. Jacob, by putting rods into the water troughs, caused the sheep of his uncle to conceive, so that he should obtain their young. With his rod the same Jacob boasts that he had crossed the river. He said that he had seen a ladder, and the Scripture has declared that God stood above it.

" But that this was not the Father we have proved from the Scriptures. And Jacob having poured oil on a stone in the same place is testified to by the very God who appeared to him, that he had anointed a pillar to the God who appeared to him. And that the stone symbolically proclaimed Christ, we have also proved by many Scriptures ; and that the unguent, whether it was of oil or of stacte, or of any other compounded sweet balsams, had reference to Him we have also proved, inasmuch as the word says, ' Therefore God, even thy God, hath anointed thee with the oil of gladness above thy fellows.' For indeed all kings and anointed persons obtained from Him their share in the names of kings and anointed ; just as he himself received from the Father the titles of King, and Christ, and Priest, and Angel, and such like other titles which He bears or did bear. Aaron's rod which blossomed, declared him to be the high priest. Isaiah prophesied that a rod would come forth from the root of Jesse [and this was] Christ. And David says that the righteous man is ' like the tree that is planted by the channels of waters, which should yield its fruit in its season, and whose leaf should not fade.' Again, the righteous is said to flourish like the palm tree. God appeared from a tree to Abraham, as it is written, near the oak in Mamre. The people found seventy willows and twelve springs after crossing the Jordan. David affirms that God comforted him with a rod and staff. Elisha, by casting a stick into the river Jordan, recovered the iron part of the axe with which the sons of the prophets had gone to cut down trees to build the house, in which they wished to read and study the law and commandments of God; even as our Christ, by being crucified on the tree, and by purifying [us] with water, has redeemed us, though plunged in the direst offences, which we have committed, and has made [us] a house of prayer and adoration. Moreover, it was a rod that pointed out Judah to be the father of Tamar's sons by a great mystery." [1]

Still more confusing fancies, under the name of exegesis, appear near the close of the *Dialogue.* Witness the following:

" 'You know then, sirs,' I said, 'that God has said in Isaiah to Jerusalem, "I saved thee in the deluge of Noah." [2] By this, which God said, was meant that the mystery of saved men appeared in the deluge. For righteous Noah, along with the other mortals at the deluge, *i. e.,* with his own wife, his three sons, and their wives, being eight in number, were a symbol of the eighth day wherein Christ appeared when He rose from the dead, forever the first in power. For Christ being the first-born of every creature, became again the chief of another race regenerated by Himself through water, and faith, and wood, containing the mystery of the cross; even as Noah was saved by wood when he rode over the

[1] *Dialogue with Trypho,* chap. lxxxvi.

[2] Isaiah liv., 9, may be referred to here, but there is nothing in Isaiah or elsewhere in the Bible like what Justin here asserts.

waters with his household. Accordingly, when the prophet says, " I saved thee in the times of Noah," as I have already remarked, he addresses the people who are equally faithful to God, and possess the same signs. For when Moses had the rod in his hands he led your nation through the sea. And you believe that this was spoken to your nation only, or to the land. But the whole earth, as the Scripture says, was inundated, and the water rose in height fifteen cubits above all the mountains ; so that it is evident this was not spoken to the land, but to the people who obeyed Him, for whom also He had before prepared a resting-place in Jerusalem, as was previously demonstrated by all the symbols of the deluge ; I mean that by water, faith, and wood, those who are afore prepared, and who repent of the sins which they have committed, shall escape from the impending judgment of God.' " [1]

Another illustration of the utterly unmeaning and fanciful interpretations of Scripture is found in *Fragments from Commentaries on Various Books of Scripture*, by HIPPOLYTUS, Bishop of Rome. He is explaining why there are one hundred and fifty psalms. The main reason adduced is that fifty is a sacred number, and the Psalms, on account of the destruction of God's enemies, should contain not only one set of fifty, but three such, for the name of the Father, and Son, and Holy Spirit. The sacred character of the number fifty is explained as follows :

[1] *Dialogue*, etc., chap. cxxxviii.

" The number fifty, moreover, contains seven sevens, or a Sabbath of Sabbaths, and also over and above these full Sabbaths, a new beginning in the eighth, of a really new rest that remains above the Sabbaths. And let any one who is able observe this [as it is carried out] in the Psalms with more, indeed, than human accuracy, so as to find out the reasons in each case, as we shall set them forth. Thus, for instance, it is not without a purpose that the eighth Psalm has the inscription, *on the wine presses,* as it comprehends the perfection of fruits in the eighth ; for the time for the enjoyment of the fruits of the true vine could not be before the eighth. And again, the second Psalm inscribed, *on the wine presses,* is the eightieth, containing another eighth number, viz., in the tenth multiple. The eighty-third again is made up by the union of two holy numbers, viz., the eighth in the tenth multiple, and the three in the first multiple. And the fiftieth Psalm is a prayer for the remission of sins, and a confession. For, as according to the Gospel, the fiftieth obtained remission confirming thereby that understanding of the jubilee, so he who offers up such petitions in full confession hopes to gain remission in no other number than the fiftieth. And again there are also certain others which are called *songs of degrees,* in number fifteen, as was also the number of the steps of the temple, and which show thereby, perhaps, that the *steps* (or *degrees*) are comprehended within the number seven and the number eight. And these songs of degrees begin after the one hundred and twentieth Psalm, which is called simply a *Psalm,* as the more accurate copies give it. And this is the number of the perfection of the life of man. And the hundredth Psalm, which begins thus, *I will sing of mercy and judgment, O Lord,* embraces the life of the saint in fellowship with God. And the one hundred and fiftieth ends with these words, *Let everything that hath breath praise the Lord.*" [1]

CLEMENT OF ROME, one of the earliest Fathers from whom anything genuine has come to our time, presents other prominent examples of myth and allegory, as follows :

" Let us consider that wonderful sign [of the resurrection] which takes place in Eastern lands, that is, in Arabia, and the countries round about. There is a certain bird which is called a phœnix. This is the only one of its kind, and lives five hundred years. And when the time of its dissolution draws near that it must die, it builds itself a nest of frankincense, and myrrh, and other spices, into which, when the time is fulfilled, it enters and dies. But as the flesh decays, a certain kind of worm is produced, which, being nourished by the juices of the dead bird, brings forth feathers. Then when it has acquired strength, it takes up that nest in which are the bones of its parent, and, bearing these, it passes from the land of Arabia into Egypt, to the city called Heliopolis. And in open day, flying in the sight of all men, it places them on the altar of the sun, and, having done this, hastens back to its former abode. The priests then inspect the registers of the dates, and finds that it has returned exactly as the five hundredth year was completed." [2]

[1] *Ante-Nicene Library*, T. & T. Clarke, vol. vi., p. 500.
[2] *Epistle of Clement*, chap. xxv.

Here is a pagan sun-myth gravely set forth as fact, and made to illustrate a Christian truth; an example of what was common in the writings and theories of those who became leaders in the Church.

The Bible, with its simple truths and plain ethical teachings, was an insipid book to men whose tastes had become abnormal and perverted through feeding on such pagan fancies and superstitions.

One more example from CLEMENT OF ALEXANDRIA. It must be remembered that the "Christian" writers who condemn gnosticism as a heresy still claimed that there was a "true Christian gnosticism"; the difference between them and those whom they condemned was in degree more than in kind. The following extracts are from Clement's *Gnostic Exposition of the Decalogue.* It needs little to show that when the law of God was thus expounded, its power and authority were practically destroyed. Such expositions were part and parcel of the lawlessness which was the unavoidable fruitage of gnosticism. Clement says:

"And the Decalogue, viewed as an image of heaven, embraces sun and moon, stars, clouds, light, wind, water, air, darkness, fire. This is the physical Decalogue of the heaven.

"And the representation of the earth contains men, cattle, reptiles, wild beasts; and of the inhabitants of the water, fishes and whales; and again of the winged tribes, those that are carnivorous, and those that use mild food;

and of plants likewise, both fruit-bearing and barren. This is the physical Decalogue of the earth.

"And there is a ten in man himself : the five senses and the power of speech, and that of reproduction ; and the eighth is the spiritual principle communicated at his creation ; and the ninth, the ruling faculty of the soul ; and tenth, there is the distinctive characteristic of the Holy Spirit, which comes to him through faith.

"Besides, in addition to these ten human parts, the law appears to give its injunctions to sight and hearing, and smell and touch and taste, and to the organs subservient to these, which are double the hands and the feet. For such is the formation of man. And the soul is introduced, and previous to it the ruling faculty, by which we reason, not produced in procreation ; so that without it there is made up the number ten, of the faculties by which all the activity of man is carried out. . . .

"Is not man, then rightly said ' to have been made in the image of God '?—not in the form of his [corporeal] structure ; but inasmuch as God creates all things by the Word (λόγῳ) and the man who has become a Gnostic performs good actions by the faculty of reason (τῷ λογικῷ) properly therefore the two tables are also said to mean the commandments that were given to the twofold spirits —those communicated before the law to that which was created, and to the ruling faculty ; and the movements of the senses are both copied in the mind, and manifested in the activity which proceeds from the body."[1]

Even TERTULLIAN, who inveighed so strongly against certain phases of gnosticism, as repre-

[1] *Stromata*, bk. vi., ch. xvi.

sented in the Alexandrian schools, has given interpretations which are no less unreliable and fanciful
than those which he condemns.

Hear him on " Types."

" *Types of the Death of Christ : Isaac, Joseph ; Jacob
against Simeon and Levi ; Moses praying against Amalek;
the Brazen Serpent.*

" On the subject of his death, I suppose you endeavor
to introduce a diversity of opinion, simply because you
deny that the suffering of the cross was predicted of the
Christ of the Creator, and because you contend, moreover, that it is not to be believed that the Creator would
expose His son to that kind of death on which He had
Himself pronounced a curse. 'Cursed,' says he, 'is
every one who hangeth on a tree.' But what is meant by
this curse, worthy as it is of the simple prediction of the
cross, of which we are now mainly inquiring, I defer to
consider, because in another passage, we have given the
reason of the thing preceded by proof. First, I shall
offer a full explanation of the types. And no doubt it
was proper that this mystery should be prophetically set
forth by types, and indeed chiefly by that method ; for
in proportion to its incredibility would it be a stumbling
block, if it were set forth in bare prophecy ; and in proportion, too, to its grandeur, was the need of obscuring it
in shadow, that the difficulty of understanding it might
lead to prayer for the grace of God. First, then, Isaac,
when he was given up by his father, as an offering, himself carried the wood for his own death. By this act he
even then was setting forth the death of Christ, who was
destined by his Father as a sacrifice, and carried the cross

whereon he suffered. Joseph, likewise, was a type of Christ, not, indeed, on this ground (that I may not delay my course) that he suffered persecution for the cause of God from his brethren, as Christ did from his brethren after the flesh, the Jews; but when he is blessed by his father in these words, 'His glory is that of a bullock; his horns are the horns of a unicorn; with them shall he push the nations to the very ends of the earth,'—he was not, of course, designated as a mere unicorn with its one horn, or a minotaur with two; but Christ was indicated in him—a bullock in respect of both His characteristics; to some as severe as a judge, to others gentle as a Saviour, whose horns were the extremities of his cross. For of the antenna, which is a part of a cross, the ends are called horns; while the midway stake of the whole frame is the unicorn. By this virtue, then, of His cross, and in this manner horned, He is both now pushing all nations through faith, bearing them away from earth to heaven; and will then push them through judgment, casting them down from heaven to earth. He will also, according to another passage in the same Scripture, be a bullock when he is spiritually interpreted to be Jacob against Simeon and Levi, which means against the scribes and the pharisees; for it was from them that these last derived their origin. [Like] Simeon and Levi, they consummated their wickedness by their heresy, with which they persecuted Christ. 'Into their counsel let not my soul enter; to their assembly let not my heart be united; for in their anger they slew men,' that is, the prophets; 'and in their self-will they hacked the sinews of a bullock,' that is, of Christ. For against Him did they wreak their fury, after they had slain His prophets, even by affixing Him with nails to the cross. Otherwise it is an idle thing, when, after slaying men, he inveighs against them for the torture of a bullock. Again, in the case of Moses, wherefore did he at that moment particularly, when Joshua was fighting Amalek, pray in a sitting posture with outstretched hands, when in such a conflict it would surely have been more seemly to have bent the knee, and smitten the breast, and to have fallen on the face to the ground, and in such prostration to have offered prayer? Wherefore, but because in a battle fought in the name of that Lord who was one day to fight against the devil, the shape was necessary of that very cross through which Jesus was to win the victory? Why, once more, did the same Moses, after prohibiting the likeness of everything, set up the golden serpent on the pole, and, as it hung there, propose it as an object to be looked at for a cure? Did he not here also intend to show the power of our Lord's cross, whereby that old serpent, the devil, was vanquished—whereby also to every man who was bitten by spiritual serpents, but who yet turned with an eye of faith to it, was proclaimed a cure from the bite of sin, and health for evermore?"[1]

The allegorizing method continued with great pertinacity. AUGUSTINE, the master mind of the fifth century, whose influence yet abounds in the doctrines of both Catholics and Protestants, was under its sway. With him, as with those who preceded him, this allegorical interpretation perverted the Scriptures and obscured truth. A single instance must suffice :

[1] *Against Marcion*, book iii., chapter xviii.

" Hence, also, in the number of the large fishes which our Lord, after His resurrection, showing this new life, commanded to be taken on the right side of the ship, there is found the number fifty, three times multiplied with the addition of three more [the symbol of the Trinity] to make the holy mystery more apparent ; and the disciples' nets were not broken, because in that new life there shall be no schism, caused by the disquiet of heretics. Then [in this new life] man, made perfect and at rest, purified in body and in soul, by the pure words of God which are like silver purged from its dross, seven times refined, shall receive his reward, the denarius. So that with that reward the numbers ten and seven meet in Him. For in this number seventeen [there is found] as in other numbers representing a combination of symbols, a wonderful mystery. Nor is it without good reason that the seventeenth Psalm is the only one which is given complete in the Book of Kings, because it signifies that kingdom in which we shall have no enemy. For its title is, 'A Psalm of David in the day that the Lord delivered him from the hand of all his enemies and from the hand of Saul.' For of whom is David the type, but of Him who, according to the flesh, was born of the seed of David? He, in His church, that is, in His body, still endures the malice of enemies. Therefore the words which from heaven fell upon the ear of that persecutor whom Jesus slew by His voice, and whom He transformed into a part of His body (as the food which we use becomes a part of ourselves), were these : ' Saul, Saul, why persecutest thou me?' And when shall this His body be finally delivered from enemies? Is it not when the last enemy, death, shall be destroyed? It is to that time that the number of the

5

one hundred and fifty-three fishes pertains. For if the number seventeen itself be the side of an arithmetical triangle, formed by placing above each other rows of units, increasing in number from one to seventeen, the whole sum of these units is one hundred and fifty-three: since one and two make three; three and three, six; six and four, ten; ten and five, fifteen; fifteen and six, twenty-one; and so on: continue this up to seventeen, the total one hundred and fifty-three." [1]

The foregoing examples are neither isolated nor peculiar. They represent fully and fairly the prevailing methods of exegesis, falsely so called. Such men shaped the faith and governed the thought of Christianity west of Palestine after the middle of the second century. Other fruitage of their system will be found in another chapter, in the Antinomian and anti-Sabbath doctrines by which the authority of Jehovah and His word were still further undermined. A careful examination of the entire group of "Christian writings" of the first five centuries shows that the age was uncritical and utterly wanting in the learning and habits of thought which prepare men to interpret the Bible. It was brought down to the level of the pagan books with which these men were familiar, both as to its authority and as to the methods by which its meaning was sought. Indeed, its real meaning

[1] Letter lv., chapter xvii., par. 31.

was not sought; the main effort was to show how it accorded with pagan books, and with the philosophical speculations which were popular. If, in any case, it was recognized as the supreme authority, the prevailing methods of interpretation obscured and perverted its meaning, so that men were not governed by what it really taught. Men who did not have clear and correct views of the Bible could not impart them to others. The masses did not possess copies of the Bible, and could not have interpreted it critically had it been in their hands. KILLEN declares these Fathers to be untrustworthy and incompetent interpreters of the Bible. These are his words:

" Earlier writers, such as Origen or Clement of Alexandria, frequently expounded the word of God in the way in which Neo-Platonists explained the pagan mythology —that is, they regard it as an allegory from which they extract whatever meaning happens to be most agreeable to themselves—and too many continued to adopt the same system of interpretation. But among the Fathers of the fourth century there were some who followed sounder principles of exegesis, and carefully investigated the literal sense of the holy oracles. Still, comparatively few of the Christian writers even of this period are very valuable as biblical interpreters. These authors occasionally contradict themselves, and, without acknowledgment, copy most slavishly from each other. Jerome argues that the great duty of an expositor is, not so much to exhibit

the mind of the Spirit, as to set before the reader the con-
flicting sentiments of interpreters.   .   .   .

" But though we discover in these Fathers so many
traces of human infirmity, we must make allowance for
the time in which they lived, and for the prejudices in
which they were educated. Christianity passed through
a terrible ordeal when it suddenly became the religion of
the Empire. Society was by no means prepared for so
vast a change. Already the Gospel had suffered sadly
from adulteration, and now it was more rapidly deterio-
rated. Many who were quite uninstructed became pastors
of the Church; pagan forms and ceremonies were incor-
porated with its ritual; pagan superstitions were recognized as principles of action; and pagan philosophy
corrupted theological science. A dense cloud of errors
soon overspread the whole spiritual firmament." [1]

This chapter may well close with the following quotation from UHLHORN, which shows how
nearly Christianity was ruined through the prevalence of this gnostic allegorizing system, which
obscured or perverted the meaning of the Scriptures, and destroyed their authority.   He says :

" I have already called gnosticism the antipode of
montanism. Such indeed it was. If montanism was
over-narrow, here we find an all-embracing breadth.
Gnosticism knew how to utilize every mental product of
the age. Elements, Oriental and Occidental, in a curious
medley, philosophy and popular superstition—all were

[1] *The Old Catholic Church*, by W. D. Killen, D.D., pp. 99, 100, Edinburgh, 1871.

collected and used as materials for the building of gnostic systems. The myths of the heathen may be found side by side with the Gospel histories, which were only myths to the gnostic. One proof text is taken from the Bible, and the next from Homer or Hesiod, and both alike are used by an allegorical exegesis to support the ready-made creations of the author's fancy. Breadth enough, too, in morality ; no trembling fear of pollution, no anxious care to exclude the influence of heathenism. It was no fiction inspired by the hatred of heresy, when the gnostics were said to be very lax in their adhesion to the laws of morality. Many of them expressly permitted flight from persecution.

"Gnosticism extended far and wide in the second century. There was something very imposing in those mighty systems which embraced heaven and earth. How plain and meagre in comparison seemed simple Christianity! There was something remarkably attractive in the breadth and liberality of gnosticism. It seemed completely to have reconciled Christianity with culture. How narrow the Christian Church appeared! Even noble souls might be captivated by the hope of winning the world over to Christianity in this way ; while the multitude was attracted by the dealing in mysteries with which the gnostic sects fortified themselves by offering mighty spells and amulets, thus pandering to the popular taste. Finally some were no doubt drawn in by the fact that less strictness of life was required, and that they could thus be Christians without suffering martyrdom.

"But the victory of gnosticism would have been the ruin of Christianity. Christianity would have split into a hundred sects, its line of division from heathenism would have been erased, its inmost essence would have been lost, and instead of producing something really new, it would have become only an element of the melting mass, an additional ingredient in the fermenting chaos of religions which characterized the age." [1]

When the fountain of formative Christianity was thus widely and early corrupted, what wonder that the banks of the stream are covered with pagan *débris*, and that the waters are yet turbid from its sediment?

[1] *Conflict of Christianity with Heathenism*, pp. 346, 347.

CHAPTER III.

ASIATIC PAGAN WATER-WORSHIP.

Fundamental Corruption of Christian Baptism through Pagan Water-Worship—"Baptismal Regeneration," the Product of Paganism—Spiritual Purity Sought through Pagan Baptism—Testimonies from Jamblicus, Virgil, Ovid, Herodotus, Juvenal, and others—Baptism and Serpent-Worship—Baptism and Egyptian Sun-Worship—The Sacred Nile—The Prevalence of Water-Worship in India—Sacred Wells—Sacred Rivers—Modern Buddhistic and Modern Hindu Baptism.

Corrupting Influence of Pagan Water-Worship.

THE work of corrupting Christianity went forward systematically, as though an enemy planned to undermine its fundamental truths and ruin the Church through internal errors. When allegorical methods had shorn the Bible of authority, and pushed God, as represented in his word, far away from men, the next important step was to corrupt the developing Church by a false standard of membership, thus planting a sure seed of decay in its heart. In New Testament Christianity, baptism—submersion in water—was the outward symbol of a new spiritual life, beginning through faith and repentance. As such it had a specific mean-

71

ing, and from the earliest times formed the door to membership in the Christian communities. He who accepted Christ as the Messiah, testified such acceptance by being "buried with him in baptism." This was the sign of an inward purity which entitled the believer to a place in the community, and to the fellowship of "those who believed."

It was not the agent by which purity was produced, nor the source from which the new spiritual life sprung. All this was changed by introducing the pagan idea. The materials for such a corrupting process were fully developed in the pagan world.

Various forms of baptism, and the doctrine of baptismal regeneration, were common characteristics of pagan religion before the birth of Christ.

The pagan water-worship cult is secondary only to sun-worship, in age and extent. Its native home was in the East, but it appears in all periods and on both hemispheres. It had two phases: water as an object of worship, and as a means of inspiration; and water used in religious ceremonies to produce spiritual purity. These phases often mingle with each other.

This reverence for water, and faith in its cleansing efficacy, arose from the idea that it was permeated by the divine essence, from which it had supernatural power to enlighten and purify the soul, without regard to the spiritual state of the candidate. This doctrine of baptismal regeneration was transferred to Christianity before the close of the second century, and through it the Church was filled rapidly with baptized but unconverted pagans.

Sun-worship and water-worship were closely united in the pagan *cultus*, as they were in the corrupted Christian baptism. For instance, one fountain noted by Jamblicus is described thus, by BRYANT :

" From this history of the place we may learn the purport of the name by which this oracular place was called. Colophon is Col-Oph-On, Tumulus Dei Solis Pythonis, and corresponds with the character given. The river into which this fountain ran was sacred, and named Halesus ; it was called Anelon, An-El-On, Fons Dei Solis. Halesus is composed of well known titles of the same God." [1]

The following are the words of JAMBLICUS :

" It is acknowledged then by all men that the oracle in Colophon gives its answers through the medium of water. For there is a fountain in a subterranean dwelling from which the prophetess drinks ; and on certain established nights after many sacred rites have been previously performed, and she has drunk of the fountain, she delivers oracles, but is not visible to those that are present. That this water, therefore, is prophetic is from hence manifest.

[1] *Analysis of Ancient Mythology*, by Jacob Bryant, third edition, six vols. London, 1807, vol. i., page 255.

But how it becomes so, this, according to the proverb, is not for every man to know. For it appears as if a certain prophetic spirit pervaded through the water. This is not, however, in reality the case. For a divine nature does not pervade through its participants in this manner, according to interval and division, but comprehends, as it were, externally, and illuminates the fountain, and fills it from itself with a prophetic power. For the inspiration which the water affords is not the whole of that which proceeds from a divine power, but the water itself only prepares us, and purifies our luciform spirit, so that we may be able to receive the divinity ; while in the meantime, there is a presence of divinity prior to this, and illuminating from on high." [1]

Of another oracle Jamblicus says :

" The prophet woman too, in Branchidæ, whether she holds in her hand a wand, which was at first received from some God, and becomes filled with a divine splendor, or whether seated on an axis, she predicts future events, or dips her feet, or the border of her garment in the water, or receives the God by imbibing the vapor of the water ; by all these she becomes adapted to partake externally of the God." [2]

Jamblicus also states that baths were a part of the preparation for being thus inspired. The same combination is shown by VIRGIL, in the following :

[1] Jamblicus—Taylor's translation,— *The Mysteries of the Egyptians, Chaldeans, and Assyrians*, p. 141, Chiswick, 1821.
[2] *Ibid.*, p. 144.

" He started up, and viewing the rising beams of the ethereal sun, in his hollow palms with pious form he raised water from the river, and poured forth to heaven these words: 'Ye nymphs, ye Laurentine nymphs, whence rivers have their origin ; and Thou, O Father Tiber, with thy sacred river, receive Æneas and defend him at length from dangers. In whatever source thy lake contains thee, compassionate to our misfortunes, from whatever soil thou springest forth most beauteous, hornbearing river, monarch of the Italian streams, ever shalt thou be honored with my veneration, ever with my offerings. O grant us thy present aid, and by nearer aid confirm thy divine oracles.' " [1]

Ovid, describing the feast of Pales, held in May, exhibits the same combination of sun and water-worship :

" Often in truth have I leaped over the fires placed in three rows, and the dripping bough of laurel has flung the sprinkled waters. . . . Shepherd, purify the full sheep at the beginning of twilight, let the water first sprinkle them, and let the broom made of twigs sweep the ground. . . . Protect thou alike the cattle, and those who tend the cattle, and let all harm fly afar, repelled from my stalls. Let that happen which I pray for, and may we at the close of the year offer cakes of goodly size to Pales, the mistress of the shepherds. With these words must the goddess be propitiated ; turning to the East, do you repeat these words three times, and in the running stream thoroughly wash your hands." [2]

[1] *Æneid*, book viii., lines 70–82.
[2] *Fasti*, book iv., between lines 728 and 779.

In another place Ovid tells us of Deucalion and Pyrrha, resolving to seek the sacred oracles, in prayer, at the temple of the goddess Themis ; he says :

" There is no delay ; together they repair to the waters of Cephissus, though not yet clear, yet now cutting their wonted channel.   Then when they had sprinkled the waters poured on their clothes and their heads, they turn their steps to the temple of the sacred goddess, the roof of which was defiled with foul moss, and whose altars were standing without fires." [1]

The same combination appears among the Persians.   HERODOTUS, describing the crossing of the Hellespont by Xerxes on his way to the invasion of Greece, says :

" That day they made preparations for the passage over ; and on the following they waited for the sun, as they wished to see it rising, in the meantime burning all sorts of perfumes on the bridges, and strewing the road with myrtle branches.   When the sun rose, Xerxes, pouring a libation into the sea out of a golden cup, offered up a prayer to the sun, that no such accident might befall him as would prevent him from subduing Europe, until he had reached its utmost limits.   After having prayed, he threw the cup into the Hellespont, and a golden bowl and a Persian sword, which they call *acinace*.   But I cannot determine with certainty, whether he dropped these things into the sea as an offering to the sun, or whether he re-

[1] *Metamorphoses*, book i., fable 10, line 651 f.

pented of having scourged the Hellespont and presented these gifts to the sea as a compensation." [1]

Purity Sought through Baptism.

The pagan conception that water produced spiritual purity was expressed in many ways. JUVENAL describes the custom of Roman women who sought to expiate their sins, committed in licentious revelries, as follows:

" She will break the ice and plunge into the river in the depth of winter, or dip three times in the Tiber at early dawn, and bathe her timid head in its very eddies, and thence emerging, will crawl on bending knees, naked and shivering, over the whole field of the haughty kings [the Campus Martius]. If white Io command, she will go to the extremity of Egypt, and bring back water fetched from scorching Meroe, to sprinkle on the temple of Isis, that rears itself hard by the sheep-fold. For she believes that the warning is given her by the voice of the goddess herself." [2]

Mithraic and Gnostic Baptism.

The conception that water cleansed from sin was a prominent feature in Mithraicism and in gnosticism. KING, who is authority on all gnostic questions, says:

[1] Herodotus, book vii., section 54, page 431, N. Y., 1848.
[2] *Satire* vii., lines 520-30, page 59, Evans' translation, Bohn, London, 1852.

" In my account of Mithraicism, notice has been taken of the very prominent part that sacraments for the remission of sin play in the ceremonial of that religion; the following extracts from the grand Gnostic text-book will serve to show how the same notions, (and probably forms) were transferred to the service of Gnosticism.

" '*Baptism Remitting Sins.*'—(*Pistis-Sophia*) (298).

" ' Then came forth Mary and said: Lord, under what form do *baptisms* remit sins? I have heard thee saying that the Ministers of Contentions (ἐριδᾶιοι)[1] follow after the soul, bearing witness against it of all the sins that it hath committed, so that they may convict it in the judgments. Now, therefore, Lord, do the mysteries of Baptism blot out the sins that be in the hands of the Receivers of Contention, so that they shall utterly forget the same? Now, therefore, Lord, tell us in what form they remit sins; for we desire to know them thoroughly. Then the Saviour answered and said: Thou hast well spoken; of truth those Ministers are they that testify against all sins, for they abide constantly in the places of judgment, laying hold upon the souls, convicting all the souls of sinners who have not received the mystery, and they keep them fast in chaos tormenting them. But these contentious ones cannot pass over chaos so as to enter into the courses that be above chaos; in order to convict the souls therefore receiving the mysteries, it is not lawful for them to force so as to drag them down into chaos, where the Contentious Receivers may convict them. But the souls of such as have not received the mysteries, these

---

[1] The Cabiri, " punishers of the ancient mythology, performing their former duties under the new dispensation."

do they desire and hail into chaos; whereas the souls that have received the mysteries, they have no means of convicting, seeing that they cannot get out of their own place, and even if they did come forth, they could not stop those souls, neither shut them up in their chaos. Hearken, therefore, I will declare to you in truth in what form the mystery of Baptism remitteth sins. If the souls when yet living in the world have been sinful, the Contentious Receivers verily do come, that they may bear witness of all the sins they have committed, but they can by no means come forth out of the regions of chaos, so as to convict the soul in the places of judgment that be beyond chaos. But the counterfeit of the spirit testifies against all the sins of the soul, in order to convict it in the places of judgment that be beyond chaos. Not only doth it testify, but also sets a *seal* upon all the sins of the soul, so as to print them firmly upon the soul, that all the Rulers of the judgment place of the sinners may know that it is the soul of a sinner, and likewise know the *number* of sins which it hath committed from the seals that the counterfeit of the spirit hath imprinted upon it, so that they may punish the soul according to the number of its sins; this is the manner in which they treat the soul of a sinner. (300) Now, therefore, if any one hath received the mysteries of Baptism, *those mysteries become a great fire*, exceeding strong and wise, so as to burn up all the sins; and the Fire entereth into the soul secretly, so that it may consume within it all the sins which the counterfeit of the spirit hath printed there. Likewise it entereth into the body secretly, that it may pursue all its pursuers, and divide them into parts—for it pursueth within the body, the counterfeit of the spirit, and Fate—

so that it may divide them apart from the Power and the Soul, and place them in one part of the body—so that the fire separates the counterfeit of the spirit, Fate, and the Body into one portion, and the Soul and the Power into another portion. The mystery of Baptism remaineth in the middle of them, so that it may perpetually separate them, so that it may purge and cleanse them in order that they may not be polluted by *Matter*. Now, therefore, Mary, this is the manner whereby the mystery of Baptism remitteth sins and all transgressions.

(301) " ' And when the Saviour had thus spoken, he said to his disciples : Do ye understand in what manner I speak with you ? Then came forth Mary saying : Of a truth, Lord, I perceive in reality all the things that thou hast said. Touching this matter of the Remission of Sins, thou speaketh aforetime to us in a parable, saying : I am come to bring fire upon the earth, nay more ; let it burn as much as I please. And, again thou hast set it forth openly, saying : I have a baptism wherewith I will baptize and how shall I endure until it be accomplished ? Ye think that I am come to bring peace upon the earth ? By no means so, but dissension, which I am come to bring. For from this time forth there shall be five in one house ; three shall be divided against two, and two against three. This, Lord, is the word that thou speakest openly. But concerning the word that thou spakest : I am come to bring fire upon the earth, and let it burn so much as I please ; in this thou hast spoken of the mystery of Baptism in the world, and let it burn as much as thou pleasest for to consume all the sins of the soul, that it may purge them away. And again thou hast shewn the same forth openly, saying : I have a baptism wherewith I will

baptize, and how shall I endure until it be accomplished? The which is this: Thou wilt not tarry in the world until the baptisms be accomplished to purify all the perfect souls. And again what thou spakest unto us aforetime: " Do ye suppose I am come to bring peace upon earth," etc. (302) This signifieth the mystery of Baptism which thou hast brought into the world, because it hath brought about dissension in the body of the world, because it hath divided the Counterfeit of the spirit, the Body, and the Fate thereof, into one party, and the Soul and the Power into the other party. The same is, " There shall be three against two, and two against three." And when Mary had spoken these things the Saviour said: Well done thou spiritual one in the pure light, this is the interpretation of my saying.' " [1]

The opinion of Simon Magus, a representative Gnostic, concerning baptism is expressed by King thus :

" The Kabbalists, or Jewish Gnostics, like Simon Magus, found a large portion of apostolic teaching in accordance with their own, and easily grafted upon it so much as they liked. Again the Divine power of working miracles possessed by the Apostles and their successors, naturally attracted the interest of those whose chief mystery was the practice of magic. Simon the Magician was considered by the Samaritans to be ' the great Power of God ' ; he was attracted by the miracles wrought by the Apostles, and no doubt he sincerely ' believed '—that is, after his own fashion. His notion of Holy Baptism was probably

[1] *The Gnostics and Their Remains*, pp. 141 ff.

6

an initiation into a new mystery, with a higher Gnosis than he possessed before, and by which he hoped to be endued with higher powers; and so likewise many of those who were called Gnostic Heretics by the Christian Fathers, were not Christians at all, only they adopted so much of the Christian doctrine as accorded with their system." [1]

Baptism of Blood.

The importance which the sun-worship cult attached to baptism is further shown in the baptism of blood, which formed a prominent feature in the Mithraic system of atonement and spiritual enlightenment. This is commented upon by King as follows:

" The ' Taurobolia,' or *Baptism of Blood*, during the later ages of the Western Empire, held the foremost place, as the means of purification from sin, however atrocious. Prudentius has left a minute description of this horrid rite, in which the person to be regenerated, being stripped of his clothing, descended into a pit, which was covered with planks pierced full of holes; a bull was slaughtered upon them whose hot blood, streaming down through these apertures (after the fashion of a shower-bath) thoroughly drenched the recipient below. The selection of the particular victim proves this ceremony in connection with the Mithraic, which latter, as Justin says, had a ' baptism for the remission of Sins '; and the Bull being in that religion the recognized emblem of *life*, his blood necessarily constituted the most effectual laver of regeneration. No more conclusive evidence of

[1] *Ibid.*, p. 6.

the value then attached to the Taurobolia can be adduced, than the fact mentioned by Lampridius that the priest-emperor Heliogabalus thought it necessary to submit to its performance; and a pit, constructed for the purpose as late as the fourth century, has lately been discovered within the sacred precincts of the Temple at Eleusis, the most holy spot in all Greece." [1]

Baptism at Death, and for the Dead.

The following throws light upon the pagan origin of baptism as a saving act, at death, and after death. Describing the nature of the mystic formulæ which the Gnostics used, King says:

" The motive for placing in the coffin of the defunct *illuminato* these ' words of power ' graven on scrolls of lead, plates of bronze, the gems we are considering, and doubtless to an infinitely greater extent on more perishable materials, derives much light from the description Epiphanius gives of the ceremony whereby the Heracleonitæ prepared their dying brother for the next world. They sprinkled his head with water, mingled with oil, and opobalsamum, repeating at the same time the form of words used by the Marcosians in baptism, in order that his *Inner Man*, thus provided, might escape the vigilance of the Principalities and Powers whose domains he was about to traverse, and mount up unseen by any to the Pleroma from which he had originally descended. Their priests therefore instructed the dying man that as he came before these Powers he was to address them in the following words: ' I, the son from the Father, the Father

[1] *Ibid.*, p. 154.

pre-existing, but the son in the present time, am come to behold all things, both of others and of my own, and things not altogether of others, but belonging unto Achamoth (*Wisdom*) who is feminine, and hath created them for herself. But I declare my own origin from the Pre-existing One, and I am going back unto my own from which I have descended.' By the virtue of these words he will elude the Powers and arrive at the Demiurgus in the eighth sphere, whom again he must thus address: ' I am a precious vessel, superior to the female power who made thee, inasmuch as thy mother knoweth not her own origin, whereas I know myself, and I know whence I am ; and I invoke the Incorruptible Wisdom who is in the father and in the mother of your mother who hath no father—nay, not even a male consort, but being a female sprung from a female that created thee, though she herself knows not her mother, but believes herself to exist alone. But I invoke the mother.' At this address the Demiurgus is struck with confusion (as well he might be) and forced to acknowledge the baseness of his origin; whereupon the inner man of the Gnostic casts off his bondage as well as his own *angel* or soul, which remains with the Demiurgus for further use, and ascends still higher into his proper place." [1]

We shall find that this pagan conception became very prominent in the early Church. The " being baptized for the dead," of which Paul speaks, and which was much practised after the second century, sprang from this source; also delaying baptism until the moment of death.

[1] *Ibid.,* pp. 329, 330.

Baptism and Serpent-Worship.

The serpent worshippers formed a prominent branch of the Gnostics, if they were not the originators of the system. Water-worship was a special and fundamental idea in their creed. Witness the following from King.

" The well-informed and temperate Hippolytus, writing at the most flourishing period of these transitional theosophies, thus opens his actual ' Refutation of All Heresies,' and his Fifth Book with the description ' of that sect which hath dared to boast the *Serpent* as the author of their religion, as they prove by certain arguments wherewith *he* hath inspired them. On this account the apostles and priests of this creed have been styled " Naaseni," from " Naas " the Hebrew word for *serpent ;* but subsequently they entitled themselves " The Gnostics," because they alone understood the deep things of religion. Out of this sect sprung many other teachers, who, by diversifying the original doctrines through inventions of their own, became the founders of new systems.' Further on he has a passage bearing immediately upon this subject. ' This *Naas* is the *only thing* they worship, for which reason they are called " Naaseni," (*i. e.*, Ophites, or Serpent-worshippers). From this same word *Naas*, they pretend that all the temples (*ναοί*) under Heaven derive the name. And unto this Naas are dedicated every rite, ceremony, mystery, that is ; in short, not one rite can be found under Heaven into which this Naas does not enter. For they say the Serpent signifies the element Water ; and with Thales of Miletus contend that nothing in the

Universe can subsist without it, whether of things mortal or immortal, animate or inanimate. All things are subject unto him; and he is good, and hath all good things within himself as in the horn of a unicorn, so that he imparts beauty and perfection unto all that is, inasmuch as he pervades all things, as flowing out of Eden, and divided into four heads. . . . This Naas is the "water above the firmament" and likewise "the living water" spoken of by the Saviour. Unto this *Water* all Nature is drawn, and attracts out of the same whatever is analogous to its own nature, each thing after its own kind, with more avidity than the loadstone draws the iron, the ray of the sea-hawk, gold, or amber straws. Then they go on to boast: We are the *Spiritual*, who have drawn our own portion out of the living water of the Euphrates that flows through the midst of Babylon; and who have entered in through the True Gate, the which is Jesus the Blessed. And we of all men are the *only Christians* in the Third Gate, celebrating the Mystery, being anointed with the ineffable ointment out of the *horn*, like David, not out of the *earthen vessel*, like Saul who conversed with the Evil Spirit of carnal concupiscence.'"

The conception of water as a life-producing agent appears prominently in the religion of the Egyptians. They associated it with Osiris, the

[1] *The Gnostics and Their Remains*, p. 224.

The references to Hippolytus, made by King may be found in vol. vi., Ante-Nicene Library, Edinburgh, 1877, pp. 126-194, especially 150, 151. One should read the fifth book of his "Refutation of All Heresies" to see how much water, as a divine agency and power, entered into various phases of the gnostic system. The original of the quotations from the gnostic gospel, *Pistis-Sophia*, may be found in the London edition—Latin—of 1856.

life-producing god of the sun. Speaking of this King says :

"The *symbols* of the same worship have been to some extent explained by persons writing at a time when they were still a living though fast expiring language. Of such writers the most valuable is Plutarch, who in his curious treatise *De Iside et Osiride*, has given the meaning of several of these symbols, and, as it would appear, upon very good authority. According to him, Isis sometimes signifies the Moon, in which sense she is denoted by a Crescent : sometimes the Earth as fecundated by the waters of the Nile. For this reason water, as the seed of Osiris, was carried in a vase in the processions in honor of this goddess." [1]

James Bonwick, F.R.G.S., says :

"The baptism of Egypt is known by the hieroglyphic terms of 'waters of purification.' In Egypt, as in Peru, the water so used in immersion absolutely cleansed the soul, and the person was said to be *regenerated*. The water itself was holy, and the place was known, as afterwards by the Eastern Christians, by the name of *holy bath*. The early Christians called it being 'brought anew into the world.' The ancients always gave a new name at baptism, which custom was afterwards followed by moderns. The Mithraic font for the baptism of ancient Persians is regarded as of Egyptian origin. Augustine may, then, well say that 'in many sacrilegious rites of idols, persons are reported to be baptized.'" [2]

[1] *Ibid.*, p. 106.
[2] *Egyptian Belief and Modern Thought*, p. 416, London, 1878.

The Sacred Nile.

Pagan water-worship everywhere was closely associated with sacred rivers. HARDWICK speaks of the Nile as follows :

"As the Nile, for instance, was a sacred river and as such was invoked in the Egyptian hymns among the foremost of the national gods, whatever bore directly on the culture of the soil, and the succession of the crops in every district of the Nile valley, was enforced among the duties claimed from husbandmen by that divinity. To brush its sacred surface with the balance bucket at a forbidden time was a crime equal in atrocity to that of reviling the face of a king or of a father." [1]

Water-Worship in India.

Sir MONIER-WILLIAMS describes water-worship in India as follows :

" Rivers as sources of fertility and purification were at an early date invested with a sacred character. Every great river was supposed to be permeated with the divine essence, and its waters held to cleanse from all moral guilt and contamination, and as the Ganges was the most majestic, so it soon became the holiest and most sacred of all rivers. No sin was too heinous to be removed, no character too black to be washed clean by its waters. Hence the countless temples with flights of steps lining its banks ; hence the array of priests, called ' Sons of the Ganges,' sitting on the edge of its streams, ready to aid the ablutions of conscience-stricken bathers, and stamp

[1] *Christ and Other Masters*, part iv., p. 84.

them as whitewashed when they emerge from its waters. Hence also the constant traffic carried on in transporting Ganges water in small bottles to all parts of the country."[1]

Sacred wells abound in India, especially in and around the city of Benares. Mr. Williams describes some of these as follows. The one first noted is said to be sacred, because when a certain temple was destroyed by the Mohammedans the outraged god took refuge in this well; thus it became a sacred shrine. Mr. Williams says:

"Thither, therefore, a constant throng of worshippers continually resort, bringing with them offerings of flowers, rice and other grain, which they throw into the water thirty or forty feet below the ground. A Brahman is perpetually employed in drawing up the putrid liquid, the smell or rather stench of which, from incessant admixture of decaying flowers and vegetable matter, makes the neighborhood almost unbearable. This he pours with a ladle into the hands of the expectant crowds, who either drink it with avidity, or sprinkle it reverentially over their persons. A still more sacred well, called the Manikarnika, situated on one of the chief Ghats leading to the Ganges, owes its origin, in popular belief, to the fortunate circumstance that one of Siva's earrings happened to fall on the spot. This well is near the surface and quite exposed to view. It forms a small quadrangular pool, not more than three feet deep. Four flights of steps on the four sides lead to the water, the disgusting foulness of which, in the

[1] *Brahmanism and Hinduism*, by Sir Monier-Williams, M.A., D.C.L., London, 1887, p. 172.

estimation of countless pilgrims, vastly enhances its
efficacy for the removal of sin.   The most abandoned
criminals journey from distant parts of India to the
margin of this sacred pool.   There they secure the services of Brahmans, appointed to the duty, and descending
with them into the water are made to repeat certain texts
and mutter certain mystic formulæ, the meaning of which
they are wholly unable to understand.   Then, while in the
act of repeating the words put into their mouths, they
eagerly immerse their entire persons beneath the offensive
liquid.   The longed-for dip over, a miraculous transformation is the result; for the foul water has cleansed
the still fouler soul.   Few Hindus venture to doubt that
the most depraved sinner in existence may thus be converted into an immaculate saint, worthy of being translated at once to the highest heaven of the god of Benares.

"But to return to the temple of Visvesvara.   I found
when I visited it a constant stream of worshippers
passing in and out.   In fact, Siva, in his character of the
lord of the universe, is the supreme deity of Benares.
Not that the pilgrims are prohibited from worshipping at
the shrines of other gods, but that Siva is here paramount,
and claims the first homage.   Yet this supreme god has
no image; he is represented by a plain conical stone, to
wit, the Linga or symbol of male generative power.   The
method of performing worship in this great central and
confessedly typical temple of Hinduism, appeared to me
very remarkable in its contrast with all Christian ideas
of the nature of worship.   All that each worshipper did
was to bring Ganges water with him, in a small metal
vessel, and pour the water over the stone Linga; at the
same time ringing one of the bells hanging from the roof,

to attract the god's attention towards himself, bowing low in obeisance and muttering a few texts, with the repetition of the god's name. In this way the god's symbol was kept perpetually deluged with water, while the crowds who passed in and out lingered for a time close to the shrine, talking to each other in loud tones. Nor did any idea of irreverence seem to be attached to noisy vociferation in the interior of the sanctuary itself. Nor was any objection made to an unbeliever, like myself, approaching and looking inside; whereas in the south of India I was strictly excluded from all the avenues to the inner Linga sanctuaries.[1] In the courts adjacent to the Linga were other shrines dedicated to various deities, and in a kind of cloister or gallery which encircled the temple, were thousands of stone Lingas crowded together carelessly, and apparently only intended as votive offerings. I noticed the coil of a serpent carved around one or two of the most conspicuous symbols of male generative energy, and the combination appeared to be very significant and instructive."[2]

In another work Mr. Williams says:

" Passing on to the worship of water, especially running water, it is to be observed that river-water is everywhere throughout India held to be instinct with divinity. It is not merely holy, it is especially pervaded by the divine essence. We must, however, be careful to distinguish between the mere sacredness of either fire or water, and their worship as mere personal deities. In *Rig-Veda*, X., 30, X., 9, VII., 47, and other passages of the *Veda*, the Waters are personified, deified and honored as goddesses,

[1] See p. 447.   [2] *Ibid.*, p. 437 ff.

and called the Mothers of earth. In X., 17, 10, their puri-fying power, and in VI., 50, 7, their healing power, is celebrated. They cleanse their worshippers from sin and untruthfulness (I., 6, 22, 23,) . . . The river Saras-vati—called the purifier in *Rig-Veda*, I., 3 10—was to the earlier Hindus what the Ganges was to the later. She was instinct with divinity, and her influence permeated the writers of the Vedic hymns. Sometimes she is iden-tified with the Vedic goddess, vac, speech, and invoked as the patroness of Science.[1]

The confluence of the Ganges with the Jumna and Sarasvati is one of the most hallowed spots in India. Many other rivers are held as being es-pecially sacred. The river Narboda is deemed by some to surpass all others. The mere sight of it cleanses the soul from all guilt. It makes all other waters sacred for thirty miles northward and eigh-teen southward. The banks of all the chief rivers in India are considered holy ground from their source to the sea. Pilgrimages, which continue for six years, are undertaken, the pilgrim going down one bank of the Ganges, and returning by another. Many hardships are incidental to such pilgrimages, but are counted light, and the greater the difficul-ties the greater the resultant merit.

In a still later work, Sir Williams describes the present baptismal custom in Thibet and Mongolia, as follows :

[1] *Religious Thought and Life in India*, p. 346, London, 1883.

"It is noticeable that a kind of baptism is practised in Tibet and Mongolia. It is usual to sprinkle children with consecrated water, or even to immerse them entirely on the third or tenth day after birth. This is called Khrus-sol (according to Jäschke). The priest consecrates the water by reciting some formula, while candles and incense are burning. He then dips the child three times, blesses it, and gives it a name. After performing the ceremony he draws up the infant's horoscope. Then, as soon as the child can walk and talk, a second ceremony takes place, when prayers are said for its happy life, and an amulet or little bag is hung around its neck, filled with spells and charms against evil spirits and diseases."[1]

Other writers support the foregoing, though Sir Williams is too high an authority to need confirmation. ALABASTER says:

"Baptism was a religious rite from very ancient times, the Brahmins holding that if any one who had sinned went to the banks of the Ganges and saying: 'I will not sin again,' plunged into the stream, he would rise to the surface free of sin, all his sins floating away with the water; hence it is called baptism, or the rite of washing off offences, so that they floated away. Sometimes where any one was sick unto death, his relatives would place him by the river, and give him water to drink, and pour water over him till he died, believing that he would thus die holy and go to heaven."[2]

[1] *Buddhism*, etc., p. 356, 357, New York, 1889.
[2] *The Wheel of the Law*; *Buddhism, Illustrated from Siamese Sources*, by Henry Alabaster, London, 1871, pp. 30, 31.

Mr. WILKINS says :

" Dasahara : this festival commemorates the descent of the Ganges from heaven to earth, and is called Dasahara, because bathing at this season is said to remove all the sins committed in ten births, *i. e.*, during ten different lives. This is a most interesting ceremony. Thousands upon thousands of the people bring their offerings of flowers, fruits and grain to the river-side, and then enter the sacred stream. It is a thing worthy of note that although in many places men and women bathe together, the men having simply a cloth around their loins, and the women often having the upper part of their bodies exposed, I have never seen the slightest impropriety of gestures on these occasions. In some festivals, as previously noticed, the grossest impropriety of language and gesture are freely indulged in : but at bathing festivals I have never noticed anything indecent. It is proper to bathe in the Ganges, for those who live near enough ; but other rivers may take the place of the Ganges, and legends have been manufactured to show that their virtues are even greater than those of the Ganges ; if there is no river convenient, then a tank can be substituted." [1]

Modern Buddhistic Baptism.

The modern water-worship connected with Buddhism is described by Sir Monier-Williams in his latest book [2] as follows :

[1] *Modern Hinduism*, by W. J. Wilkins, p. 219, New York, 1887. Consult also, *Religions of India*, by A. Barth, p. 278 ff., New York, 1882.

[2] *Buddhism in its Connection with Brahmanism and Hinduism, and in its Contrast with Christianity*, second edition, London, 1890.

"In Burmah, where a good type of southern Buddhism is still to be found, the New Year's festival might suitably be called a ' water festival.' It has there so little connection with the increase of the New Year's light that it often takes place as late as the early half of April.[1] It is, however, a movable feast, the date of which is regularly fixed by the astrologers of Mandalay, who ' make intricate calculations based on the position of various constellations.' The object is to determine on what precise day the king of the Naths will descend upon the earth and inaugurate the new year. When the day arrives all are on the watch, and just at the right moment, which invariably occurs at midnight, a cannon is fired off, announcing the descendant of the Nath king upon earth. Forthwith (according to Mr. Scott) men and women sally out of their houses, carrying pots full of water, consecrated by fresh leaves and twigs of a sacred tree, repeat a formal prayer, and pour out the water on the ground. At the same time all who have guns of any kind discharge them, so as to greet the new year with as much noise as possible.

" Then, ' with the first glimmer of light ' all take jars full of fresh water and carry them off to the nearest monastery. First they present them to the monks, and then proceed to bathe the images. This work is usually done by the women of the party, ' who reverently clamber up ' and empty their goblets of water over the placid features of the Buddhas and Bodhisattvas. Then begins the Saturnalia. All along the road are urchins with squirts and syringes, with which they have been furtively practising for the last few days. The skill thus acquired is exhibited by the accuracy of their aim. Cold streams of water catch

[1] See Mr. Scott's *Burmah*, ii., 48.

the ears of the passers-by. Young men and girls salute
one another with the contents of jars and goblets. Shouts
of merriment are heard in every quarter. Before breakfast
every one is soaked, but no one thinks of changing his garments, for the weather is warm and ' water is everywhere.'
The girls are the most enthusiastic, as they generally go
in bands and carry copious reservoirs along with them ;
' unprotected males' are soon routed. Then a number of
' zealous people' go down to the river, wade into the water
knee-deep, splash about, and drench one another till they
are tired. No one escapes. For three days no one likes to
be seen with dry clothes. The wetting is a compliment."[1]

"In Tibet there is a water festival in the seventh or
eighth month (about our August and September). At
this festival the Lamas go in procession to rivers and lakes
and consecrate the waters by benediction or by throwing
in offerings. Huts and tents are erected on the banks,
and people bathe and drink to wash away their sins. It
concludes with dancing, buffoonery, and masquerading."[2]

LYDIA MARIA CHILD thus describes
Baptism among the Hindus :

" Water is supposed to cleanse the soul and guard from
evil. When a child is born priests sprinkle it, and sprinkle
the dwelling, and all the inmates of the house bathe.
They do this from an idea that it keeps off evil spirits.
People perform ablutions before they eat ; and priests
purify themselves with water, accompanied with prayers,
on innumerable occasions. When a man is dying, Brahmins hasten to plunge him into a river, believing that the
departing soul may be thus freed from impurities before
it quits the body. Some rivers are deemed more pecul-

[1] Pp. 341, 342.   [2] P. 344.

iarly holy and efficacious than others, such as the Ganges, the Indus, and the Chrishna ; the water of the Ganges is used on all the most solemn occasions. Images of the deities are washed with it, and Brahmins are sprinkled with it, when inducted into the priestly office. Happy above other men is he who is drowned in that sacred stream. Once in twelve years the waters of Lake Cumbhacum are supposed to be gifted with power to cleanse from all sin. As this period approaches, Brahmins send messengers in every direction to announce when the great day of ablution will take place. The shores are crowded with a vast multitude of men, women, and children from far and near. They plunge, at a signal from the officiating Brahmin, and in the universal rush many a one is suffocated or has his limbs broken. Water from the Ganges is kept in the temples, and when the people are dying they often send from a great distance to obtain some of it. Before devotees put their feet into a river they wash their hands and utter a prayer." [1]

These witnesses show us that water-worship and baptism, the water being variously employed, by immersion, sprinkling, pouring, etc., has formed a prominent feature in Oriental paganism from the earliest time until now. It passed from the Orient to Greece and Rome. Perhaps the stream from Egypt was an independent one, which came from the south. Before considering the immediate contact of pagan water-worship with early Christianity, it is necessary to note its existence outside of the Orient and Egypt.

[1] *The Progress of Religious Ideas,* New York, 1853, vol. i., p. 124.

7

CHAPTER IV.

WATER-WORSHIP IN NORTHERN EUROPE AND IN MEXICO.

Water-Worship Prominent in Many Ways, and Associated with Holy Seasons—Infant Baptism among the Scandinavians and Teutons—Pagan "Christening of Children"—Sacred Water as a Safeguard against Disease, etc.—Virtue of Water Used for Mechanical Purposes—Water Sprites—Similarity between Roman Catholicism and Paganism of Mexico—Aztec Baptism—Prayer for "Baptismal Regeneration" of Child by Mexican Midwife.

THE existence of a widespread system of water worship in Northern Europe is attested by the direct history of paganism, by the history of Christianity at its first introduction, by the decrees of councils, capitularies, and similar documents. These sources show that the Allamanns, Franks, and others worshipped rivers and fountains, and used water in various ways for sacred purposes. They prayed upon the banks of sacred rivers and at sacred fountains. Springs which gushed from the earth were considered especially sacred, as being produced directly by divine agency. Lighted candles were used in the worship of fountains and wells. This custom continues until the present day in the semi-religious habits of the people, who gaze into wells by the light of a candle on Christmas and Easter nights. Sacred brooks and rivers were believed to have been produced from the pouring of water by the gods out of bowls and urns.

Water drawn at holy seasons, such as midnight and sunrise, has always been known as "holy water." Running spring-water gathered on holy Christmas night, while the clock strikes twelve is yet known as *heilway*, and is believed to be good for certain diseases. At the present time the common people of Northern Europe believe that between eleven and twelve on Christmas night, and on Easter night, *spring water changes into wine.* A similar faith is found as far back as the latter part of the fourth century, which is noted by Chrysostom in an Epiphany sermon preached at Antioch.

The following quotation will show that pagan water-worship was indigenous in Northern Europe as well as in the Orient :

" It is no less remarkable that a kind of infant baptism was practised in the North, long before the dawning of Christianity had reached those parts. Snorri Sturlason, in his chronicle, speaking of a Norwegian nobleman who lived in the reign of Harald Harfagra, relates that he poured water on the head of a new-born child, and called him Hakon, from the name of his father. Harald himself had been baptized in the same manner, and it is noted of King Olaf Tryggvason, that his mother, Astrida, had him thus baptized and named as soon as he was born. The Livonians observed the same ceremony, which also prevailed among the Germans, as appears from a letter which the famous Pope Gregory the third sent to their Apostle Boniface directing him expressly how to act in this respect. It is probable that all these people might intend, by such a rite, to preserve their children from the sorceries and evil charms which witched spirits might employ against them at the instant of their birth. Several nations of Asia and America have attributed such a power to ablutions of this kind ; nor were the Romans without such a custom, though they did not wholly confine it to new-born infants." [1]

S. Baring Gould testifies concerning pagan baptism in Scandinavia as follows :

" Among the Scandinavians, infant baptism was in vogue long before the introduction of Christianity, and the rite accompanied the naming of the child. Before the accomplishment of this rite, the exposition of the babe was lawful, but after the ceremony it became murder. A baptism in blood seems to have been practised by the Germans and Norsemen in remote antiquity ; to this the traditions of the horny Sigfrid, or Sigurd, and Wolfdietrich point. Dipping in water, and aspersion with water, or with blood of a victim, was also customary among the Druids, as was also the baptism of fire, perhaps borrowed by them from

[1] *Northern Antiquities of the Ancient Scandinavians*, translated from the French of P. H. Mallet by Bishop Percy, edition revised by J. A. Blackwell, London, 1847, p. 206.

the Phœnicians. This was that passing through the fire to Molech alluded to repeatedly in the Jewish Scriptures." [1]

There is an excellent picture of baptism among the pagan Teutons, by Konrad Maurer, in which the author shows, in detail, the relation between infant baptism among the Greeks, Romans, Teutonic pagans, and Teutonic Christians. *The Nation* for September 22, 1881, speaks of Mr. Maurer's work as follows [2]:

"A large portion of Maurer's monograph is devoted to showing how the ceremonies connected with heathen baptism were adopted by the Christian Church, and in tracing to a heathen source the rights and privileges secured to children by baptism in the Church. The author suggests that the laying at the breast was a recognition of the child on the mother's part, and that the granting of the right of baptism was a recognition of the child on the part of the father, and that this was the chief significance of the latter ceremony; although it would seem from Havamal, in the Elder Edda, that spiritual blessings were also secured to the infant by the sprinkling of holy water. Baptism made the child an *heir* both among the heathen and among the old Teutonic Christians, and the fact that among both it had so many things in common, that it took place soon after the birth of the child, and was connected with the naming of it; that there were god-fathers

[1] *The Origin and Development of Religious Belief*, by S. Baring Gould, M.A., London, 1869, p. 393.

[2] For details see *Uber die Wasserweihe des Germanischen Heidenthumes*, von Konrad Maurer, as found in the Transactions of the Bavarian Academy of Science for 1880.

and god-mothers, and that presents were given, makes the question an exceedingly interesting one. But the author goes farther, and proves from ancient laws of the Germans, Visigoths, and Anglo-Saxons, that the rite of baptism is to be performed within the ninth day after the birth of the child ; and here he calls attention to the ancient Roman custom of giving the name to a female infant on the eighth, and to a male infant on the ninth day after birth, and quotes Roman law to show that this naming day was of legal importance to the child. A similar custom is also found among ancient Greeks, where the seventh day after the birth of the child was celebrated with *cleansing*, gifts, sacrifices, banqueting, and other ceremonies. Maurer suggests that this seventh day of cleansing among the heathen Greeks was of the same legal value to the child as the day of sprinkling with water among the Teutons, and that it determined whether the child should live or be exposed. Roman law establishes the fact that the eighth day after birth for girls, and the ninth for boys was a *Dies lustricus*—that is, a day on which a religious rite *(lustratio)* for infants took place, and on which names were given to them, whence it was called *solonnitas nominalium*. The day was observed by bringing the infants to the temple, by banquets, etc.[1] We find, therefore, among the old Greeks, and what is of vastly more importance, in the old Roman laws, a day set apart for infants on which they get their names, and this naming connected with the observation of certain ceremonies. What the precise nature of these rites was, we are not told ; but inasmuch as the Roman documents designate

[1] See on this point Marquardt, *Das Privat-leben der Romer*, i., pp. 81, 82.

thereby the term *lustratio*, there can scarcely be room for doubt that it must have been a symbolic cleansing by means of water. And since the *Dies lustricus* confessedly secured legal rights to the infant, the question lies near at hand whether the old Teutonic heathen borrowed the baptismal right from the ancient Romans, or whether baptism was an original institution among the Aryans before they became divided into Teutons, Romans, etc. There can be no doubt, on the one hand, that the *Dies lustricus* of the Romans obtained among the Christians in fixing the day for baptism, especially since it corresponded so nearly with the Mosaic day for circumcision; and on the other hand, that just as many of the old Teutonic feasts were turned into festivals, so the form of the Teutonic baptism was largely adopted by the Christians in Northern Europe."

Baptism was undoubtedly an ancient Aryan rite, which existed before the division of the race, of which Mr. Maurer speaks. For supplementary proof of the lustration and naming of infants among the Greeks and the Romans, consult Smith's *Dictionary of Greek and Roman Antiquities*, pp. 800, 801. Also, for lustration, by holy water, of children and adults, see *The Life of Greeks and Romans*, by E. Guhl and W. Koner, p. 282, London (no date, but since 1862). See also Tertullian, *Concerning Idolatry* (chap. xvi.), for reference to pagan " Naming Festivals."

JACOB GRIMM (*Teutonic Mythology*, 4 vols., London, 1883), a most painstaking and scholarly authority, shows that the Christianity of the present century is yet deeply imbued with the residuum of the ancient pagan water-worship.   He says:

" Superstitious Christians then believed two things : a hallowing of the water at midnight of the day of baptism, and a turning of it into wine at the time of the beth-phania.   Such water the Germans called *heilawâc*, and ascribed to it a wonderful power of healing diseases and wounds, and of never spoiling.

" Possibly even in Syria an old pagan drawing of water became veiled under new Christian meanings.   In Germany other circumstances point undisguisedly to a heathen consecration of water : it was not to be drawn at midnight, but in the morning *before sunrise down stream* and *silently*, usually on *Easter Sunday*, to which the above explanations do not so well apply : this water does not spoil, it restores youth, heals eruptions, and makes the young cattle strong.   Magic water, serving for unchristian divination, is to be *collected before sunrise on a Sunday* in one glass from *three flowing springs;* and *a taper is lighted* before a glass, as before a divine being.   Here I bring in once again the Hessian custom mentioned at page 58 : On Easter Monday youths and maidens walk to the Hollow Rock in the mountains, draw *water from the cool spring in jugs to carry home*, and throw flowers in as an offering.   Apparently this water-worship was Celtic likewise.   The water of the rock spring Karnant makes a broken sword whole again.   Curious customs show us in what manner young girls in the Pyrenees country *tell their own fortunes in the spring water* on May-day morning." [1]

[1] Vol. ii., pp. 586, 587.

Water Securing Immunity from Disease.

Sacred water as a means of lustration and of immunity from disease is yet a prominent characteristic of Northern European water-worship. GRIMM thus describes it :

"In a spring near Nogent men and women bathed on St. John's eve: Holberg's comedy of *Kilde-reisen* is founded on the Copenhagen people's practice of pilgriming to a neighboring spring on *St. Hans aften* to heal and invigorate themselves in its waters. On Midsummer-eve the people of Ostergötland journeyed according to ancient custom to Lagman's bergekälla near Skeninge, and drank of the well. In many parts of Germany some clear fountain is visited at Whitsuntide, and the water drunk in jugs of a peculiar shape. Still more important is Petrarch's description of the annual bathing of the women of Cologne in the Rhine; it deserves to be quoted in full, because it plainly proves that the cult prevailed not merely at here and there a spring, but in Germany's greatest river. From the Italian's unacquaintance with the rite, one might infer that it was foreign to the country whence all Church ceremonies proceeded, and therefore altogether unchristian and heathenish. But Petrarch may not have had a minute knowledge of all the customs of his country ; after his time, at all events, we find even there a lustration on St. John's Day (described as ancient custom then dying out). And long before Petrarch, in Augustine's time, the rite was practised in Libya, and is denounced by that Father as a relic of paganism. Generally sanctioned by the Church it certainly was not, yet it might be allowed here and there, as a not unapt reminder of the Baptizer in the Jordan, and now interpreted of him, though once it had been heathen. It might easily come into extensive favor, and that not as a Christian feast alone : to our heathen forefathers St. John's Day would mean the festive middle of the year, when the sun turns, and there might be many customs connected with it. I confess, if Petrarch had witnessed the bathing in the river at some small town, I would the sooner take it for a native rite of the ancient Germani ; at Cologne, the holy city so renowned for its relics, I rather suspect it to be a custom first introduced by Christian tradition." [1]

Water used for mechanical purposes was also looked upon as possessing peculiar virtues. Down to the present time the Servians catch the water which rebounds from the paddles of mill wheels. Women go early on St. George's day, April 23d, to catch such water for bathing purposes. Some carry it home on the evening before the twenty-third and sprinkle broken bits of green herbs and boughs upon it. They believe that all evil and harm " will then glance off their bodies like water off the mill wheel," as the result of such bathing. A trace of the same superstition remains in Servia in the popular warning, " Not to flirt the water off your hands after washing in the morning," else you flirt away your luck for the day.

Many religious and superstitious practices are prevalent in Northern Europe in times of drouth,

[1] Vol. ii., pp. 588, 590.

in order to propitiate the divinities, either good or evil, and secure a rainfall. Certain goddesses which were prominent in the Northern European mythologies, especially Nerthus and Holda, were closely connected with water-worship. The former represented the earth and is spoken of as " the bath-loving Nerthus." Holda lived in wells. She was identical with the Roman Isis. " When it snows, she is making her bed, and the feathers fly. She stirs up snow as Donar does rain." In Prussia when it snows the people say: " The angels are shaking their beds, and the flakes of down drop to the earth." It was believed that Holda haunted the lakes and fountains and might be seen bathing at the hour of noon. Mortals could reach her dwelling by passing through a well. She was supposed to pass through the land at Christmas time, bringing fertility by her presence.[1]

On the fifth of August the lace-makers of Brussels pray to Mary that their work "may keep as white as snow." It was believed that Holda appeared as an ugly old woman, long-nosed, big-toothed, with bristling and thick-matted hair. The common people still say of a man whose hair is tangled and in disorder : " He has had a jaunt with Holda."

---

[1] Several attributes of the heathen goddess Holda passed over to the worship of Mary in the Roman Catholic Church.

The pagan fear of water sprites still exists in Sweden.   On crossing any water after dark it is thought advisable to *spit three times*, as a safeguard against their evil influences.[1]   It is also thought to be dangerous to draw water from a well without saluting the divinity which governs it.   This custom remains among modern Greeks.   A thief is supposed to be safe in his evil course if he sacrifices to the water sprites, by throwing a little of that which he has stolen into a stream.   In Esthonia, the newly married wife drops a present into the well of the house where she is to reside. In 1641, Hans Ohm, of Sommerpahl in Esthonia, built a mill upon a sacred stream.   Bad harvests followed for several years until the peasants fell upon the mill, burnt it down and destroyed the piles in the water.   Ohm went to law and obtained a verdict against the peasants.   But to rid himself of new and grievous persecutions, he induced pastor Gutslaff to write a treatise especially combating this superstition.   The Esthonians replied, when asked how good or bad weather could depend upon springs and brooks : " It is our ancient faith : the men of old have so taught us.   Mills have been burnt down on this brook before now."   They called it " Holy Brook," and believed that when

[1] Compare this with what is said by Pliny, and with the use of spittle by the Roman Catholics in baptism.   Chapter V. of this book.

they wanted rain it could be produced by throwing something into the stream.[1]

Many similar stories abound in the modern literature of Esthonia. Although less refined, the water-worship mythology of Northern Europe was as widespread and persistent in its influence as that of Southern Europe or of Asia. Its influence upon Christianity was not less strongly marked, and the modifications which it produced in Christian baptism continue in a great degree to the present day. The universal sway of pagan baptism and its essential unity are shown by turning from Northern Europe to the extreme point of another continent and considering

Water-Worship in Mexico.

PRESCOTT speaks of the amazement with which the early Spaniards beheld the points of similarity between the customs of the pagan Mexicans and the Roman Catholic Church ; he says :

" With the same feelings they witnessed another ceremony, that of the Aztec baptism ; in which, after a solemn invocation, the head and lips of the infant were touched with water, and a name given to it ; while the goddess Cioacoatl, who presided over childbirth, was implored that the sin which was given to us before the beginning of the

---

[1] See *A Short Account of the Holy Brook*, etc., by John Gutslaff, Pastor at Urbs in Liefland, Dorpt, 1644, pp. 25, 258.

world might not visit the child, but that, cleansed by these waters, it might live and be born anew." [1]

A full account of this pagan baptism in Mexico is given by SAHAGUN-DE-BERNARDINO, as follows:

"When everything necessary for the baptism had been made ready, all the relations of the child were assembled, and the midwife, who was the person that performed the rite of baptism, was summoned. At early dawn they met together in the court-yard of the house. When the sun had risen the midwife, taking the child in her arms, called for a little earthen vessel of water, while those about her placed the ornaments which had been prepared for the baptism in the midst of the court. To perform the rite of baptism, she placed herself with her face towards the west, and immediately began to go through certain ceremonies. . . . After this she sprinkled water on the head of the infant, saying: 'O my child! take and receive the water of the Lord of the world, which is our life, and is given for the increasing and renewing of our body. It is to wash and to purify. I pray that these heavenly drops may enter into your body and dwell there; that they may destroy and remove from you all the evil and sin which was given to you before the beginning of the world; since all of us are under its power, being all the children of Chalchivitlycue' (the goddess of water). She then washed the body of the child with water and spoke in this manner: 'Whencesoever thou comest, thou that art hurtful to this child, leave him and depart from him, for he now liveth anew and is born anew; now he is purified and cleansed afresh, and our Mother Chalchivit-

[1] *Conquest of Mexico*, vol. iii., p. 369 f., Philadelphia, J. B. Lippincott.

lycue again bringeth him into the world.' Having thus prayed, the midwife took the child in both hands, and lifting him towards heaven, said : ' O Lord, thou seest here thy creature, whom thou hast sent into this world, this place of sorrow, suffering, and penitence. Grant him, O Lord, thy gifts and thine inspiration, for thou art the great God, and with thee is the great goddess.' Torches of pine were kept burning during the performance of these ceremonies. When these things were ended, they gave the child the name of some one of his ancestors, in hope that he might shed a new lustre over it. The name was given by the same midwife or priestess who baptized him." [1]

A full discussion of baptismal ceremonies among the pagans of Mexico may be found in H. H. Bancroft's works,[2] which discussion fully supports the foregoing from Prescott and Sahagun.

[1] *Hist. de Neuva Espana*, lib. vi., cap. xxxvii.
[2] *The Native Races, Myths, and Languages*, vol. iii., p. 369 *seq.*, San Francisco, 1882.

CHAPTER V.

GREEK WATER-WORSHIP.

Sprinkling and Immersion Both Used—Prominence of "Baptismal Regeneration"—Lustral Water at Temple Doors—Baptism of Animals—Influence of "The Greek Mysteries" on Christian Baptism—Initiatory Baptisms—Scenic Illustrations—Mithraic Baptism Engrafted on Grecian—"Creed," "Symbol," Drawn from Grecian Water-Worship Cult—Identity of Grecian and Roman Catholic Forms—The Use of Spittle in Pagan Baptism.

IN our survey of the wide field, we now come to a still more specific view of the pagan cult, along the line of Hellenic thought, where it impinged most strongly upon Christianity.

POTTER writes learnedly of water-worship among the Greeks, in the following :

"At least every person who came to the solemn sacrifices was purified by water. To which end at the entrance to the temples there was commonly placed a vessel full of holy water. This water was consecrated by putting into it a burning torch taken from the altar. The same torch was sometimes made use of to sprinkle those who entered into the temple. Thus we find in Euripides, and also in Aristophanes, where the scholiast observes that this torch was used because of the quality of fire, which is thought to purify all things. Instead of the torches, they sometimes used a branch of laurel, as we find in Pliny. Thus Sozomen, where he speaks of Valentinian following Julian into a pagan temple, relates that when they were about to enter, a priest holding certain green boughs dropping water besprinkled them after the Grecian manner. Instead of laurel, olive was sometimes used. Thus we find in Virgil:

> ' Old Corianæus compassed thrice the crew,
> And dipped an olive branch in holy dew.'

"This custom of surrounding here expressed, was so constant in purifying that most of the terms which relate to any sort of purification are compounded with περι, around, thus: περιραίνειν, περιμάττεσθαι, περιθειοῦν, περιαγνίζειν, etc.

"The vessel which contained the water of purification was termed, περιρραντήριον. And the Latin word *lustrare*, which signifies to purify or expiate, came hence to be a general word for any sort of surrounding or encompassing. Thus it is used by Virgil, . . . *dum montibus umbræ lustrabunt convexo.* Spondanus tells us that before the sacrifices of the celestial gods, the worshippers had their whole bodies washed, or if that could not be, at least their hands; but for those that performed the sacred rites to the infernal gods, a small sprinkling was sufficient. Sometimes the feet were washed as well as the hands; whence came the proverbs, ανιπτοις χερσιν and ανιπτοις ποσιν. In Latin *illotis manibus*, and *illotis pedibus*,—which are usually applied to men who undertake anything without due care and preparation. Porphyry tells us there was a programme fixed up, that no man should go beyond the περιρραντήριον till he had washed his hands; so great a crime was it counted to omit this ceremony, that

8

Timarchides hath related a story of one Asterius, who was struck dead with thunder because he had approached the altar of Jupiter with unwashed hands. Nor was this custom only used at solemn sacrifices, but also at the smallest parts of their worship. Hector tells us that he was afraid to make so much as a libation to Jupiter before he had washed.

> ' I dread with unwashed hands to bring,
> My incensed wine to Jove, an offering.'

" And Telemachus is said, in Homer's *Odysseis*, to have washed his hands before he ventured to pray to the gods. This they did out of a conceit that thereby they were purified from their sins ; and withal signifying that nothing impure ought to approach the deities. On the same account, they sometimes washed their clothes, as Homer relates of Penelope, before she offered prayers to the gods. The water used in purification was required to be clear, and without mud and all other impurities. It was commonly fetched from fountains and rivers. The water of lakes or standing ponds was unfit for this purpose. So also was the purest stream if it had been a considerable time separated from its source." [1]

Baring Gould gives another picture of baptism and lustration among the Greeks :

" Among the Greeks, the mysteries of Cotys commenced with a purification, a sort of baptism, and the priests of the Thracian Goddess derived from this their title of βάπται. But Apollo, from a supposed derivation of his

[1] *Antiquities of Greece*, by John Potter, D.D., vol. i., pp. 261-263, Edinburgh, 1832.

name from ἀπολούω to purify, was the special god of
expiation by baptismal acts. In Thessaly was yearly
celebrated a great festival of cleansing. A work bearing
the name of *Musæus* was a complete ritual of purifications.
It distinguished the ceremonies into two orders, τελεταί
and καθαρμοί. The latter were purifications and expia-
tions accomplished by special sacrifices. The former
resembled the purifications performed in the Mysteries.
The usual mode of purification was dipping in water, or
it was performed by aspersion. The baptism of immersion was called λοῦτρον, the other περίῤῥανσις. These
sacraments were held to have virtue independent of the
disposition of the candidate, an opinion which called forth
the sneer of Diogenes when he saw some one undergoing
baptism by aspersion: 'Poor wretch! do you not see
that, since these sprinklings cannot repair your gram-
matical errors, they cannot repair either the faults of
your life?'

"Lustral water was placed at the temple doors, with
which the profane were purified by the priests. Usually,
before entering a temple, the hands and feet were washed.
At Athens, when the prœdrai had opened the assembly,
the peristiarch offered a sacrifice, and then with the blood
of the victim sprinkled the seats. The herald then took
the place of the peristiarch, and continued the lustration
by burning incense; for fumigations (περιθειώσεις), constituted another means of purification. In default of water,
sand was used, and salt, which, as a symbol of incorruption,
was regarded as possessed of purificatory virtue. Every
impure act, murder, the touch of a corpse, illegitimate
commerce, even the conjugal act, demanded purification.
In like manner, baptism was practised by the Romans,

and Juvenal satirizes those who washed away their sins by dipping the head thrice in the morning into the waters of the Tiber.[1]

"On the feast of Pales, the goddess of flocks, the shepherds purified themselves by washing their hands thrice in new fallen dew; or a lustration was effected by aspersion with consecrated water shaken from a branch of laurel or olive; in reference to which rite Propertius prays, much as once did David: '*Spargite me lymphis.*'"[2]

The Grecian idea of baptism is well set forth by OVID, in the following lines :

> "From Greece the custom came, for Greece esteems
> Those free from guilt who bathe in sacred streams.
> Thus did old Pelius once Patroclus lave,
> And free from stain in the Hæmonian wave :
> As, in that same Hæmonian stream before,
> Acastus, Pelius freed from Phocus' gore.
> The Phasian sorceress, in her fiery car,
> Borne by yoked dragons through the liquid air,
> To credulous Ægeus supplication made,
> And from him won an undeservèd aid.
> In Naupactoan Achelous' flood,
> His horrid hands stained with his mother's blood,
> Alcæmon bathed ; 'Cleanse me from crime,' he cried,
> Nor by the stream was his request denied.
> Ah, vain the hope, and far to easy they,
> Who think the water takes such guilt away."
>
> *Fasti*, book ii., line 58 ff.

[1] See Satire vi., line 522.
[2] *The Origin and Development of Religious Belief*, by S. Baring Gould, M.A., vol. i., p. 397, London, 1869.

Influence of the " Greek Mysteries."

The influence of the Greek mysteries in corrupting Christian baptism is more plainly seen than that of any other specific department of the pagan cult. These mysteries were the remnant of the oldest religion known to the Greeks. They embodied the worship of the gods of the productive forces in nature, and of the gods of death. The most important centre of this cult was at Eleusis, where the worship was celebrated in the largest temple in Greece. The chief elements in the cult were initiation, sacrifice, and scenic representations of the great facts in the processes of nature and in human life. The main conception in the initiation was that the candidate must be purified before he could approach God. The initiated, being thus purified, were inducted to a divine life and to the hope of a resurrection. The ceremonial began with the proclamation : " Let no one enter whose hands are not clean, and whose tongue is not prudent." [1]

Confession was followed by a kind of baptism. [2] The candidates for initiation bathed in the pure waters of the sea. The manner of bathing and the

[1] See Keil, *Attische Cults aus Inschriften*, *Phlologus*, bd. xxiii., 212, 259, 592, 622 ; also Weingarten, *Histor. Zeitschrift*, bd. xlv., 1881, p. 441 ff.

[2] See Tertullian, *De Baptismo*, chap. v. ; and Clem. of Alex., *Strom.*, book v., chap. iv.

number of immersions varied with the degree of
guilt which they had confessed. They came from
the bath new men. It was a *κάθαρσις,* a *λουτρὸν,* a
"laver of regeneration." Certain forms of abstinence were imposed; they had to fast; and when
they ate they had to abstain from certain kinds of
food.[1]

After this purification came a *σωτήρια,* "a great
public sacrifice of salvation"; also personal sacrifices. After an interval of two days still more
sacrifices, shows, and "processions" followed. The
initiated carried lighted torches and sang "loud
peans in honor of the God."[2] Then came the
scenic representations at night. The initiated stood
outside the temple in deep darkness. Suddenly the
door opened, and in a blaze of light the drama of
Demeter and Kore appeared—in which the loss of
the daughter, the wanderings of the mother, and
the birth of the child, were enacted. This symbol-
ized the earth in its great experiences, as well as the
corresponding experiences in human life. All this
was enacted in silence. Each man saw and medi-
tated for himself. It was believed that this gave
purity to the initiated, changed their relations to
the gods, and made them "partakers of a life to

---

[1] *Cf.* Hatch, *Influence of Greek Ideas and Usages upon the Christian
Church.*

[2] *Cf.* Clem. of Alex., *Exhortation to the Heathen,* chap. xii.

come."[1]   Mithraicism had a similar form of initiation, a prominent feature of which was a sacred meal, upon a "holy table," of which the initiated took part after they were purified.   The societies which practised these mysteries existed on a large scale during the earliest centuries of our era, and had a marked influence upon the earliest Christian communities, and upon the subsequent church. HATCH thus describes these effects :

"It was inevitable when a new group of associations came to exist side by side with a large existing body of associations, from which it was continually detaching members, introducing them into its own midst, with the practices of their original societies impressed upon their minds, that this new group should tend to assimilate, with the assimilation of their members, some of the elements of these existing groups.

"This is what we find to have been in fact the case.   It is possible that they made the Christian associations more secret than before.   Up to a certain time there is no evidence that Christianity had any secrets.   It was preached openly to the world.   It guarded worship by imposing a moral bar to admission.   But its rites were simple and its teaching was public.   After a certain time all is changed ; mysteries have arisen in the once open and easily accessible faith, and there are doctrines which must not be declared in the hearing of the uninitiated."[2]

---

[1] *Cf*. Hatch as above ; and Lenormant, in *Contemporary Review* for September, 1880.

[2] "The objection which Celsus makes (c. *Cels.*, i., 1, Keim, p. 3) to the secrecy of the Christian associations would hardly have held good in the apostolic age.

The effect of these pagan mysteries upon Christian baptism, and upon the Lord's Supper also, will be more clearly seen when we remember how simple a ceremony New Testament baptism was. It followed immediately upon confession of faith in Christ. There was no preparatory ceremony, no ritual, only the simple formula. There was no confusion or controversy concerning the "mode," for submersion alone was known within Christian circles.

When the current of history emerges at and after the middle of the second century, marked changes appear which are so identical with gnosticism and the Greek mysteries that there can be no question as to their source.[1] Among these changes were the following:

The name is changed, and the new terms used come directly from the familiar mysteries. Justin

Origen admits (c. *Cels.*, i., 7) that there are exoteric and esoteric doctrines in Christianity, and justifies it by (1) the philosophies, (2) the mysteries. On the rise of this conception of Christian teaching as something to be hidden from the mass, *cf.* the Valentians in Tert., c. *Valent.*, i., where there is a direct parallel drawn between them and the mysteries ; also the distinction of men into two classes—πνευματικοὶ and ψυχικοὶ or ὑλικοί,—among the Gnostics. Yet this very secrecy was naturalized in the Church. *Cf.* Cyril Hier., *Catech.*, vi., 30 ; Aug. in *Psalm* ciii. ; *Hom.*, xcvi., in *Joan ;* Theodoret, *Quæst.* xv., *in Num.*, and *Dial.*, ii., *(Inconfusus) ;* Chry., *Hom.*, xix., *in Matt.* Sozomen's (i., 20, 3) reason for not giving the Nicene creed is significant alike as regards motive and language."—Hibbert Lectures, 1888, p. 293 and footnote.

[1] *Cf.* Hatch, p. 294 ff.

calls it φωτισμός, φωτιξεσθαι, " enlightenment."[1]
Those who had passed the tests were " sealed,"
φραγις—a term from the mysteries.[2] It was also
called μυστήριον,[3] "Mysteries" and many other terms,
all of which sprung from the " mysteries of Greek
paganism, rather than from the New Testament."

The time of baptism of adults was changed to
meet the pagan conception of it as a purifying and
saving act. A long preparation was demanded,
and, to meet the pagan idea that it removed sins,
it was often deferred until near the close of life in
order to make the most of both worlds.[4] The initiated in the Greek mysteries were given a pass-
word : σύμβολον or σύνθημα. " So the catechumens
had a formula which was only entrusted to them in
the last days of their catechumenate, the baptismal
formula itself, and the Lord's Prayer."[5] A special
rite accompanied the giving of this formula. Otherwise both the Lord's Prayer and the Creed were
kept as " mysteries"; the technical name for creed
remains to this day as σύμβολον " symbol."[6]

Hatch quotes a description of baptism in the
Roman Catholic Church, which shows every essen-

[1] *Apol.*, i., 61.
[2] *Cf*. Clem. of Alex., *Stroma.*, bk. ii., chap. iii.
[3] Chrysostom, *Hom.*, 85, in *Joan*, xix., 34.
[4] *Cf. Apostol. Const.* and *Bingham Antiq. in loco.*
[5] Hatch, p. 298.
[6] *Cf. Dic. Chris. Antiq.*, " Baptism " and " Creed."

tial feature of the Eleusinian mysteries transferred to "Christian baptism," falsely so called. The account is taken from Mabillon.[1]   He writes thus:

"I will abridge the account which is given of the practice at Rome so late as the ninth century. Preparation went on through the greater part of Lent. The candidates were examined and tested; they fasted; they received the secret symbols, the Creed and the Lord's Prayer. On Easter eve, as the day declined towards afternoon, they assembled in the Church of St. John Lateran. The rites of exorcism and renunciation were gone through in solemn form, and the rituals survive. The Pope and his priests come forth in their sacred vestments, with lights carried in front of them, which the Pope then blesses; there is a reading of lessons and a singing of psalms. And then, while they chant a litany, there is a procession to the great bath of baptism, and the water is blest. The baptized come forth from the water, are signed with the cross, and are presented to the Pope one by one, who vests them in a white robe and signs their foreheads again with the cross. They are arranged in a great circle, and each of them carries a light. Then a vast array of lights is kindled; the blaze of them, says a Greek Father, makes night continuous with dawn. It is the beginning of a new life. The mass is celebrated—the mystic offering on the cross is represented in figure; but for the newly baptized the chalice is filled, not with wine, but with milk and honey, that they may understand, says an old writer, that they have entered already upon the promised land. And there was one more symbolical rite

[1] Com. Praev. Ad. Ord. Rom. Museum, Ital., ii., xcix.

in that early Easter sacrament, the mention of which is often suppressed—a lamb was offered on the altar, afterwards, cakes in the shape of a lamb. It was simply the ritual which we have seen already in the mysteries. The purified crowd at Eleusis saw a blaze of light, and in the light were represented in symbol life and death and resurrection.[1]

Anointing and Baptism.

The use of anointing oil in baptism was borrowed directly from paganism. To economize space, and fortify by the power of a great name, we again quote from Hatch :

"The general inference of the large influence of the Gnostics on baptism, is confirmed by the fact that another element, which certainly came through them, though its source is not certain, and is more likely to have been Oriental than Greek, has maintained a permanent place in most rituals—the element of anointing. There were two customs in this matter, one more characteristic of the East, the other of the West—the anointing with (1) the oil of exorcism before baptism and after the renunciation of the devil, and (2) the oil of thanksgiving, which was used immediately after baptism, first by the presbyter and then by the bishop, who then sealed the candidate on the forehead. The very variety of the custom shows how deep and yet natural the action of the Gnostic systems, with the mystic and magic customs of the Gnostic societies or associations, had been on the practices and ceremonies of the Church."[2]

[1] Hatch, p. 299.   [2] Pp. 307–308.

Use of Spittle in Baptism.

The pagan doctrine of exorcism was carried still further, and baptism was corrupted yet more by adding the use of human saliva as a " charm." This arose from the general use of spittle by the pagans as a talisman against harm and evil influences. Rev. JOHN JAMES BLUNT says:

" Human saliva was heretofore very generally used as a charm, and was thought particularly efficacious against the venom of poisonous animals. Pliny quotes some authorities to prove that the pernicious powers of toads and frogs may be disarmed by this means, and that serpents may be rendered innoxious by spitting into their mouths. The testimony of Varro is also cited by the naturalist to show that there were people in the Hellespont, near Pasium, who could cure the bite of snakes by their saliva. . . . It is remarkable that in administering the rite of baptism the priest, among other ceremonies, moistens a napkin with his own saliva, and then touches with it the eyes and nose of the child, accompanying the action by the word *Ephphatha*. It was with a similar rite that Roman infants received their names on the *Dies Lustricus*." [1]

The Satirists were not slow in holding up these various superstitions to deserved ridicule. PERSEUS touches the spittle superstition in the following stanza :

[1] *Vestiges of Ancient Manners and Customs in Italy and Sicily*, by John James Blunt, pp. 164, 165, and 167. London, 1823.

> "Lo! from his little crib the grandam hoar,
> Or aunt, well-versed in superstitious lore,
> Snatches the babe ; in lustral spittle dips
> Her middle finger, and anoints his lips
> And forehead." [1]

PLINY supports the statement of Blunt as follows :

" The Marsi, in Italy, are still in possession of the same power, for which it is said they are indebted to their origin from the son of Circe, from whom they acquired it as a natural quality. But the fact is, that all men possess in their bodies a poison which acts upon serpents, and the human saliva, it is said, makes them take to flight as though they had been touched with boiling water. The same substance, it is said, destroys them as soon as it enters their throat, and more particularly so, if it should happen to be the saliva of a man who is fasting." [2]

In another place Pliny enumerates many uses to which spittle is put :

" But it is the fasting spittle of a human being that is, as already stated by us, the sovereign preservative against the poison of serpents : while, at the same time, our daily experience may recognize its efficacy and utility in many other respects. We are in the habit of spitting, for instance, as a preservative from epilepsy, or, in other words, we repel contagion thereby ; in a similar manner, too, we repel fascinations, and the evil presages attendant upon meeting a person who is lame in the right leg. We ask pardon of the gods, by spitting in the lap, for entertain-

[1] Perseus, Satire ii., 31.
[2] *Natural History*, book vii., chap. ii., vol. ii., p. 126. London, edition 1856.

ing some too presumptuous hope or expectation. On the same principle, it is the practice, in all cases where medicine is employed, to spit three times on the ground, and to conjure the malady as often, the object being to aid the operation of the remedy employed. It is usual, too, to mark a boil, when it first makes its appearance, three times with fasting spittle. What we are going to say is marvellous, but it may easily be tested by experiment : if a person repents of a blow given to another, either by hand or with a missile, he has nothing to do but to spit at once in the palm of the hand which has inflicted the blow, and all feelings of resentment will be instantly alleviated in the person struck. This, too, is often verified in the case of a beast of burden when brought on its haunches with blows ; for upon this remedy being adopted, the animal will immediately step out and mend its pace. Some persons, however, before making an effort, spit into the hand in the manner above stated, in order to make the blow more heavy. We may well believe, then, that lichens and leprous spots may be removed by a constant application of fasting spittle ; that ophthalmia may be cured by anointing, as it were, the eyes every morning with fasting spittle ; that carcinomata may be effectually treated by kneading the root of the plant known as 'apple of the earth ' with human spittle ; that crick in the neck may be got rid of by carrying fasting spittle to the right knee with the right hand, and to the left knee with the left ; and when an insect has got into the ear it is quite sufficient to spit into that organ to make it come out. Among the counter-charms, too, are reckoned the practice of spitting into the urine the moment it is voided, of spitting into the shoe of the right foot before putting it on, and of spitting while a person is passing a place in which he has incurred any kind of peril.

"Marcion, of Smyrna, who has written a work on the virtues of simples, informs that the sea scolopendra will burst asunder if spit upon ; and that the same is the case with bramble frogs, and other kinds of frogs. Opilius says that serpents will do the same if a person spits into their open mouth ; and Salpe tells us that when any part of the body is asleep the numbness may be got rid of by the person spitting into his lap, or touching the upper eyelid with his spittle. If we are ready to give faith to such statements as these, we must believe also in the efficacy of the following practices : upon the entrance of a stranger, or when a person looks at an infant while asleep, it is usual for the nurse to spit three times upon the ground ; and this, although infants are under the special guardianship of the god Fascinus, the protector, not of infants only, but of generals as well, and a divinity whose worship is entrusted to the vestal virgins, and forms a part of the Roman rites." [1]

[1] *Natural History*, book xxviii., chap. vii., vol. v., pp. 288-90. London, 1856.

CHAPTER VI.

PAGAN WATER-WORSHIP TRANSFERRED TO CHRISTIANITY.

Testimony from Tertullian, Barnabas, Justin, Methodius, the Apostolic Constitutions, etc.—Holy Water, or Repeated Baptism, Borrowed without Change—Magical Effects of Holy Water, the Same in Christian as in Pagan Cult—Baptism of Animals by Holy Water, to Produce Magical Results—Holy Water Prepared after the Pagan Method—Consecration of Baptismal Waters Borrowed from Pagan Combination of Sun- and Water-Worship—The Church Filled with Baptized but Unconverted Pagans, and so Passed under Pagan Control.

Baptism in the Early Church.

TURNING to the earlier Church fathers, who formulated much which has come to us as Christian doctrine, we find the pagan idea of baptism repeated in all its essential characteristics. We have seen that the Greek fathers came to Christianity by way of Neo-Platonism rather than the New Testament. They accepted Christianity as containing many excellent things, but not as the only authoritative system of faith. They followed the popular syncretic tendency, and combined Christianity with the pagan faith in which they had been educated.

128

Tertullian wrote a special treatise on the question of baptism, which represents the pagano-Christian creed in fulness and in detail. I transcribe his words in part, and call attention to the similarity and the points of identity between these and the pagan theories already presented. Chapter i. of the treatise opens with these words :

" Happy is the sacrament of our water, in that, by washing away the sins of our early blindness, we are set free [and admitted] into eternal life ! . . . But we, little fishes, after the example of our Ιχθυς, Jesus Christ, are born in water, nor have we safety in any other way than by permanently abiding in [that] water." [1]

In the succeeding chapters Tertullian goes on to show that water was " chosen as a vehicle of divine operation " because it was the element over which the divine spirit brooded in creation. He says :

" *Why should WATER be chosen as a vehicle of divine operation ? Its prominence first of all in Creation.—* Mindful of this declaration as of a conclusive prescript, we nevertheless [proceed to] treat [the question], ' How *foolish* and *impossible* it is to be formed anew by water. In what respect, pray, has this material substance merited an office of so high dignity ? ' The authority, I suppose, of the liquid element has to be examined. This, however, is found in abundance, and that from the very beginning. For [water] is one of those things, which, before all the furnishing of the world, were quiescent with God in a yet

[1] *On Baptism*, Ante-Nicene Library, vol. xi., p. 231 ff.

9

unshapen state.   In the first beginning, saith [Scripture],
'God made the heaven and the earth.   But the earth was
invisible, and unorganized, and darkness was over the
abyss; and the Spirit of the Lord was hovering over the
waters.'   The first thing, oh man, which you have to
venerate, is the *age* of the waters, in that their substance
is ancient; the second, their *dignity*, in that they were
the seat of the Divine Spirit, more pleasing [to him], no
doubt, than all the other then existing elements.   For the
darkness was total thus far, shapeless, without the ornament of stars; and the abyss gloomy; and the earth
unfurnished; and the heaven unwrought; water alone
—always a perfect, gladsome, simple material substance,
pure in itself—supplied a worthy vehicle to God.   What
[of the fact] that waters were in some way the regulating
powers by which the disposition of the world thencefor-
ward was constituted by God?   For the suspension of
the celestial firmament in the midst He caused by
' dividing the waters '; the suspension of ' the dry land,'
He accomplished by ' separating the waters.'   After the
world had been hereupon set in order through [its] elements, when inhabitants were given it, ' the waters ' were
the first to receive the precept, ' to bring forth living
creatures.'   Water was the first to produce that which
had life, that it might be no wonder in baptism if waters
know how to give life.   For was not the work of fashion-
ing man himself also achieved with the aid of waters?
Suitable material is found in the *earth*, yet not apt for the
purpose unless it be moist and juicy; which [earth] ' the
waters ' separated the fourth day before into their own
place, temper with their remaining moisture to a clayey
consistency.   If, from that time onward, I go forward in

recounting universally, or at more length [than I have already done] the evidences of the 'authority' of this element which I can adduce to show how great is its power or its grace; how many ingenious devices, how many functions, how useful an instrumentality, it affords the world, I fear I may seem to have collected rather the praises of water than the reasons of baptism; although I should [thereby] teach all the more fully, that it is not to be doubted that God has made the material substance which he has disposed throughout all his products and works, obey him also in his own peculiar sacraments; that [the material substance] which governs terrestrial life acts as agent likewise in the celestial."

The title of chapter iv. is:

" *The primeval hovering of the Spirit of God over the waters typical of baptism. The universal element of water thus made a channel of sanctification. Resemblance between the outward sign and the inward grace.*"

In this chapter Tertullian teaches that the divine power hovering over the water, in creation, made it "holy" as well as life-producing, and that these qualities continue to exist in all water. He says:

" Thus the nature of the waters, sanctified by the Holy One, itself conceived withal the power of sanctifying. Let no one say, 'Why, then, are we, pray, baptized with the very waters which then existed in the first beginning?' Not with those very waters, of course, except in so far as the *genus* indeed is one, but the *species* very many. But what is an attribute to the *genus* reappears likewise in the *species.* And accordingly it makes no difference whether a man be washed in a sea or a pool, a stream or a font, a lake or a trough; nor is there any distinction between those whom John baptized in the Jordan and those whom Peter baptized in the Tiber, unless withal [it be thought that] the eunuch whom Philip baptized in the midst of his journeys with chance water, derived [therefrom] more or less of salvation [than others]. All waters, therefore, in virtue of the pristine privilege of their origin, do, after invocation of God, attain the sacramental power of sanctification; for the Spirit immediately supervenes from the heavens, and rests over the waters, sanctifying them from himself; and being thus sanctified, they imbibe at the same time the power of sanctifying."

In chapter v. Tertullian discusses the pagan theory as embodied in the rites of Isis, Mithra, the Apollinarian and the Eleusinian games, and attempts to show that cleansing cannot come through these rites, because idols cannot imbue the water with sanctifying power, and evil spirits can impart only evil influences. He expresses faith in their power to do this, thus showing that he still held to the fundamental features of the pagan system, and made them the basis of his theory of Christian baptism.

The Epistle of Barnabas presents a similar combination of fact and fancy concerning baptism. The pagan idea of water as a regenerating power underlies the theory set forth, and the reader will see how Scripture is misquoted and misapplied in the effort to give a scriptural coloring to the pagan theory. Chapter xi. of the epistle is entitled :

"*Baptism and the Cross Prefigured in the Old Testament.*— Let us further inquire whether the Lord took any care to foreshadow the water [of baptism] and the cross. Concerning the water, indeed, it is written, in reference to the Israelites, that they should not receive that baptism which leads to the remission of sins, but should procure another for themselves. The prophet therefore declares: ' Be astonished, O heaven, and let the earth tremble at this, because this people hath committed two great evils ; they have forsaken me, a living fountain, and have hewn out for themselves broken cisterns. Is my holy hill Zion a desolate rock ? For ye shall be as the fledglings of a bird, which fly away when the nest is removed.' And again saith the prophet : ' I will go before thee and make level the mountains, and will break the brazen gates, and bruise in pieces the iron bars ; and I will give thee the secret, hidden, invisible treasures, that they may know that I am the Lord God.' And, ' He shall dwell in a lofty cave of the strong rock.' Furthermore, what saith He in reference to the Son ? ' His water is sure ; ye shall see the King in His glory, and your soul shall meditate on the fear of the Lord.' And again He saith in another prophet : ' The man who doeth these things shall be like a tree planted by the courses of waters, which shall yield its fruit in due season ; and his leaf shall not fade, and all that he doeth shall prosper. Not so are the ungodly, not so, but even as chaff, which the wind sweeps away from the face of the earth. Therefore the ungodly shall not stand in judgment, nor sinners in the counsel of the just; for the Lord knoweth the way of the righteous, but the way of the ungodly shall perish.' Mark how He has described at once both the water and the cross. For these words imply, Blessed are they who, placing their trust in the cross, have gone down into the water; for, says He, they shall receive their reward in due time; then He declares, I will recompense them. But now He saith, ' Their leaves shall not fade.' This meaneth that every word which proceedeth out of your mouth in faith and love shall tend to bring conversion and hope to many. Again, another prophet saith, ' And the land of Jacob shall be extolled above every land.' This meaneth the vessel of His Spirit, which He shall glorify. Further, what says He? ' And there was a river flowing on the right, and from it arose beautiful trees; and whosoever shall eat of them shall live forever.' This meaneth that we indeed descend into the water full of sins and defilement, but come up bearing fruit in our heart, having the fear [of God] and trust in Jesus in our spirit. ' And whosoever shall eat of these shall live forever.' This meaneth : Whosoever, He declares, shall hear thee speaking, and believe, shall live forever." [1]

JUSTIN MARTYR combines his theory with his description of the rite of baptism as follows. Note the misquotation of Scripture :

" I will also relate the manner in which we dedicated ourselves to God when we had been made new through Christ; lest, if we omit this, we seem to be unfair in the

[1] *Epistle of Barnabas*, chap. xi., Ante-Nicene Library, vol. i., pp. 120, 121.

explanation we are making. As many as are persuaded and believe that what we teach and say is true, and undertake to be able to live accordingly, are instructed to pray and to entreat God, with fasting, for the remission of their sins that are past, we praying and fasting with them. Then they are brought by us where there is water, and are regenerated in the same manner in which we were ourselves regenerated. For, in the name of God, the Father and Lord of the universe, and of our Saviour, Jesus Christ, and of the Holy Spirit, they then receive the washing with water. For Christ also said: 'Except ye be born again, ye shall not enter into the kingdom of heaven.' Now, that it is impossible for those who have once been born to enter into their mother's womb, is manifest to all. And how those who have sinned and repent shall escape their sins is declared by Esaias, the prophet, as I wrote above; he thus speaks: 'Wash you, make you clean; put away the evil of your doings from your souls; learn to do well; judge the fatherless, and plead for the widow; and come and let us reason together, saith the Lord. And though your sins be as scarlet, I will make them white like wool; and though they be as crimson, I will make them white as snow. But if ye refuse and rebel, the sword shall devour you; for the mouth of the Lord hath spoken it.' And for this [rite] we have learned from the apostles this reason. Since at our birth we were born without our own knowledge or choice, by our parents coming together, and were brought up in bad habits and wicked training; in order that we may not remain the children of necessity and of ignorance, but may become the children of choice and knowledge, and may obtain in the water the remission of sins formerly committed, there is pronounced over him who chooses to be born again, and has repented of his sins, the name of God, the Father and Lord of the universe ; he who leads to the laver the person that is to be washed, calling him by this name alone. For no one can utter the name of the ineffable God ; and if anyone dare to say that there is a name, he raves with a hopeless madness. And this washing is called illumination, because they who learn these things are illuminated in their understandings. And in the name of Jesus Christ, who was crucified under Pontius Pilate, and in the name of the Holy Ghost, who, through the prophets, foretold all things about Jesus, he who is illuminated is washed." [1]

The pagano-Christian theory of baptism and baptismal regeneration, variously expressed, is found in Methodius, *The Banquet of the Ten Virgins*, chapter vi ; in Clement of Alexandria, *The Instructor*, chapter xii ; in Tertullian, *Against Marcion*, book i., chapter xxviii ; in Cyprian, *Epistles*,[2]—1, *To Donatus ;* 22, *To Clergy at Rome ;* 51, *To Antonianus ;* and 75, *To Magnus ;* also *Testimonies against the Jews*, paragraph 65 ; also, *A Treatise on Re-baptism*, by an unknown author, published in connection with Cyprian's writings, on page 402 of Clark's edition Ante-Nicene Library, vol. xiii.

The *Apostolic Constitutions* clearly set forth the

[1] *First Apology*, ch. li, Ante-Nicene Library, vol. ii., p. 59. T. & T. Clark.
[2] Numbering as found in vol. viii. of Ante-Nicene Library. Clark's edition.

result of this perversion of New Testament doctrines concerning baptism. The late Baron BUN-
SEN, one of the most eminent of German scholars
and statesmen, has grouped the teachings of the
Constitutions upon the question of baptism in
such a way as to give the reader a better view
than is possible by quoting these writings ver-
batim. Although these *Constitutions* are not the
work of the apostles, they are of great historic
value in presenting a picture of the practices of
the early Church. Bunsen thinks that the *Constitutions* present "a genuine, though not textual,
picture of the Ante-Nicene Church." He says :

"As soon as we take away what belongs to the bad taste
of the fiction, all the ethic introductions and occasional
moralizing conclusions, and, in general, all which manifestly is re-written with literary pretension, and lastly, as
soon as we expunge some easily discernible interpolations
of the fourth and fifth centuries, we find ourselves unmistakably in the midst of the life of the Church of the
second and third centuries." [1]

The summary made by Bunsen is given below.
By analyzing it the reader will see how much that
is extra-scriptural, and anti-scriptural, was associated with baptism thus early. By comparison
with the pagan water *cultus*, the source of these
errors is plainly apparent.

[1] Vol. ii. of *Hippolytus and His Age*, page 236.

" And at the time of the crowing of the cock let them first pray over the water. Let the water be drawn into the font, or flowing into it. And let it be thus if they have no scarcity. But if there be a scarcity, let them pour the water which shall be found into the font; and let them undress themselves, and the young shall be first baptized. And all who are able to answer for themselves, let them answer. But those who are not able to answer, let their parents answer for them, or one other numbered amongst their relations. And after the great men have been baptized, at the last the women, they having loosed all their hair, and having laid aside the ornaments of gold and silver which were on them. Let not anyone take a strange garment with him into the water.

" And at the time which is appointed for the baptism, let the bishop give thanks over the oil, which, putting into a vessel, he shall call the oil of thanksgiving. Again, he shall take other oil, and exorcising over it, he shall call it the oil of exorcism. And a deacon shall bear the oil of exorcism and stand on the left hand of the presbyter. Another deacon shall take the oil of thanksgiving and stand on the right hand of the presbyter.

" And when the presbyter has taken hold of each one of those who are about to receive baptism, let him command him to renounce, saying: 'I will renounce thee, Satan, and all thy service, and all thy works.' And when he has renounced all these, let him anoint him with the oil of exorcism, saying: 'Let every spirit depart from thee.'

" And let the bishop or the presbyter receive him thus unclothed, to place him in the water of baptism. Also let the deacon go with him into the water, and let him say to him, helping him that he may say: 'I believe in the only true God, the Father Almighty, and in his only begotten Son, Jesus Christ, our Lord and Saviour, and in the Holy Spirit, the Quickener, [the Consubstantial Trinity]. One Sovereignty, one Kingdom, one Faith, one Baptism; in the Holy Catholic Apostolic Church, in the life everlasting. Amen.'

"And let him who receives (baptism) repeat after all these: 'I believe thus.' And he who bestows it shall lay his hand upon the head of him who receives, dipping him three times, confessing these things each time.

"And afterwards, let him say again: 'Dost thou believe in our Lord Jesus Christ, the only Son of God, the Father; that he became man in a wonderful manner for us, in an incomprehensible unity, by his Holy Spirit, of Mary, the Holy Virgin, without the seed of man; and that he was crucified for us under Pontius Pilate, died of his own will, once for our redemption, rose on the third day, loosening the bonds (of death), he ascended up into heaven, sat on the right hand of his good Father on high, and he cometh again to judge the living and the dead at his appearing and his kingdom? And dost thou believe in the Holy Good Spirit and Quickener, who wholly purifieth; and in the Holy Church?'

"Let him say again: 'I believe.'

"And let them go up out of the water, and the presbyter shall anoint him with the oil of thanksgiving, saying: 'I anoint thee with holy anointing oil in the name of Jesus Christ.' Thus he shall anoint every one of the rest, and clothe them as the rest, and they shall enter into the Church."[1]

[1] *Hippolytus and His Age*, by C. C. J. Bunsen, D.C.L., vol. ii., pp. 321–7. London, 1852.

After entering the church the candidate was anointed a second time, in connection with the "prayer of blessing" and the "kiss of peace." This was followed by the service of the communion, which included bread, wine, *milk and honey*, showing that the Lord's Supper, as well as baptism, was corrupted with pagan elements.

Holy Water.

The use of holy water formed an important part of the pagan system. It was a sort of continuous baptism, a succession of baptismal acts. That it is wholly unscriptural, and in every way foreign to Christian baptism, is too obvious to need statement. There are abundant evidences of its pagan origin ; among them are the following :

"Some persons derive the use of holy water in the churches from the Jews ; but that it has been derived from the ancient heathens of Rome is now very generally believed, and, indeed, is warmly defended by the intelligent Ecclesiastics at Rome, on the principle that, as the heathen temples have been turned into Christian churches, so it was well to lay hold of the heathen practices and turn them into Christian customs, thus reconciling the heathen to a change of religion, seeing it did not change their favorite rites and customs. At the entrance of the heathen temples there were vessels of water with which the votaries sprinkled themselves as they entered to worship, and as it seemed desirable to make as little difference as possible, so as to induce the heathen to conform the more readily to Christian worship, similar vessels of water consecrated or made holy, were placed at the entrance of the Christian churches, and thus the custom has continued. Such at least is the origin generally ascribed at Rome to this practice, and such the principle on which it is defended by the men of mind and judgment among the priesthood." [1]

Dr. JOSEPH PRIESTLEY thus supplements Mr. Seymore's statements :

"In Popish churches the first thing that we are struck with is a vessel of what is called *holy water*, into which those who enter dip their fingers, and then mark their foreheads with the sign of the cross. This holy water, there can be no doubt, came from the *lustral water* of the pagans, as, indeed, learned Catholics allow. This water was also placed at the entrance of the heathen temples, and those who entered were sprinkled with it." [2]

CONYERS MIDDLETON attests the pagan origin of holy water :

" The next thing that will of course strike one's imagination is their use of holy water ; for nobody ever goes in or out of a church but is either sprinkled by the priest, who attends for that purpose on solemn days, or else serves himself with it from a vessel, usually of marble, placed just at the door, not unlike to one of our baptismal fonts. Now, this ceremony is so notoriously and directly transmitted to them from paganism, that their own writers

---

[1] *A Pilgrimage to Rome*, by Rev. M. Hobart Seymore, M.A., p. 537. London, 1848.

[2] *History of the Corruption of Christianity*, by Joseph Priestley, LL.D., F.R.S., vol. ii., p. 111. Birmingham, 1782.

make not the least scruple to own it. The Jesuit la Cerda, in his notes on a passage of Virgil, where this practice is mentioned, says : ' Hence was derived the custom of Holy Church to provide purifying or holy water at the entrance of their Churches.' ' *Aquaminarium* or *Amula*,' says the learned Montfaucon, ' was a vase of holy water, placed by the Heathen at the entrance of their Temples to sprinkle themselves with.' The same vessel was by the Greeks called περιρραντηριον; two of which, the one of gold, the other of silver, were given by Crœsus to the Temple of Apollo at Delphi ; and the custom of sprinkling themselves was so necessary a part of all their religious offices, that the method of excommunication seems to have been by prohibiting to offenders the approach and use of the holy water-pot. The very composition of this holy water was the same also among the Heathens, as it is now among the Papists, being nothing more than a mixture of salt with common water ; and the form of the sprinkling brush, called by the ancients *aspersorium* or *aspergillum* (which is much the same with what the priests now make use of), may be seen in bas-reliefs, or ancient coins, wherever the insignia, or emblems of the Pagan priesthood, are described, of which it is generally one.

" Palatina, in his lives of the popes, and other authors, ascribes the institution of this holy water to Pope Alexander the First ; who is said to have lived about the year of Christ 113 ; but it could not have been introduced so early, since, for some ages after, we find the primitive fathers speaking of it as a custom purely heathenish, and condemning it as impious, and detestable. Justin Martyr says that it was invented by demons, in imitation of the true baptism signified by the Prophets, that their votaries might also have their pretended purifications by water; and the Emperor Julian, out of spite to the Christians, used to order the victuals in the markets to be sprinkled with holy water, on purpose either to starve, or force them to eat what by their own principles they esteemed polluted.

"Thus we see what contrary notions the Primitive and Romish Church have of this ceremony: the first condemns it as superstitious, abominable, and irreconcilable with Christianity; the latter adopts it as highly edifying and applicable to the improvement of Christian piety: the one looks upon it as the contrivance of the Devil to delude mankind; the other as the security of mankind against the delusions of the Devil. But what is still more ridiculous than even the ceremony itself, is to see their learned writers gravely reckoning up the several virtues and benefits, derived from the use of it, both to the soul and the body; and to crown all, producing a long roll of miracles, to attest the certainty of each virtue, which they ascribe to it. Why may we not, then, justly apply to the present people of Rome what was said by the Poet of its old inhabitants, for the use of this very ceremony?

> "'Ah, easy Fools, to think that a whole Flood
> Of water e'er can purge the Stain of Blood!'
> Ovid, *Fasti*, ii., 45.[1]

Mr. Middleton wrote as a polemist against Romanism, and hence he took especial pains to apply

[1] A letter from Rome, by Conyers Middleton, D.D., *Works*, vol. iii., p. 71 ff. London, 1752.

these facts to that system of Christianity exclusively. Such an application is manifestly unjust, since baptism was fully corrupted before the formal establishment of the Papacy, and many corrupt elements are yet retained in Protestantism. Mr. Middleton's suggestion that men were debarred from the use of holy water as a punishment is sustained by the following from ÆSCHINES. In his speech against Ctesiphon he said :

" Now the said law-giver (Solon) excludes as well the fearful, and him that refuses to serve in war, as him that deserts his rank in battle, from the privilege of holy lustration, and from the assembly of the people." [1]

The magical virtues which Christians came to ascribe to holy water are essentially identical with those which the pagans attributed to it. Mr. Seymore, whom we have already quoted, gives a catalogue of the uses and virtues of holy water, which he found in the chapel of St. Carlo Borromeo at Rome. Similar virtues are still attributed to it by modern Catholics.[2] The catalogue is as follows :

" Holy water possesses much usefulness when Christians sprinkle themselves with it with due reverence and devotion. The Holy Church proposes it as a remedy and

[1] *Orations,* etc., p. 115. Oxford, 1755.
[2] See *The Church Progress and Catholic World*, St. Louis, Mo., July 5, 1890.

assistant in many circumstances, both spiritual and corporeal, but especially in these following :

" *Its spiritual usefulness.*

" 1. It drives away devils from places and persons.

" 2. It affords great assistance against fears and diabolical illusions.

" 3. It cancels venial sins.

" 4. It imparts strength to resist temptation and occasions to sin.

" 5. It drives away wicked thoughts.

" 6. It preserves safely from the passing snares of the devil, both internally and externally.

" 7. It obtains the favor and presence of the Holy Ghost by which the soul is consoled, rejoiced, excited to devotion, and disposed to prayer.

" 8. It prepares the human mind for a better attendance on the divine mysteries, and receiving piously and worthily the most holy sacrament.

" *Its corporeal usefulness.*

" 1. It is a remedy against barrenness, both in woman and in beast.

" 2. It is a preservation from sickness.

" 3. It heals the infirmities both of the mind and of the body.

" 4. It purifies infected air, and drives away plague and contagion.

" Such is this document. It is the only authorized one I have seen respecting holy water ; and this extraordinary statement stands as publicly in the church as do the ten commandments in a church in England. It is affixed separately over each of the vessels containing the Holy Water ; and as every member of the congregation must

10

have sprinkled himself with the water as he entered the church, so he may have seen and read these, its uses." [1]

Holy water was also used to sprinkle animals. This custom continues in the Roman Church. The counterpart is found in several pagan customs which are described by Ovid in *Fasti*, as already quoted, and further as shown in book i., line 669. Speaking of animals, Mr. Seymore says :

"It was supposed to guard them [horses] against evil genii as they ran the race; and a legend is told of the horses of some Christians having outstripped all the horses of the heathen, owing to their being sprinkled with holy water. Such a legend serves as a sanction of primitive Christianity to horse-races, quite as well as to the use of holy water. The pagan custom soon became a papal custom, and falling in with the humor of the people, and the patronage of St. Anthony, who is usually pictured accompanied by a pig, and being conducive to the pecuniary interests of the convent of St. Anthony, the custom was continued under a new name, and 'St. Anthony's day' and the 'blessing of the horses' are thus identified." [2]

Roman Catholics Defend this Use.

Dr. WISEMAN, who stands high as a Roman Catholic authority, in his third letter, in reply to Poynder's *Pagano-Papismus* defends the use of holy water :

[1] *Pilgrimage*, etc., p. 527.   [2] *Ibid.* p. 535.

" But did not the ancient Christians use holy water ? Indeed they did, and that in a manner to shame us. They did not sprinkle themselves with it, to be sure, or help themselves from a vessel at the door, as you express it ; they did more than either, *they bathed in it.* Read Pacciandi, *De Sacris Christianorum Balneis*, Rome, 1758, and you will find much to instruct you on this subject. You will see how the ancient Christians used to bathe themselves before going to church after the commission of any sin. 'Why do you run to the bath after sin?' asks St. John Chrysostom. 'Is it not because you consider yourselves dirtier than any filth?' And Theophylactus writes in a similar strain. An ancient Christian bath was discovered by Ciampini among the ruins of Rome. But what is more to our purpose, the ancient Christians never went to receive the Eucharist, or even to pray in their churches, without washing their hands. 'What propriety is there,' says Tertullian, 'to go to prayer with washed hands and yet with an unclean spirit?' St. Chrysostom is still stronger: 'Thou darest not touch the sacred victim with unwashed hands, although pressed by extreme necessity; approach not, therefore, with an unwashed soul.' To supply the necessary convenience for this rite, a fountain or basin was provided at the church porch at which the faithful washed, as St. Paulinus of Nola several times described in the churches which he built. . . . St. Leo the Great built one at the gate of St. Paul's Church which was celebrated by Ennodius of Pavia in eight verses. . . . The same was the practice of the Greek Church ; for Eusebius tells us with commendation how Paulinus, Bishop of Tyre, placed in the porch of a splendid church which he built, the symbols of sacred purification, that is, fountains which gave, by their abundant supply, means of washing themselves to those who entered the temple.[1]

" In fact, we have several of the old lustral vases with early Christian symbols and inscriptions, belonging to both the churches, as a celebrated Latin one at Pesaro, and a Greek one at Venice, drawings of both of which you will find in Pacciandi's work with an ample description."

Preparing Holy Water.

The corrupting presence of paganism is shown in the preparation of water for purification and for baptism quite as much as in its use. The following description is from Foy, *Romish Rites*, as quoted by Brock :

" It appears that there are three kinds of holy water, two of which are used for the consecration of churches. Of these two, the first is considered to be inferior, since nothing but salt is used in its preparation—'salt exorcised for the salvation of those that believe.' It serves for sprinkling the building. The other is made up by a mixture of salt, ashes, and wine—all blessed, of course. This appears to be the holier of the two, and is used for the consecration of the altar. The third class of holy water, that which is referred to above as being consecrated on 'Holy

[1] Eusebius, *Ecc. Hist.*, vi., x.

This reference to Eusebius should be book x., chap. iv., p. 375 of vol. i. Christian Literature Company's publications, second series. The description given by Eusebius shows that holy water played an important part in the Christian Church at Tyre, as early as 315 A.D. See also Bingham, *Antiquities*, book viii., chap. iii. The church buildings described by Eusebius and Bingham contained many prominent elements of sun-worship, associated with the water-worship emblems.

Saturday,' is used for baptisms during the following year; and also, as I gather, for sprinkling generally. In its preparation—amid many exorcisms of devils and evil spirits, and forms of prayer—the following ceremonies are observed: The priest divides the water in the font with his hand, in the shape of a cross. In exorcising the water he touches it with his hand. In blessing it, he thrice makes over it the sign of the cross. In dividing it, he pours it toward the four quarters of heaven. He breathes thrice into it in the form of a cross. He lets down the great Paschal candle a little into it, and says: 'The might of the Holy Ghost descend into this fountain —plentitude.' *In hanc plentitudinem fontis.*

"Then he takes the candle from the water and again merges it more deeply, saying the same words as before, but in a higher tone. The third time he plunges it to the bottom, again repeating the formula with a still louder voice. Then blowing—*sufflans*—thrice into the water in the form of the Greek letter Psi, he says: 'Impregnate with regenerating efficacy the whole substance of this water'; and so takes the candle out of the font. Besides these doings, various oils are poured into the water and mixed with the hand; and still more strange, spittle is mingled with it, as I have once seen with my own eyes in the grand baptistery at St. John Lateran in Rome.

"'*The might of the Holy Ghost descend into this fountain —plentitude, and impregnate with regenerating efficacy the whole substance of this water.*' Such is the spell. Exorcisms first chase all evil spirits from the water, then incantations and charms—dividings, oils, crossings, breathings, candle plungings, and other things—cause the might of the Holy Ghost to descend and impregnate the water with regenerating efficacy. It is no longer ordinary water, such as that wherein the eunuch or Cornelius and his friends were baptized ; but, by the power of charms, it has become an ecclesiastical compound, and those to whom it is administered are made new creatures and regenerate, not—so far as I understand—because they are brought by faith to Christ, but through the mere application of the fluid impregnated with virtue by an ecclesiastical process. And the only man who can make and apply this ' Elixir of Life,'—of eternal life,—is the priest." [1]

Sun-Worship and Water-Worship.

We have already shown that the sun-worship *cultus* and water-worship were united from the beginning. This union was made anterior to Grecian or Roman times, and much of the sacredness of water arose from it. HISLOP describes this connection in the sanctifying of water, as follows :

" In Egypt, as we have seen, Osiris, as identified with Noah, was represented when overcome by his grand enemy, Typhon, or the ' Evil One,' as passing through the waters. The poets represented Semiramis as sharing in his distress, and likewise seeking safety in the same way. We have seen already that under the name of Astarte she was said to have come forth from the wondrous egg that was found floating on the waters of the Euphrates. Now, Manilius tells, in his *Astronomical Poetics*, what induced her to take refuge in these waters.

[1] *Rome, Pagan and Papal*, by Mourant Brock, M.A., p. 107 ff. London, 1883.

'Venus plunged into the Babylonian waters,' says he, 'to shun the fury of the snake-footed Typhon.' When Venus Urania, or Dione, the 'Heavenly Dove,' plunged in deep distress into these waters of Babylon, be it observed what, according to the Chaldean doctrine, this amounted to. It was neither more nor less than saying that the Holy Ghost incarnate, in deep tribulation, entered these waters, and that on purpose that these might be fit, not only by the temporary abode of the Messiah in the midst of them, but by the spirit's efficacy thus imparted to them, for giving new life and regeneration, *by baptism,* to the worshippers of the Chaldean Madonna. We have evidence that the purifying virtue of the waters, which, in pagan esteem, had such efficacy in cleansing from guilt and regenerating the soul, was derived in part from the passing of the mediatorial god, the sun-god, and god of fire, through these waters during his humiliation and sojourn in the midst of them ; and that the Papacy at this day retains the very custom which had sprung up from that persuasion. So far as heathenism is concerned, the following extracts from Potter and Athenæus speak distinctly enough : 'Every person,' says the former, 'who came to the solemn sacrifices [of the Greeks] was purified by water. To which end, at the entrance of the temples, there was commonly placed a vessel full of holy water.' How did this water get its holiness? This water 'was consecrated,' says Athenæus, 'by putting into it a Burning Torch taken from the Altar.' The *burning torch* was the express symbol of the god of fire ; and by the light of this torch, so indispensable for consecrating the 'holy water,' we may easily see whence came one great part of the purifying virtue of 'the water of the loud resounding sea,' which was held to be so efficacious in purging away the guilt and stain of sin,—even from the sun-god having taken refuge in its waters. Now this very same method is used in the Romish Church for consecrating the water for baptism. The unsuspicious testimony of Bishop Hay leaves no doubt on this point. 'It,' [the water kept in the baptismal font] says he, 'is blessed on the eve of Pentecost, because it is the Holy Ghost who gives to the waters of baptism the power and efficacy of sanctifying our souls, and because the baptism of Christ is with the Holy Ghost and with fire.'[1] In blessing the waters a Lighted Torch is put into the font.

" Here, then, it is manifest that the baptismal *regenerating* water of Rome is consecrated just as the *regenerating* and *purifying* water of the pagans was. Of what avail is it for Bishop Hay to say, with a view of sanctifying superstition and 'making apostasy plausible,' that this is done ' to represent the fire of divine love, which is communicated to the soul by baptism and the light of good example, which all who are baptized ought to give.' This is the fair face put on the matter; but the fact still remains that while the Romish doctrine in regard to baptism is purely pagan, in the ceremonies connected with the papal baptism one of the essential rites of the ancient fire-worship is still practised at this day, just as it was practised by the worshippers of Bacchus, the Babylonian Messiah. As Rome keeps up the remembrance of the fire-god passing through the waters and giving virtue to them, so when it speaks of the ' Holy Ghost *suffering* for us in baptism,' it in like manner commemorates the part which paganism assigned to the Babylonian goddess when

[1] Matt. iii., 11.

she plunged into the waters. The sorrows of Nimrod, or Bacchus, when in the waters, were meritorious sorrows. The sorrows of his wife, in whom the Holy Ghost miraculously dwelt, were the same. The sorrows of the Madonna, then, when in these waters, fleeing from Typhon's rage, were the birth-throes by which children were born to God. And thus, even in the Far West, Chalchivitlycue, the Mexican 'goddess of the waters' and 'mother' of all the regenerate, was represented as purging the new-born infant from original sin, and 'bringing it anew into the world.'" [1]

Summary.

1. The worship of water as a divine element or agent, and hence its use as a protection against evil, and, in baptism, as a means of producing spiritual purity, forms a prominent feature of pagan religions.

2. Pagan water-worship was associated with the higher forms of sun-worship in various ways, and notably with that lower phase, Phallicism, with the obscene rites of which it is yet closely connected in India. In Mexico the cross was the special symbol of the water-worship cult.

3. In pagan water-worship the sacred fluid was applied in many ways—by immersion, by bathing, by sprinkling; in the latter use, the water was sprinkled upon the candidate from a sacred sprink-

[1] *The Two Babylons*, by Rev. Alexander Hislop, p. 142 ff., seventh edition, London.

ling-brush, or from a bough of some sacred tree; it was sometimes poured upon the candidate from a cup made from the bark of a sacred tree; trine immersion appears in some instances. Inspiration was sought from sacred water, by drinking, by bathing, by sitting over it, and by inhaling its vapors.

4. Water for religious purposes was taken from sacred streams, fountains, and wells; or it was made holy by exorcisms and by the use of salt; it was carried to remote points and preserved for a long time. The ancient Druids caught rain-water in receptacles on the hill-tops and carried it to their altars through necessary aqueducts.

5. The fundamental errors of the pagan water-worship cult appeared in Western Christianity as early as the middle of the second century; this resulted in the baptism of the sick, baptism of infants, baptism for the dead, the delaying of baptism until the approach of death in order to make the most of both worlds, and the doctrine of penance to atone for sins committed after baptism; all these followed as a legitimate result.

6. As baptism was the door to Church membership, the Church was soon filled with "baptized pagans," who were Christians in name only; by this means New Testament Christianity was rapidly perverted.

7. Whoever will seek the ultimate facts must confess that the Christianity of the third and the succeeding centuries was far removed from the New Testament standard. Protestants are returning to that standard all too slowly and unwillingly. Many are drifting farther away.

It is scarcely necessary to add that every form of baptism except submersion was borrowed from paganism ; that faith in baptism as producing spiritual purity, and hence as a " saving ordinance," was borrowed from paganism : the notion that only the baptized can be saved was borrowed from paganism ; the use of oil, of spittle, of the sign of the cross, of lights, of white robes, is a remnant of paganism ; baptising for the dead, and delaying baptism until near death, are a part of the pagan residuum ; faith in water from the Jordan or elsewhere is paganism. The naming of children at baptism was a direct importation from paganism. In so far as any of these false elements are yet retained by Roman Catholics, Greeks, or Protestants, thus far does paganism dominate Christian thought and practice.

CHAPTER VII.

PAGAN SUN-WORSHIP.

Sun-Worship the Oldest and Most Widely Diffused Form of Paganism—
Gnostic Antinomianism or Lawlessness—Anti-Judaism, Mainly of Pa-
gan Origin—Anti-Sabbathism and Sunday Observance Synchronous—
Anti-Lawism and Anti-Sabbathism Unscriptural—Christ's Teachings
Concerning the Law of God ; Paul's Teachings on the Same—Destruc-
tive Effect of Pagan Lawlessness on Christianity.

THE sun-god, under various names, Mithras, Baal, Apollo, etc., was the chief god of the heathen pantheon. A direct conflict between him and Jehovah appears wherever paganism and revealed religion came in contact. As "Baal," "Lord" of the universe and of the productive forces in nature and in man, this sun-god was the pre-eminent divinity in ancient Palestine and throughout Phœnicia. The chosen people of God were assailed and corrupted by this cult, even while they were in the desert,[1] being led away by the women of Moab. During the period of the Judges, Baal-worship was the besetting sin of Israel, which the most vigorous measures could not eradicate.[2]

[1] Numbers xxv.
[2] Judges ii., 13 ; iii., 7 ; vi., 25 ff.; x., 6 ; 1 Sam. vii., 4 ; xii. 10.

A reformation came under Saul and David, only to be followed by a relapse under Solomon, which culminated in the exclusion of Jehovah-worship under Ahab.[1] Jehu broke the power of the cult, for a time, but the people soon returned to it.[2] It also spread like a virus through Judah ; repressed by Hezekiah, but continued by Manasseh.[3]

This worship of the sun-god was a sign of disloyalty to Jehovah, and formed the certain road to wickedness and impurity.[4]

In its lowest forms it was so closely allied to sex-worship, Phallicism, that it lent great power to that debasing licentiousness, which sanctified lust, and made prostitution of virtue a religious duty. Sun-worship was both powerful and popular in the Roman Empire when Christianity came into contact with Western thought. It furnished abundant material for the corrupting process. We have seen in a former chapter that several minor elements of sun-worship mingled with pagan water-worship : such as turning to the west to renounce evil, and turning to the east to promise allegiance to Christ and Light, before baptism; "Orientation"—building

---

[1] 1 Kings xvi., 31 ff., and xix., 10.

[2] 2 Kings x., 18–28, and xvii., 16.

[3] 2 Kings xviii., 4, and xxi., 3.

[4] When Joshua, the servant of Jehovah, commanded the sun to stand still, there was given an ocular demonstration of the power of the God who made the heavens and the earth, over the sun-god, in whom the pagan enemies of Israel trusted.

churches with the altar so that men should worship toward the east—was another element, while the extinguishing of a torch or a candle in the font, in the preparation of holy water, was a direct importation from this cult. But these were of little account in extent or influence, when compared with the corruption which came through the introduction of Baal's and Apollo's day, " Sunday," in place of the Sabbath, which had always represented, and yet represents, Jehovah, maker of heaven and earth. The introduction of Sunday into Christianity was a continuation of the old-time conflict between Baal and Jehovah.

The definite and systematic manner in which the corrupting process was carried forward is clearly seen by the preparatory steps which opened the way for paganism to thrust the sun's day upon Christianity. We have seen how the foundation of God's authority was undermined by the gnostic opposition to the Old Testament, and by the allegorizing of both Old and New ; how a false " baptismal-regeneration " theory filled the church with baptized but unconverted heathens. These were not enough to complete the corrupting process. While men still had regard for the Sabbath, they could not entirely give up the law of Jehovah on which it was based, and thus the fundamental doctrines of paganism were still held in check.

The Simultaneous Development of Anti-Sabbathism and of Sunday Observance.

Gnosticism was *antinomian* from the core. All knowledge, and hence all authority, was in the heart of the "true Gnostic." The "initiated" were divinely enlightened, were a law unto themselves. This was doubly true when they came into contact with a law promulgated by the "inferior God of the Jews," the weak Creator of matter, and hence a God in league with evil. Such opposition was natural, was unavoidable, from the gnostic standpoint. Coupled with the allegorical method of interpretation, it was an easy task for this opposition to create a violent anti-Jewish prejudice, and a combined no-lawism, and no-Sabbathism, which became the main factor in sundering the Jewish and Gentile churches, and introducing the reign of "*lawlessness*," of which Paul wrote in the second chapter of Thessalonians. This anti-lawism and anti-Sabbathism appear in JUSTIN, the first pagano-Christian writer of whom we have sufficient definite knowledge to gain a picture of the incipient results of pagan influence on Christianity. He accepted Christianity after reaching mature life, but retained his "philosopher's cloak" as he did many of his pagan ideas. His theories are a compound of pagan philosophy and Christianity. He was furiously opposed to all that savored of Judaism. His interpretations of Scripture and his religious opinions are all strongly colored by this anti-Jewish spirit. His *Dialogue with Trypho the Jew*, whether Trypho were a real or an imaginary character, is the special exponent of anti-Judaism. The following examples show how he confounded the moral laws and the ceremonial code of the Jews, and set forth baneful no-lawism and no-Sabbathism, which grew in virulence and destroyed the authority of the Old Testament wherever his influence was felt. His special anti-Jewish treatise is entitled, *Dialogue of Justin, Philosopher and Martyr, with Trypho, a Jew.* It opens as follows:

"While I was going about one morning in the walks of the Xystus, a certain man, with others in his company, having met me said, 'Hail, O Philosopher!' And immediately after saying this, he turned round and walked along with me; his friends likewise followed him. And I, in turn having addressed him, said, 'What is there important?'

"And he replied: 'I was instructed,' says he, 'by Corinthus, the Socratic in Argos, that I ought not to despise or treat with indifference those who array themselves in this dress, but to show them all kindness, and to associate with them, as perhaps some advantage would spring from the intercourse either to some such man or to myself. It is good, moreover, for both, if either the one or the other be benefited.'

"On this account, therefore, whenever I see any one in such costume, I gladly approach him, and now, for the same reason, have I willingly accosted you; and these accompany me, in the expectation of hearing for themselves something profitable from you."

This opening shows Justin in his true character, as a philosopher who has united certain elements of Christianity (see *Dialogue*, ch. viii.) with his pagan theories, and is now to defend this product as Christianity. In chapter x., Trypho states his case against Christians in the following words :

"Moreover I am aware that your precepts in the so-called Gospel are so wonderful and so great, that I suspect no one can keep them; for I have carefully read them. But this is what we are most at a loss about; that you, professing to be pious, and supposing yourselves better than others, are not in any particular separated from them, and do not alter your mode of living from the nations, in that you observe no festivals or Sabbaths, and do not have the rite of circumcision; and further, resting your hopes on a man that was crucified, you yet expect to obtain some good thing from God, while you do not obey His commandments. Have you not read, that that soul shall be cut off from his people who shall not have been circumcised on the eighth day? And this has been ordained for strangers and for slaves equally. But you, despising this covenant rashly, reject the consequent duties, and attempt to persuade yourselves that you know God, when, however, you perform none of those things which they do who fear God. If, therefore, you can defend yourself on these points, and make it manifest in what way you hope for any thing whatsoever, even though

11

you do not observe the law, this we would very gladly hear from you, and we shall make other similar investigations." [1]

Justin answers Trypho in the next chapter, (chapter xi), which is entitled : " *The Law Abrogated ; The New Testament Promised and Given of God.*"

Note the following from this, and subsequent chapters :

" For the law promulgated on Horeb is now old, and belongs to yourselves alone ; but this is for all universally. Now law placed against law has abrogated that which is before it, and a covenant which comes after in like manner has put an end to the previous one ; and an eternal and final law—namely Christ—has been given to us, and the covenant is trustworthy, after which there shall be no law, no commandment, no ordinance." [2]

" You have now need of a second circumcision, though you glory greatly in the flesh. The new law requires you to keep perpetual Sabbath, and you, because you are idle for one day, suppose you are pious, not discerning why this has been commanded you ; and if you eat unleavened bread, you say the will of God has been fulfilled. The Lord our God does not take pleasure in such observances ; if there is any perjured person, or a thief among you, let him cease to be so ; if any adulterer, let him repent ; then he has kept the sweet and true Sabbaths of God. If any one has impure hands, let him wash and be pure. [3]

[1] *Dialogue with Trypho*, chap. x.

[2] *Ibid.*, chap. xi.   [3] *Ibid.*, chap. xii.

" For we too would observe the fleshly circumcision, and the Sabbaths, and in short all the feasts, if we did not know for what reason they were enjoined you— namely on account of your transgressions and the hardness of your hearts.   For if we patiently endure all things contrived against us by wicked men and demons, so that even amid cruelties unutterable, death and torments, we pray for mercy to those who inflict such things upon us, and do not wish to give the least retort to any one even as the new Lawgiver commanded us; how is it, Trypho, that we would not observe those rites which do not harm us—I speak of fleshly circumcision, and Sabbaths and feasts ? " [1]

In many different forms Justin Martyr repeats his theory, that the ten commandments and the ceremonial economy of the Jews were abrogated, and that there is no written law regulating conduct on the part of the Christians.

TERTULLIAN also taught the temporary character of the Decalogue, and no-lawism, as the following shows :

" Whence we understand that God's law was anterior even to Moses, and was not first [given] in Horeb, or in Sinai, and in the desert, but was more ancient ; [existing] first in paradise, subsequently reformed for the patriarchs, and so again for the Jews, at definite periods ; so that we are not to give heed to Moses' law as to the primitive law, but as to a subsequent, which at a definite period, God has set forth to the Gentiles too, and, after repeatedly promising so to do, through the prophets, has re-formed

[1] *Dialogue*, etc., chap. xviii.

for the better; and has premonished [men] that it should come to pass that, 'just as the law was given through Moses,' at a definite time, so it should be believed to have been temporarily observed and kept. And let us not annul this power which God has, which reforms the law's precepts answerably to the circumstances of the times, with a view to man's salvation. In fine, let him who contends that the Sabbath is still to be observed as a balm of salvation, and circumcision on the eighth day because of the threat of death, teach us that, for the time past, righteous men kept the Sabbath, or practised circumcision, and were thus rendered 'friends of God.' For if circumcision purges a man, since God made Adam uncircumcised, why did he not circumcise him, even after his sinning, if circumcision purges? At all events, in settling him in paradise, He appointed one uncircumcised as colonist of paradise. Therefore since God originated Adam uncircumcised, and inobservant of the Sabbath, consequently his offspring also, Abel, offering Him sacrifices, uncircumcised and inobservant of the Sabbath, was by Him commended; while He accepted what he was offering in simplicity of heart, and reprobated the sacrifice of his brother Cain, who was not rightly dividing what he was offering. Noah, also, uncircumcised,—yes, and inobservant of the Sabbath—God freed from the deluge. For Enoch, too, most righteous man, uncircumcised and inobservant of the Sabbath, He translated from this world; [Enoch] who did not first taste death, in order that, being a candidate for eternal life, he might by this time show us that we also may, without the burden of the law of Moses, please God. Melchizedek, also, 'the priest of the most high God,' uncircumcised and inobservant of the Sabbath, was chosen to the priesthood of God. Lot, withal, the brother of Abraham, proves that it was for the merits of righteousness, without observance of the law, that he was freed from the conflagration of the Sodomites. . . .

" Therefore, since it is manifest that a Sabbath temporal was shown, and a Sabbath eternal foretold, and a circumcision carnal foretold, and a circumcision spiritual pre-indicated; a law temporal and a law eternal formally declared; sacrifices carnal and sacrifices spiritual foreshown; it follows that, after all these precepts had been given carnally, in time preceding, to the people of Israel, there was to supervene a time whereat the precepts of the ancient law, and of the old ceremonies would cease, and the promise of the new law, and the recognition of spiritual sacrifices, and the promise of the New Testament, supervene; while the light from on high would beam upon us who were sitting in darkness, and were being detained in the shadow of death. And so there is incumbent on us a necessity, binding us, since we have premised that a new law was predicted by the prophets, and that not such as had been already given to their fathers, at the time when He led them forth from the land of Egypt, to show and prove, on the one hand, that that old law has ceased, and on the other, that the promised new law is now in operation." [1]

These examples must suffice, since all who are familiar with Patristic literature know that its general trend, and its openly avowed opposition to Judaism and all things connected with the Old

[1] *Against the Jews*, chapters ii. and vi.

Testament and the Decalogue, place it beyond controversy, that the prevailing type of Christianity during the third, fourth, and succeeding centuries, was anti-Sabbatic, and antinomian.   There were practical exceptions among the more common people, but the prevailing thought, and hence the strong tendency, was away from the Sabbath, and from Sabbathism.   He who questions this shows himself ignorant in the premises.   This growing disregard for the authority of the Sabbath law, and the steady development of anti-Sabbathism, prepared the way for a vast system of semi-religious pagan days, with the Sun's day at their head.

Antinomianism and Anti-Sabbathism Unscriptural.

Before we inquire how Sunday was introduced, it will be well to consider the unscriptural and destructive nature of the theories by which the Decalogue and the Sabbath were dethroned, through false teachings.

Christ is the central figure in both dispensations. If new expressions of the Father's will are to be made in connection with the work of Christ on earth, they must be made by the " Immanuel," who is thus "reconciling the world unto himself."   Did Christ teach the abrogation of the Decalogue, of which the Sabbath law is a part?   Let His own words answer:

" Think not that I came to destroy the law or the prophets. I came not to destroy, but to fulfil. For verily I say unto you, till heaven and earth pass away, one jot or one tittle shall in no wise pass away from the law, till all things be accomplished. Whosoever, therefore, shall break one of these least commandments, and shall teach men so, shall be called least in the kingdom of heaven ; but whosoever shall do and teach them, he shall be called great in the kingdom of heaven." [1]

When Christ speaks of the law (τὸν νόμον) in these emphatic words, He cannot mean the ceremonial code, for these ceremonies were typical of Him and must pass away with His death. Besides this, the word fulfil (πληρῶσαι) means the opposite of destruction (καταλῦσαι). Christ fulfilled the law by perfect obedience to it. He corrected false interpretations, and intensified its claims. He taught obedience to it in the spirit as well as the letter, and urged obedience from love rather than fear. Such a work could not have been done in connection with the dying ceremonies of the Jewish system. Such a work Christ did do with reference to the Decalogue. In connection with the passage above quoted Christ immediately refers to two laws from the Decalogue, explains and enforces their meaning in a way far more broad and deep than those who listened to Him were wont to conceive of them.

[1] Matthew v., 17-19.

On another occasion[1] a certain shrewd lawyer sought to entrap the Saviour by asking "which is the greatest commandment in the law." The question has no meaning unless it be applied to the Decalogue. Christ's answer includes all the commandments of the Decalogue, and thus avoids the trap designed by the questioner, who sought to lead Him into some distinction between laws known to be equal in their nature and extent.

In the sixteenth chapter of Luke,[2] Christ again affirms in the strongest language, that "It is easier for heaven and earth to pass, than one tittle of the law to fail." Language could not be plainer than that which is used in these statements.

These sentiments accord fully with the practice of Christ relative to the Sabbath. He boldly condemned the unjust requirements which the Jews had attached to the observance of it, and taught that works of mercy were to be freely done on that day; that it was made for man's good, and not his injury. But He never taught that because it was "made for man" therefore it was to be abrogated, or unsanctified. Neither did He delegate to His disciples any power to teach the abrogation of the law, or of the Sabbath. On the contrary, their representative writings contain the same clear testimony in favor of the perpetuity of the law, and

---

[1] Matthew xxii., 35–40.   [2] 17th verse

show the same practical observance of the Sabbath. Paul, the great reasoner among the Apostles, after an exhaustive discussion concerning the relations between the law and the Gospel, concludes the whole matter in these words:

"Do we then make the law of none effect through faith? God forbid! Nay, we establish the law." [1]

Again in the same epistle [2] he presents a conclusive argument, starting from the axiom that "where there is no law there is no sin." Showing that since death, which came by sin, reigned from Adam to Moses, therefore the law then existed, and, by the same reasoning that if there be no law under the Gospel dispensation, there can be no sin ; if no sin, then no Saviour from sin, and Christ died in vain, if by His death he destroyed the law. In another place Paul contrasts the Decalogue with the ceremonial code, and declares the worthlessness of the one and the binding character of the other, in these words:

"Circumcision is nothing, and uncircumcision is nothing, but the keeping of the commandments of God." [3]

Thus, in a plain and unequivocal way, Paul teaches as his Master taught.

[1] Romans iii., 31.

[2] Romans v., 13, 14.

[3] The example of Christ and His Apostles concerning Sabbath observance is discussed in detail in *Biblical Teachings*, etc., by the writer, pp. 26–44.

In view of Christ's words, and Paul's sharp logic, the following conclusions are unavoidable. They annihilate the no-law theory.

1. If the Decalogue was abolished by the death of Christ, then Christ by His death prevented the possibility of sin, to redeem man from which He died.

2. "Sin is not imputed where there is no law,"[1] hence the consciousness of sin which men feel under the claims of the Gospel is a mockery, and all faith in Christ is a farce. It only increases the difficulty to say that the law is written in the hearts of believers. If that be true, then :

3. None but believers in Christ can be convicted of sin, for no others can know the law which convicts of sin. Therefore those who reject Christ become, at least negatively, *righteous* by refusing to come where they can be convicted of sin. Thus does the no-Sabbath theory make infidelity better than belief, and *rejection of Christ the only means of salvation*. It leads to endless absurdities, and the overthrow of all moral government. It contradicts the plain words of God, and puts darkness for light. Its fruitage in human life has been only bitterness and ashes.

[1] Romans v., 13.

CHAPTER VIII.

SUNDAY OBSERVANCE UNKNOWN TO CHRISTIANITY BEFORE THE MIDDLE OF THE SECOND CENTURY.

Mistaken Notions Concerning the Beginning of Sunday Observance—No Sunday Observance in the New Testament—Sunday Directly Referred to but Three Times—It is Never Spoken of as a Sabbath, nor as Commemorative of Christ's Resurrection—The Bible does not State that Christ Rose on Sunday—Christ and His Disciples Always Observed the Sabbath—The "Change of the Sabbath" Unknown in the New Testament—The Sabbath Never Called "Jewish" in the Scriptures, nor by Any Writer until after Paganism had Invaded the Church—Origin of Sunday Observance Found in Paganism—First Reference to Sunday Observance about 150 A.D.—No Writer of the Early Centuries Claimed Scriptural Reasons for Its Observance—Pagan Reasons and Arguments Adduced in Its Support; a Day of "Indulgence to the Flesh"—Pretended Scriptural Reasons, *ex post facto*.

THERE are few if any questions concerning which popular notions and ultimate facts are more at variance than the question of the early observance of Sunday. It is not uncommon for men to assert that "Sunday has been observed as the Christian Sabbath ever since the resurrection of Christ"; while the fact is, that the first authentic and definite statement concerning Sunday observance was made by Justin Martyr as late as 150 A.D. Even if we accept the passage quoted from

171

the *Didache*, the portion of that document in which the reference occurs cannot be placed earlier than 150, and it is probably much later. Since the facts as they appear in the New Testament can be easily obtained, I shall take only space enough to state them briefly.

" The first day of the week," Sunday, is definitely referred to but three times in the New Testament. Each of the Evangelists speaks of the day on which Christ's resurrection was made known to His disciples. These references are all to the same day.[1] The book of Acts has but one reference to Sunday[2]; and there is but one in all the Epistles.[3] Three other passages are quoted in favor of Sunday observance.[4]

It is so easy for the reader to examine these passages, and to compare them with popular notions and with what is said here, that I shall be content with the following summary of facts touching Sunday observance in the New Testament:

Six passages are quoted in favor of such observance. Only *three* of these passages mention the first day of the week in any manner. Neither of them speaks of it as sabbatic, or as commemorative of any event, or sacred, or to be regarded above

[1] Matt. xxviii., 1–8 ; Mark xvi., 2 ; Luke xxiv., 1–3 ; John xx., 1.
[2] Acts xx., 7.
[3] I. Cor. xvi., 2.
[4] John xix., 23 and 26, and Rev. i., 10.

other days, and it is only by vague and illogical inferences that either of them is made to produce a shadow of proof for such a change. Concerning the other three, it is only *supposed* by the advocates of the popular theory, that they in some way refer to the first day. To this, therefore, does the "argument from example" come, when carefully examined. The New Testament never speaks of, or hints at, a change of the Sabbath; it contains no notice of any commemorative or sabbatic observance of Sunday. It does tell of the repeated and continued observance of the Sabbath by Christ and His Apostles. Will the reader please examine the Bible to see whether these things are so. Sunday is a myth, as far as the Bible is concerned, and the theory of a "change of the Sabbath by divine authority," had its birth with English Puritanism less than three hundred years ago.

Christ's Resurrection and Sunday.

Another popular notion is equally unsupported by New Testament history. The Bible never associates the observance of Sunday, or of any other day, with the resurrection of Christ. The Bible does not state that Christ rose from the grave on Sunday. The most that can be said on this point is, that when the friends of Christ first came to the tomb it was empty. He had risen and gone. Matthew xxviii., 1, shows that the first visit was made 'late on the Sabbath," *i. e.* on Saturday afternoon before sunset, at which time the tomb was empty.[1]

All references to Sunday are fully accounted for on other considerations than that it was a sacred or a commemorative day. New Testament arguments in favor of Sunday observance are all *ex post facto ;* they were developed after the practice had been initiated for other reasons.

The Sabbath in the New Testament.

The history of the Sabbath in the New Testament is as much at variance with popular notions as is the history of Sunday. The statement sometimes made that " The Sabbath was never observed after the resurrection of Christ," contains as much error as can be put into that number of words. Since the facts are in the hands of every reader of the New Testament, only a general summary of them is given here.

Collating the facts, and summing up the case as regards the example of Christ and His Apostles, it stands as follows :

1. During the life of Christ the Sabbath was always observed by Him and by His followers.

---

[1] For discussion of the time of Christ's resurrection, see *Biblical Teachings*, etc., by the writer.

He corrected the errors and false notions which were held concerning it, but gave no hint that it was to be abrogated.

2. The book of Acts gives a connected history of the recognition and observance of the Sabbath by the Apostles while they were organizing many of the churches spoken of in the New Testament. These references extend over a period of eight or nine years, the last of them being at least twenty years after the resurrection.

3. In all the history of the doings and teachings of the Apostles, there is not the remotest reference to the abrogation of the Sabbath.

Had there been any change made or beginning to be made, or any authority for the abrogation of the Sabbath law, the Apostles must have known it. To claim that there was is therefore to charge them with studiously *concealing the truth.* And also, with recognizing and calling a day the Sabbath which *was not the Sabbath.*

Add to these considerations the following facts :

(*a*) The latest books of the New Testament, including the Gospel of John, were written about the year ninety-five or later. In none of these is there any trace of the change of the Sabbath, nor is the abrogation of the Sabbath law taught in them.

(*b*) The Sabbath is mentioned in the New Testament sixty times, and always in its appropriate character.

Thus the law and the gospel are in harmony, and teach that " the seventh day is the Sabbath of the Lord thy God."

But some will say, " Christ and His Apostles did all this as Jews, simply." If this be true, then Christ lived and taught simply as a *Jew* and not as the *Saviour of the world.* On the contrary, He was at war with the false and extravagant notions of Judaism concerning questions of truth and duty. If Christ were not a " Christian," but a " Jew," what becomes of the system which He taught ? If His first followers, who perilled all for Him and sealed their faith with their blood, were only Jews, or worse, were dissemblers, doing that which Christians ought not to do, for sake of policy, where shall Christians be found ? The assumption dies of its own inconsistency. More than this, New Testament history repeatedly states that the Greeks were taught on the Sabbath the same as the Jews ; and in those churches where the Greek element predominated there is no trace of any different teaching or custom on this point. The Jewish Christians kept up their *national* institutions, for a time, such as circumcision and the passover, while all Christians accepted the Sabbath as a part of the law of God. The popular outcry against the Sabbath as " Jewish" is unscriptural. Christ was in all respects, as regards nationality, a Jew. So were all the writers of the Old Testament, and all the writers of the New Testament. God has given the world no word of inspiration in the Bible, from Gentile pen, or Gentile lips. Is the Bible therefore "Jewish"? The Sabbath, if possible, is less Jewish than the Bible. It had its beginning long before a Jew was born. It is God's day marked by His own example, and sanctified by His blessing, for the race of man, beginning when the race began, and can end only when the race shall cease to exist. Christ recognized it under the Gospel as He recognized each of the other eternal laws with which it is associated in the Decalogue; recognized them as the everlasting words of His Father, whose law He came to magnify and fulfil. It is manifestly unjust and unchristian to attempt to thrust out and stigmatize any part of God's truth as "Jewish," when all of God's promises and all Bible truths have come to us through the Hebrew nation.[1]

As we were compelled to go outside the Bible to find the influences which undermined the Decalogue and the Sabbath, so we must seek for the origin of Sunday observance outside of that book.

[1] The reader will find this question discussed in detail in "*Biblical Teachings Concerning the Sabbath and the Sunday*," p. 26 ff. If that is not at hand, take your Bible and Concordance, and examine each passage in the New Testament where "Sabbath" occurs. *Cf.* also *Sabbath Commentary*, by Bailey.

12

We find the first mention of such observance, and of reasons therefor, in the same author, Justin, who we have seen was the first to formulate the anti-law and anti-Sabbath doctrines which have already been examined.[1]

This earliest reference to Sunday observance is found in Justin's *Apology* as follows :

" On the day called Sunday, all who live in cities or in the Country, gather together to one place, and the memoirs of the apostles or the writings of the prophets are read as long as time permits ; then when the reader has ceased, the president verbally instructs and exhorts to the imitation of these good things. Then we all rise together and pray, and, as we before said, when our prayer is ended, bread, and wine, and water are brought, and the president in like manner offers prayers and thanksgivings, according to his ability, and the people assent saying Amen ; and there is a distribution to each, and a participation of that over which thanks have been given, and to those who are absent a portion is sent by the deacons. And they who are well to do, and willing, give what each thinks fit ; and what is collected is deposited with the president, who succours the orphans and widows, and those who, through sickness or any other cause, are in want, and those who are in bonds, and the strangers sojourning among us, and in a word takes care of all who are in need. But Sunday is the day on which we all hold

[1] For an examination of the writings, genuine and spurious, which are adduced in favor of Sunday observance, before the time of Justin Martyr, consult *A Critical History of the Sabbath and Sunday in the Christian Church*, by the writer, pp. 33–69.

our common assembly, because it is the first day on which God, having wrought a change in the darkness and matter, made the world ; and Jesus Christ our Saviour on the same day rose from the dead. For He was crucified on the day before that of Saturn (Saturday) ; and on the day after that of Saturn which is the day of the Sun, having appeared to His apostles and disciples, He taught them these things, which we have submitted to you also for your consideration." [1]

There is nothing scriptural in the reasons given by Justin ; the first is purely fanciful, and is in accord with the prevailing gnostic speculations of those times. His statement that Christ was crucified on Friday is the beginning of a popular error, which has come down, not unchallenged, but largely uninvestigated. Some writers claim that the last clause intends to state that Christ taught His disciples when He first appeared to them, what Justin had written concerning the Sunday ; but one has only to read Justin's words to see how entirely unfounded such a claim is. At all events, there is not a word in Scripture to support the reasons adduced by Justin for Sunday observance.

It is important that the reader note carefully what sort of Sunday observance Justin describes. Laying aside all "suppositions," and "inferences," and *ex-post-facto* conclusions, we learn from him

[1] Chap. lxvii.

that at the middle of the second century a form of religious service was held on Sunday. But it is equally evident that there was no sabbatic regard for the day. Sir WILLIAM DOMVILLE summarizes the case as follows :

" This inference appears irresistible when we further consider that Justin, in this part of his *Apology*, is professedly intending to describe the mode in which Christians observed the Sunday. . . . He evidently intends to give all information requisite to an accurate knowledge of the subject he treats upon. He is even so particular as to tell the Emperor why the Sunday was observed ; and he does, in fact, specify every active duty belonging to the day, the Scripture reading, the exhortation, the public prayer, the Sacrament, and the alms-giving : why then should he not also inform the Emperor of the one inactive duty of the day, the duty of abstaining from doing in it any manner of work ? The Emperor well knew that such abstinence was the custom of all his Jewish subjects on the Saturday (*die Saturni*), and could readily have understood it to be the custom of his Christian subjects on the Sunday (*die Solis*, as Justin calls it in his *Apology*), and, therefore, if such was the custom of Christians in Justin's time, his description of their Sunday duties was essentially defective. It is not, however, at all probable that he would intend to omit noticing so important a characteristic of the day, as the Sabbatical observance of it, if it was in fact Sabbatically observed. But even were it probable he should intend to omit all mention of it in his Apology to the Emperor, it would be impossible to imagine any sufficient cause for his remaining silent on the subject in his *Dialogue* with Trypho the Jew ; and this whether the *Dialogue* was real or imaginary, for if the latter, Justin would still, as Dr. Lardner has observed, ' choose to write in character.' . . . The testimony of Justin, therefore, proves most clearly two facts of great importance in the Sabbath controversy : the one, that the Christians in his time observed the Sunday as a prayer day ; the other, that they did not observe it as a Sabbath-day." [1]

Such is the summary of the case at the year 150 A.D. No-Sabbathism and a form of Sunday observance were born at the same time. Trained in heathen philosophies until manhood, Justin accepted Christianity as a better philosophy than he had before found. Such a man and those like him could scarcely do other than build a system quite unlike apostolic Christianity. That which they did build was a paganized rather than an apostolic type.

Pagan Reasons for Observing Sunday.

Pagan philosophy as a source of argument in favor of the observance of Sunday is made still more prominent by CLEMENT of Alexandria, as follows :

" And the Lord's day Plato prophetically speaks of in the tenth book of the *Republic*, in these words : ' And when seven days have passed to each of them in the

---

[1] *Sabbath : An Examination of the Six Texts*, p. 274 *seq.*, London, 1849.

meadow, on the eighth they are to set out and arrive in four days.' By the meadow is to be understood the fixed sphere, as being a mild and genial spot, and the locality of the pious; and by the seven days each motion of the seven planets, and the whole practical art which speeds to the end of rest. But after the wandering orbs the journey leads to heaven, that is, to the eighth motion and day. And he says that souls are gone on the fourth day, pointing out the passage through the four elements. But the seventh day is recognized as sacred, not by the Hebrews only, but also by the Greeks; according to which the whole world of all animals and plants revolve. Hesiod says of it:

"' The first, and fourth, and seventh day were held sacred.'

" And again :

"'And on the seventh the sun's resplendent orb.'

" And Homer :

"' And on the seventh, then came the sacred day.'

" And :

"' The seventh was sacred.'

" And again :

"' It was the seventh day, and all things were accomplished.'

" And again :

"' And on the seventh morn we leave the stream of Acheron.'

" Callimachus the poet also writes :

"' It was the seventh morn, and they had all things done.'

" And again :

"' Among good days is the seventh day, and the seventh race.'

" And :

"' The seventh is among the prime, and the seventh is perfect.'

" And :

> " ' Now all the seven were made in starry heaven,
>   In circles shining as the years appear.'

"The *Elegies of Solon*, too, intensely deify the seventh day. And how? Is it not similar to Scripture when it says, ' Let us remove the righteous man from us, because he is troublesome to us?' When Plato, all but predicting the economy of salvation, says in the second book of the *Republic*, as follows: ' Thus he who is constituted just shall be scourged, shall be stretched on the rack, shall be bound, have his eyes put out; and, at last, having suffered all evils, shall be crucified.' "[1]

A similar combination of pagan error and wild speculation is found in another of Clement's works, where he discusses reasons for fasting on Wednesday and on Friday, and also considers how one may keep Sunday. Writing of the " True Gnostic," Clement says:

" He knows also the enigmas of the fasting of those days—I mean the Fourth and the Preparation. For the one has its name from Hermes, and the other from Aphrodite. He fasts in his life, in respect of covetousness and voluptuousness, from which all the vices grow. For we have already often above shown the three varieties of fornication, according to the apostle—love of pleasure, love of money, idolatry. He fasts then, according to the law, abstaining from bad deeds, and according to the perfection of the Gospel, from evil thoughts. Temptations are applied to him, not for his purification, but, as we have

---

[1] *Stromata*, book v., chap. xiv.

said, for the good of his neighbors, if, making trial of toils and pains, he has despised and passed them by.

"The same holds of pleasure. For it is the highest achievement for one who has had trial of it, afterwards to abstain. For what great thing is it, if a man restrains himself in what he knows not? He, in fulfilment of the precept according to the Gospel, keeps the Lord's day, when he abandons an evil disposition, and assumes that of the Gnostic, glorifying the Lord's resurrection in himself. Further also when he has received the comprehension of scientific speculation, he deems that he sees the Lord, directing his eyes towards things invisible, although he seems to look on what he does not wish to look on; chastising the faculty of vision, when he perceives himself pleasurably affected by the application of his eyes; since he wishes to see and hear that alone which concerns him."[1]

Clement on the Sabbath Law.

Prominent examples of paganism are found in Clement's *Gnostic Exposition of the Decalogue.* Discoursing upon the Fourth Commandment, he says:

"Having reached this point, we must mention these things by the way, since the discourse has turned on the seventh and the eighth. For the eighth may possibly turn out to be properly the seventh, and the seventh manifestly the sixth, and the latter properly the Sabbath, and the seventh a day of work. For the creation of the world was concluded in six days. For the motion of the

[1] *Stromata*, book vii., chap. xii.

sun from solstice to solstice is completed in six months, in the course of which, at one time the leaves fall, and at another plants bud and seeds come to maturity. And they say that the embryo is perfected exactly in the sixth month, that is, in one hundred and eighty days in addition to the two and a half, as Polybus the physician relates in his book *On the Eighth Month*, and Aristotle the philosopher in his book *On Nature*. Hence the Pythagoreans, as I think, reckon six the perfect number, from the creation of the world, according to the prophet, and call it Meseuthys and Marriage, from its being the middle of the even numbers, that is, of ten and two. For it is manifestly at an equal distance from both." [1]

The next paragraph is too gross to appear in this place. Toward the close of this learned (?) "exposition," Clement gives birth to the following curious argument from the Psalms :

" And the blessed David delivers clearly to those who know the mystic account of seven and eight, praising thus : ' Our years were exercised like a spider. The days of our years in them are seventy years ; but if in strength, eighty years. And that will be to reign.' That, then, we may be taught that the world was originated, and not suppose that God made it in time, prophecy adds : ' This is the book of the generation, also of the things in them, when they were created in the day that God made heaven and earth.' For the expression, ' when they were created ' intimates an indefinite and dateless production. But the expression ' in the day that God made,' that is, in and by

[1] *Stromata*, book vii., chap. xvi.

which God made 'all things," and 'without which not even one thing was made,' points out the activity exerted by the Son. As David says, 'This is the day which the Lord hath made ; let us be glad and rejoice in it '; that is, in consequence of the knowledge imparted by Him, let us celebrate the divine festival ; for the Word that throws light on things hidden, and by whom each created thing came into life and being, is called day. And in fine, the Decalogue, by the letter *Iota*, signifies the blessed name, presenting Jesus, who is the Word." [1]

Pagan nonsense could scarcely go further, and yet this man wielded a prominent influence in developing the doctrine of Sunday Observance.

Tertullian on the Sabbath.

TERTULLIAN was a prolific writer, and one not noted for consistency. He taught the abolition of the Sabbath (see *Against the Jews*, chapter iv.), and refers to the observance of Sunday without giving formal reasons therefor. But incidental references which he makes show how the Sunday, although it had then come to be called the " Lord's Day," still bore the heathen characteristics. Witness the following :

" The Holy Spirit upbraids the Jews with their holy-days. 'Your Sabbaths, and new moons, and ceremonies,' says He, ' My soul hateth.' By us, to whom Sabbaths are strange, and the new moons and festivals formerly beloved

[1] *Stromata*, book vi., chap. xvi.

by God, the *Saturnalia* and *New-Years* and *Midwinter's* festivals and *Matronalia* are frequented—presents come and go—New-Year's Gifts—games join their noise—banquets join their din! Oh, better fidelity of the nations to their own sect, which claims no solemnity of the Christians for itself! Not the Lord's day, not Pentecost, even if they had known them, would they have shared with us; for they would not fear lest they would seem to be Christians. *We* are not apprehensive least we seem to be *heathens!* If any indulgence is to be granted to the flesh, you have it. I will not say your own days, but more too; for to the *heathens*, each festive day occurs but once annually; *you* have a festive day every eighth day. Call out the individual solemnities of the nations and set them out into a row, they will not be able to make up a Pentecost." [1]

Here we have the native character of the Sunday truly set forth; a day of "indulgence to the flesh." Such was the legitimate, the unavoidable fruitage of this semi-pagan festivalism, a fruitage which poisoned the Church rapidly and almost fatally.

It is enough to add under this head, that *no writer of the first three hundred years gives, or attempts to give,* a scriptural reason for observing Sunday. There are no such reasons to give.

[1] *De Idolatria*, chap. xiv.

CHAPTER IX.

STATE RELIGION A PAGAN INSTITUTION.

Christ's Attitude toward the State — The Roman Conception of Religion as a Department of the State—Roman Civil Law Created and Regulated All Religious Duties—Effect of the Pagan Doctrine of Religious Syncretism on Christianity—The Emperor a Demi-God, Entitled to Worship, and, *ex officio*, the Supreme Authority in Religion—The Deep Corruption of Roman Morals and Social Life under Pagan State Religion.

THREE fundamental points at which Christianity was corrupted by heathenism have been examined. It remains to consider another which was not less fundamental, and has not been less persistent—viz., the *Union of Christianity with the State.*

Christ's Attitude Toward the State.

Christ taught the infinite worth of man as an individual. The divine priesthood of every believer in Christ, and his absolute spiritual kingship over himself, under God, is a fundamental doctrine of the Gospel. On such a platform, Christ proclaimed the absolute separation of Church and State. "My kingdom is not of this world" was the keynote in His proclamation. His kingdom knew neither Jew nor Greek, Roman nor Egyptian, bondman nor freeman. Ethnic distinctions and lines of caste were unknown to the world's Redeemer. Wherever a heart bowed in simple faith and loyal obedience, there Christ's kingdom was set up. Placed alongside the state-church theory of Rome, the doctrine of Christ's kingdom was noonday by the side of midnight. It was a diamond among pebbles. It was the proclamation of a brotherhood all-embracing and eternal. This kingdom rendered unto Cæsar the little that was due him, and demanded the fullest and highest allegiance to the invisible but not unknown God. It sought only simple protection from the civil power, and patiently suffered wrong, even unto death, when this was denied. Such a kingdom found its first adherents among those who were least entangled in the meshes of the state religions, and whose hearts opened most loyal to the one God, and His Son, the Christ. These were naturally the common people, who heard gladly, and entered joyfully into the heavenly citizenship. Thus the Church of Christ, like Himself, was born among the lowly, and wholly independent of the state. Such a spiritual kingdom could not be brought under the control of the civil power, and that a pagan power, without being corrupted, if not destroyed.

Roman Conception of Religion.

The reader will be better prepared to understand how Christianity became corrupted along this line, by considering the genius of the Roman nation, and its conception of religion. The idea of law as the embodiment of absolute power pervaded the Roman mind. Men were important only as citizens. Separate from the state, man was nothing. " To be a Roman, was greater than a king." Every personal right, every interest was subservient to the state. This conception of power was the source of Roman greatness, prowess, and success. It conscripted the legions, conquered the world, and made all roads lead to Rome. Previous to Christianity, all religion was ethnic. To the Roman, religion was a part of the civil code. It was a system of contracts between men and the gods, through the civil law. The head of the State was, *ex officio*, the head of the Department of Religion. There was no place in heathen theories for the Gospel idea of the Church. Speaking on this point, Dr. SCHAFF says :

" Of a separation of religion and politics, of the spiritual power from the temporal, heathen antiquity knew nothing, because it regarded religion itself only from a natural point of view, and subjected it to the purposes of the all-ruling state, the highest known form of human society.

The Egyptian kings, as Plutarch tells us, were at the same time priests, or were received into the priesthood at their election. In Greece the civil magistrate had supervision of the priests and sanctuaries. In Rome, after the time of Numa, this supervision was intrusted to a senator, and afterward united with the imperial office. All the pagan emperors, from Augustus to Julian the Apostate, were at the same time supreme pontiffs (Pontifices Maximi), the heads of the state religion, emperor-popes. As such they could not only perform all priestly functions, even to offering sacrifices, when superstition or policy prompted them to do so, but they also stood at the head of the highest sacerdotal college (of fifteen or more Pontifices), which in turn regulated and superintended the three lower classes of priests (the Epulones, Quindecemviri, and Augures), the temples and altars, the sacrifices, divinations, feasts and ceremonies, the exposition of the Sibylline books, the calendar, in short, all public worship, and in part even the affairs of marriage and inheritance." [1]

That Christianity must needs become paganized if it became a religion of the state, is shown further by the following, from an editor of *Justinian's Institutes :*

" What was most peculiar in the religion of Rome was its intimate connection with the civil polity. The heads of religion were not a priestly caste, but were citizens, in all other respects like their fellows, except that they were invested with peculiar sacred offices. The king was at

[1] *Church History*, vol. iii., pp. 131, 132, New York, 1884.

the head of the religious body, and beneath him were augurs and other functionaries of the ceremonies of religion. The whole body of the *populus* had a place in the religious system of the state. The mere fact of birth in one of the *familiæ* forming part of a *gens* gave admittance to a sacred circle which was closed to all besides. Those in this circle were surrounded by religious ceremonies from their cradle to their grave. Every important act of their life was sanctioned by solemn rites. Every division and subdivision of the state to which they belonged had its own peculiar ceremonies. The individual, the family, the *gens*, were all under the guardianship of their respective tutelar deities. Every locality with which they were familiar was sacred to some patron god. The calendar was marked out by the services of religion. The pleasure of the gods arranged the times of business and leisure; and a constantly superintending Providence watched over the councils of the state, and showed, by signs which the wise could understand, approval or displeasure of all that was undertaken." [1]

The fundamental difference between New Testament Christianity and the Roman idea of religion is further shown by the following from Reville and Tiele :

REVILLE says :

" In Rome religious tradition was an affair of the state, like the priesthood itself. The senate was by right its guardian. That body legislated for religion as for everything

---

[1] *The Institutes of Justinian*, by Thomas Collett Sandars, Oxford, Eng., Introduction, p. 4, Chicago, 1876.

else ; and when the Greco-Roman paganism persecuted, it did so from essentially political motives."

TIELE says :

" Much greater weight was attached by the practical Roman to the cultus than to the doctrines of religion. This was the one point of supreme importance ; in his view the truly devout man was he who punctually performed his religious obligations, who was pious according to law. There was a debt to be paid to the gods, which must be discharged, but it was settled if the letter of the contract was fulfilled, and the symbol was given in place of the reality. The animistic conception that the gods might be employed as instruments for securing practical advantages, lies at the basis of the whole Roman cultus. In the earliest times, therefore, it was quite simple, so far as regards the absence of images or temples, but it was at the same time exceedingly complicated and burdened with all kinds of ceremonies and symbolic actions, and the least neglect destroyed the efficacy of the sacrifice. This necessitated the assistance of priests acquainted with the whole ritual, not to serve as mediators, for the approach to the deity was open to all, but to see that pious action failed in no essential element. . . . Everything was regulated with precision by the government, and the fact that the highest of the priests was always under the control of the state, prevented the rise of a priestly supremacy, the absence of which in Greece was due to other causes ; but the consequence was that the Roman religion remained dry and formal and was external rather than

[1] *Prolegomena of the History of Religions*, by Albert Reville, D.D., p. 169, London, 1884.

13

inward. Even the purity (*castitas*) on which great stress was laid, was only sacerdotal, and was attained by lustration, sprinkling, and fumigation, and the great value attached to prayer, so that a single error had to be atoned for as a neglect, had its basis in the superstitious belief that it possessed a high magic power."[1]

Religious Syncretism.

The prevailing tendency to religious syncretism in the Roman empire paved the way for corrupting Christianity by union with the State.

The doctrine of courtesy in religious matters had risen in the Roman mind, to a theory of religious syncretism, which offered recognition to other religions outside the Roman. The religions of the Orient and of Egypt already had a place and protection at Rome. These, like the citizens of the lands whence they came, were taken in charge by the laws of the Mistress of the World. By the opening of the fourth century, Christianity had gained such influence and standing that, although it had no claims as an ethnic religion, it was too promising a waif to be longer unnoticed. The great empire was conscious of present decline and coming decay. New blood was an imperative necessity ; perhaps this new religion, that had given

[1] *Outlines of the History of Religions,* C. P. Tiele, Boston, 1877, pp. 237, 238.

such power of endurance to its votaries, would furnish the needful help.

This recognition, at first, was not in any true sense toleration, nor a full recognition of the freedom of conscience. It was rather such recognition as the foreman gives to the apprentice : "Come in and show what you can do." In this recognition Rome adopted no new policy, neither gave evidence of any genuine faith in Apostolic Christianity. As late as 321 A.D., not more than one-twentieth part of the people were Christians ; and Constantine, erroneously called " The first Christian emperor," did not make an open confession of Christianity, until he lay on his death-bed in 337 A.D. Christianity was taken under the protection of the empire, to be cared for and controlled according to the genius of Roman history and Roman law. The "Christian emperors," from Constantine to Gratian (312–383), retained the title of " Pontifex Maximus." The visiting of heathen temples for religious purposes, and the performance of heathen rites in private, were not prohibited by imperial law until 391–393 A.D. by Theodosius. Nor were these laws then enforced where the heathen element was in the ascendency. Theodosius himself was not deemed an enemy of the old religion ; he stood in such favor that the senate enrolled him among the gods, after his death, in 395 A.D.

Instead of developing normally, after the simple New Testament model, the Roman church was modelled largely after the Roman empire. The union once begun, political intrigue and religious degeneracy followed in rapid succession. All civil legislation in matters of religion pushes the divine authority aside, and substitutes the human. This creates conscience, if at all, toward the state alone, and so remains on heathen ground.

Thus, by descending from the high ground of the Apostolic period, from the immediate control and direction of the Holy Spirit, to the control of a heathen state-system, and being already weakened by the false philosophies which had driven out the authority of the Word, Christianity was turned far away from its true status and character. The legislation which followed, concerning festivals, ceremonies, and doctrines, was a medley of paganism and Christianity, truth and error, widely removed from the Sermon on the Mount, and the epistles of Paul. The kernel of Papal error, and the fountain which was the source of the Dark Ages, are both involved in the fundamental perversions of Apostolic Christianity.

Since the emperor was, *ex officio*, the head of the Department of Religion, it was comparatively easy to accomplish the amalgamation of the different systems. Gibbon gives an outline picture of this tendency as it prevailed during the third century. It was the more destructive to Christianity because of the degraded character of the emperors and those who controlled the public life of the empire. The emperor of whom Gibbon writes below, is described by Schaff as follows :

" The abandoned youth El-Gabal, or Heliogabalus (218–222), who polluted the throne by the blackest vices and follies, tolerated all the religions in the hope of at last merging them in his favorite Syrian worship of the sun, with its abominable excesses. He himself was a priest of the god of the sun, and thence took his name.

" His far more worthy cousin and successor, Alexander Severus (222–235), was addicted to a higher kind of religious eclecticism and syncretism, a pantheistic hero-worship. He placed the busts of Abraham and Christ in his domestic chapel, with those of Orpheus, Apollonius of Tyana, and the better Roman emperors, and had the Gospel rule, ' As ye would that men should do to you, do ye even so to them,' engraven on the walls of his palace and on public monuments. His mother, Julia Mammæa, was a patroness of Origen."

Gibbon says of this period :

" The sun was worshipped at Emesa, under the name of Elagabalus, and under the form of a black conical stone, which, as it was universally believed, had fallen from heaven on that sacred place. To this protecting deity Antoninus, not without some reason, ascribed his eleva-

---

[1] Schaff, *History of the Christian Church*, vol. ii., pp. 58, 59.

tion to the throne. The display of superstitious gratitude was the only serious business of his reign. The triumph of the god of Emesa over all the religions of the earth. was the great object of his zeal and vanity; and the appellation of Elagabalus (for he presumed, as pontiff and favorite to adopt that sacred name) was dearer to him than all the titles of Imperial greatness. In a solemn procession through the streets of Rome, the way was strewed with gold-dust; the black stone, set in precious gems, was placed on a chariot, drawn by six milk-white horses, richly caparisoned. The pious emperor held the reins, and supported by his ministers, moved slowly backwards, that he might perpetually enjoy the felicity of the divine presence. In a magnificent temple raised on the Palatine Mount, the sacrifices of the god Elagabalus were celebrated with every circumstance of cost and solemnity. The richest wines, the most extraordinary victims, and the rarest aromatics, were profusely consumed on his altar. Around the altar, a chorus of Syrian damsels performed their lascivious dances to the sound of barbarian music, whilst the gravest personages of the state and army, clothed in long Phœnician tunics, officiated in the meanest functions, with affected zeal and secret indignation.

" To this temple, as to the common center of religious worship, the Imperial fanatic attempted to remove the Ancilia, the Palladium, and all the sacred pledges of the faith of Numa. A crowd of inferior deities attended in various stations the majesty of the god of Emesa; but his court was still imperfect, till a female of distinguished rank was admitted to his bed. Pallas had been first chosen for his consort; but, as it was dreaded lest her warlike terrors might affright the soft delicacy of a Syrian deity, the Moon, adored by the Africans under the name of Astarte, was deemed a more suitable companion for the Sun. Her image, with the rich offerings of her temple as a marriage portion, was transported with solemn pomp from Carthage to Rome, and the day of these mystic nuptials was a general festival in the capital and throughout the empire." [1]

Elagabalus reigned from 218 to 222 A.D. The foregoing facts show that the empire was practically prostituted, and given over to the lowest forms of sun-worship during his reign. It was the triumph of Orientalism in the West. The same devotion to sun-worship appears in other emperors, toward the close of the third century.

Aurelian reigned from 270 to 276 A.D. Speaking of the magnificent " Triumph " of this emperor in 274 A.D., Gibbon says :

"So long and so various was the pomp of Aurelian's triumph, that, although it opened with the dawn of day, the slow majesty of the procession ascended not the Capitol before the ninth hour ; and it was already dark when the emperor returned to the palace. The festival was protracted by theatrical representations, the games of the circus, the hunting of wild beasts, combats of gladiators, and naval engagements. Liberal donatives were distributed to the army, and people, and several institutions agreeable or beneficial to the city, contributed to perpetuate the glory of Aurelian.

[1] *Decline*, etc., vol. i., pp. 170, 171, New York, 1883.

" A considerable portion of his oriental spoils was consecrated to the gods of Rome; the Capitol, and every other temple, glittered with the offerings of his ostentatious piety; and the temple of the Sun alone received above fifteen thousand pounds of gold. This last was a magnificent structure, erected by the emperor on the side of the Quirinal hill, and dedicated, soon after the triumph, to that deity whom Aurelian adored as the parent of his life and fortunes. His mother had been an inferior priestess in a chapel of the Sun; a peculiar devotion to the god of Light was a sentiment which the fortunate peasant imbibed in his infancy; and every step of his elevation, every victory of his reign, fortified superstition by gratitude." [1]

Speaking of Diocletian, who reigned from 284 to 305, MILMAN says:

" Diocletian himself, though he paid so much deference to the older faith as to assume the title of Jovius, as belonging to the Lord of the world, yet, on his accession, when he would exculpate himself from all concern in the murder of his predecessor Numerian, appealed in the face of the army to the all-seeing deity of the sun. It is the oracle of Apollo of Miletus, consulted by the hesitating emperor, which is to decide the fate of Christianity. The metaphorical language of Christianity had unconsciously lent strength to this new adversary; and, in adoring the visible orb, some, no doubt, supposed that they were not departing far from the worship of the " Sun of Righteousness."

[1] *Ibid.*, vol. i., p. 361.

In a foot-note, Milman quotes:

" Hermogenes, one of the older heresiarchs, applied the text, ' He has placed his tabernacle in the sun,' to Christ, and asserted that Christ had put off his body in the sun." [1]

Dr. GEIKIE touches the point, and shows in a few words how Christianity yielded to paganism and its corrupting results; he says:

" Helios, the sun, was the great object of worship, and so deep-rooted was this idolatry that the early Christian missionaries knew no other way of overthrowing it than by changing it into the name of Elias, and turning the temples into churches dedicated to him." [2]

Two important factors touching the union of Christianity and the state are now before the reader.

1. Under the Roman empire all recognized religions were controlled by the civil law. The persecution of Christians was based upon the idea that their worship was illegal; or rather that their refusal to worship the national gods, according to the legal *cultus*, was an offence against the commonwealth.

2. Sun-worship in its higher and lower forms was the prevailing and popular cult at Rome in the third and fourth centuries of Christian history.

[1] *Hist. Christianity*, book ii., chap. ix.
[2] *Life and Words of Christ*, vol. i., pp. 53, 54. Appleton & Co., 1883.

The emperors were devotees of this cult. It was therefore a foregone necessity that when Christianity grew strong enough to be entitled to recognition rather than persecution, it should be adopted by the state, and further commingled with the prevailing sun-worship. The next chapter will show how this was accomplished.

CHAPTER X.

THE CONTROL OF CHRISTIANITY BY THE STATE UNDER CONSTANTINE AND HIS SUCCESSORS.

A New Epoch in the Paganizing of Christianity—Paganism Seeking a New God, Strong enough to Save the Empire—Constantine not a "Christian Emperor," but Superstitious, Time-Serving, and Ambitious—Murdering his Kindred while Promoting Christianity as a rising Political Influence —Seeking Christianity mainly for Ambitious Ends—Professing Christianity only on his Death-Bed—Making the Most of Both Worlds—Constantine Corrupted and Perverted Christianity More than he Aided it.

THE opening of the fourth century marks a new era in the process by which paganism poisoned Christianity, by applying to it the pagan theory set forth in the last chapter. Though sadly weakened and corrupted by these influences, Christianity was a growing power in the empire. On the other hand, paganism was declining, and the fortunes of the disintegrating empire seemed to be going down with the national religious cult. Pagan superstition looked upon all the fortunes of the empire as the direct work of the gods, and as misfortunes piled up around the empire, it was natural to think that the old gods were deserting it, and that new gods must be sought. When the empire became subdivided under different rulers, the rivalry between them, and the varying success which attended the efforts of each, naturally associated success and failure with the gods to whom each was devoted. The firmness of the Christians under persecution was looked upon by the pagans as evidence that the Christian's God had great power to help those who worshipped him. In this way many were brought to consider the idea of adding this God to the catalogue of those whom they already worshipped.

The severe edicts of Diocletian against the Christians, issued in 303 A.D., spread desolation far and wide. In Gaul, Britain, and Spain, where Constantius Chlorus and Constantine his son reigned, the edict was tamely enforced, they preferring to favor the Christians. The bitterness of the persecutions in other parts of the empire inflamed the zeal of Christians, and martyrdom was sought by many, not so much from calm faith as from fanatical zeal.[1] This cruel persecution was the last direct effort of paganism to destroy Christianity by the sword. The fortunes which befell the leaders in the persecution increased superstitious regard for the God of the martyrs, who was thought to be like the gods of the pagans, only more powerful.

[1] See Schaff, vol. ii., chap. 64 *ff.*

Galerius, who was the leader in the horrid work, being striken by a terrible disease, was overcome with fear, and, in connection with Constantine and Licinius, ordered the persecutions to cease, by an edict in 311 A.D. This edict was to the effect that since punishment had not reclaimed the Christians, they might now hold their assemblies, providing they did not disturb the order of the state. The real animus of the edict is seen in its closing words, in which Galerius suggested that " after this manifestation of grace, Christians ought to pray to their God for the welfare of the Emperors and of the State." Constantine attributed the military success which finally made him sole ruler in 323 A.D. to the help of the Christians' God. All parties looked upon the issue as a political struggle between Jupiter and Jehovah, in which the latter was victorious.

Boissier, a late, learned French writer, says :

" Constantine recalled that of all the princes that he had known, the only one who had lived prosperously, without eclipse, was his father Constance, who had protected the Christians; while nearly all those who had persecuted them had ended their lives miserably." [1]

---

[1] *La Fin du Paganisme :* Étude sur les Dernières Luttes Religieuses en Occident, au Quatrième Siècle. Par Gaston Boissier, de l'Académie Française, et de l'Académie des Inscriptions et Belles Lettres. Tome premier, p. 28, Paris 1891.

Character of Constantine.

Constantine has been called the "first Christian Emperor"; how unjustly will be seen in what follows.   In a certain sense, Christianity ascended the throne of the Cæsars with Constantine.   It was a political triumph, but a spiritual defeat. That we may the better understand the case, the reader needs to look carefully into the character of this first representative of the pagan state-church policy, and of the subordinating of Christianity to the political power.   The reader will be permitted to make this survey mainly through the eyes of other writers, which I think will be more satisfactory than any picture that I might draw.

KILLEN thus summarizes the character of Constantine :

"The personal conduct of Constantine in advanced life did not exhibit Christianity as a religion fitted to effect a marked improvement in the spirit and character.   In A.D. 326, he put to death his son Crispus, a youth of the highest promise, who had in some way disturbed his suspicious temper.   His nephew Licinius and his own wife Fausta shared the same fate.   His growing passion for gaudy dress betrayed pitiable vanity in an old man of sixty; and towards the end of his reign, the general extravagance of his expenditure led to an increase of taxation of which his subjects complained.   He desired to be a dictator of the Church, rather than a disciple; and with a view to share its privileges without submitting to its discipline, deferred his baptism until the near approach of death. He then received the ordinance from the Arian bishop of Nicomedia.

" The defects in the religious character of Constantine greatly impaired his moral influence. Though he did much to promote the extension of the visible Church, his reign forms an era in the history of ecclesiastical corrupt-tion. His own Christianity was so loose and accommo-dating that it seemed to consist chiefly in the admiration of a new ritual ; and the courtiers who surrounded him and who complimented him by the adoption of his creed, seldom seemed to feel that it taught the necessity of per-sonal reformation. All at once, the profession of the Gospel became fashionable ; crowds of merely nominal converts presented themselves at the baptismal font ; and many even entered the clerical office who had no higher object in view than an honorable or a lucrative position. Ecclesiastical discipline was relaxed ; and that the hea-then might be induced to conform to the religion of the emperor, many of their ceremonies were introduced into the worship of the Church. The manner in which Constantine intermeddled with ecclesiastical affairs was extremely objectionable. He undertook not only to preach, but also to dicate to aged and learned ministers. Had any other individual who had never been baptized appeared in the Nicene synod, and ventured to give counsel to the assembled fathers, he would have been speedily rebuked for his presumption ; but all were so delighted to see a great prince among them, that there was a general unwillingness to challenge his intrusion. He sometimes indeed declared, that he left spiritual matters to Church courts ; but his conduct demonstrated how little he observed such an arrangement. He con-vened synods by his own authority; took a personal share in their discussions; required their members to appear before him, and submit their proceedings to his review; and inflicted on them civil penalties when their official acts did not meet his approval. Had Constantine given his sanction and encouragement to the Church, and yet permitted her to pursue her noble mission in the full enjoyment of the right of self government, he might have contributed greatly to promote her safe and vigorous development; but by usurping the place of her chief ruler, and bearing down with the weight of the civil power on all who refused to do his pleasure, he secularized her spirit, robbed her of her freedom, and converted her divine framework into a piece of political machinery." [1]

Rev. E. EDWIN HALL, who was for many years chaplain of the American Legation at Rome, Italy, also chaplain of the American Church at Florence, made a careful study of the early history and of the modern characteristics of Roman Catholicism. In July, 1889, a paper from his pen was published in the *Outlook*, a Sabbath quarterly from which the following is taken :

" Soon after the so-called conversion of Constantine, when he became sole emperor, the Church entered on its apostasy from the primitive simplicity and purity which marked its earlier history. Pagans in vast multitudes pressed into the Christian fold, bringing with them old

[1] *The Old Catholic Church*, etc., by W. D. Killen, D.D., pp. 70-72, Edinburgh, 1871.

practices and customs, and filling the places of Christian worship with the pageantry and the ornaments which characterized the worship of the gods in heathen temples. These unconverted millions became only nominally Christian, impressing their character together with the doctrines, rites and forms of pagan religion upon the Christian Church. Gibbon, speaking of these innovations, shows that : ' Rites and ceremonies were introduced which seemed most powerfully to affect the senses of the people. If in the beginning of the 5th century Tertullian or Lactantius had been suddenly raised from the dead, to assist at the festival of some popular saint or martyr, they would have gazed with astonishment and indignation on the profane spectacle which had succeeded the pure and spiritual worship of a Christian congregation. As soon as the doors of the church were thrown open, they must have been offended at the smoke of incense, the perfume of flowers, the glare of lamps and tapers which diffused at noonday, in their opinions, a gaudy, superfluous, and sacrilegious light. They would see a prostrate crowd of worshipers devoutly kissing the walls and pavement of the sacred edifice, their fervent prayers directed to the bones, the blood, or ashes of the saints, the walls covered with votive offerings, representing the favors received from saints in answer to their prayers and illustrating the abuse of indiscreet or idolatrous devotion, in recognition of the image, the attributes, and the miracles of the tutelar saint, which had the same value to their mind as a local divinity in the pagan religion. The ministers of various names in the Catholic Church imitated the profane model which they should have been impatient to destroy. So the religion of Constantine achieved, in less than a century, the

14

final conquest of the Roman Empire, but the victors themselves were insensibly subdued by the acts of their vanquished rivals.' [1]

" From that time the worship of the Roman Catholic Church, in its forms and ceremonies, has been more clearly identified with the paganism of ancient Rome than with the religion of the New Testament. The customs of pagan religion were only baptized with Christian names. Gregory the Great in the latter part of the 6th century, ignoring the sovereignty of the Holy Spirit and the power of the Gospel, directed the Monk Augustine, whom he sent to convert the idolaters of England, ' not to suspend or abolish the pagan festivals, nor the customs of their worship, but rather retain them, contenting himself with substituting for the names of false gods, the names of saints borne by their temples, and whose relics were deposited in them.' " [2]

F. W. MAURICE aptly describes the Christianity of Constantine's time as follows :

" And to the gloss of civilisation had been added the gloss of Christianity. The Emperor had believed, when other help was failing, that in the might of the Cross he might still conquer. The sign was indeed there, but it was marked upon the standard, not written upon the hearts, of those rulers of the world. They saw not what it meant ; how it interpreted and crowned all that had been great in their history hitherto ; how it separated the real great from the real little ; how it sanctified all those feelings of obedience, duty, reverence for unseen law, self-

---

[1] *Decline*, etc., c. xxviii.

[2] *Beda*, lib. i., c. xxx.

devotion, by which the city had risen from nothing ; how it poured contempt upon dominion, except as an instrument by which the highest might serve the lowest, upon glory, except as it grew out of humiliation, and was the exaltation of man above himself. The civilised Christian Roman had lost the heart, the reverence, the faith which belonged to his rude Pagan ancestors ; that Christianity and civilisation might be victorious, the miserable patrons of both were swept away." [1]

Speaking of the effect of Constantine's attitude in favoring Christianity as a rising influence in the nation, MERIVALE says :

"We may suppose, indeed, that the favor thus unexpectedly showered on the new faith by the Imperial government would tend inevitably to reverse the proportions of the two persuasions, or rather of the two parties, which now divided the Roman world. Powerful as the example of rulers has always been in such matters, it would never, perhaps, be more so than at the moment when paganism, corrupt and effete, had lost all the spirit of a real faith, and when, as we shall see, Christianity was only too ready to accept overtures to the easy compromise which its rivals soon began to offer it. Nevertheless, the progress of the Church of Christ was really slower and less complete than might have been expected. Some allowance, as we have seen, must be made for the spirit of pique and the wounded pride of a class so deeply prejudiced on all matters of sentiment as the magnates of Roman society. But paganism, it must be added, developed at her last

---

[1] *The Religions of the World*, by F. W. Maurice, p. 185, London, 1886.

gasp a new principle of vitality, and nerved herself for a desperate conflict along her whole line."[1]

Concerning the overthrow of paganism, as late as the time of Gratian, 375–383 A.D., Merivale says :

"It seems clear that, as might indeed be expected, the earliest edicts for the confiscation of the temple-endowments under Gratian, big and stern as they look in the codes or statute-book, were practically of little effect. If many temples were really closed, as we may readily believe, though certainly by no means all or the greater number of them, we must suppose that the lordly holders of their property contrived to retain the enjoyment of the funds, while they, not unwillingly perhaps, relieved themselves from the services for which these funds had been originally given. Theodosius found the pagan priesthood despoiled of their wealth in name only, and however earnest he might be in his Christian profession, he long abstained, both in policy and mercy, from asserting the full authority of previous enactments."[2]

ALZOG, a modern Roman Catholic Church historian, though laboring hard to set forth Constantine as the first Christian emperor, and a "saint" of the Roman Catholic Church, is forced to say :

"The law said to have been published by Constantine, A.D. 335, prohibiting all pagan sacrifices, is of doubtful authenticity, and, if authentic, is of very little importance, for like a great many others of a similar nature, it was

---

[1] *Four Lectures on Early Church History*, by Charles Merivale, D.D., pp. 13, 14, New York.
[2] *Ibid.* p. 45.

never enforced. The execution of such laws met with a determined resistance in many places, and particularly at Rome." Constantine, although professing to be a Christian, lived pretty much the same sort of life he had lived while a pagan, and even stained his reputation by the commission of deeds of murder. "

"Licinius was executed A.D. 324, and Licinianus, his son, who appears to have excited the fears of Constantine, shortly afterward met the fate of his father. Constantine also had Crispus, his son by his first wife, Minervina, apprehended in the midst of a solemn festival and exiled him to the shore of Istria, where he perished by an obscure death. Learning afterward, as it is supposed, that Fausta, his second wife, the daughter of Maximianus Herculeus, had been instrumental in causing the death of his brave and illustrious son Crispus, he had her strangled in a bath of warm water heated to an insupportable temperature. It may be that these murders, in which the designing policy of Fausta played so conspicuous a part, prompted Constantine to delay his entrance into the Church, and to put off his baptism till the hour of his death. He was, moreover, influenced by the prevailing prejudice relative to the sacrament of baptism, and also wished to be baptized in the river Jordan, which, however, 'God did not permit.'"[1]

Dr. SCHAFF describes Constantine's relation to Christianity as follows :

"Constantine adopted Christianity first as a superstition, and put it by the side of his heathen supersition, till

---

[1] *Universal Church History*, by Rev. Dr. John Alzog, vol. i., p. 471, Cincinnati, 1874.

finally, in his conviction, the Christian vanquished the pagan, though without itself developing into a pure and enlightened faith."

"At first Constantine, like his father, in the spirit of the Neo-Platonic syncretism of dying heathendom, reverenced all the Gods as mysterious powers; especially Apollo, the god of the sun, to whom in the year 308 he presented munificent gifts. Nay, so late as the year 321 he enjoined regular consultation of the soothsayers in public misfortunes, according to ancient heathen usage; even later, he placed his new residence, Byzantium, under the protection of the God of the Martyrs and the heathen goddess of Fortune; and down to the end of his life he retained the title and the dignity of a *Pontifex Maximus*, or high-priest of the heathen hierarchy. His coins bore on the one side the letters of the name of Christ, on the other the figure of the Sun-God, and the inscription "*Sol invictus.*" Of course these inconsistencies may be referred also to policy and accommodation to the toleration edict in 313. Nor is it difficult to adduce parallels of persons who in passing from Judaism to Christianity, or from Romanism to Protestantism have so wavered between their old and their new position that they might be claimed by both. With his every victory over his pagan rivals, Galerius, Maxentius, and Licinius, his personal leaning to Christianity and his confidence in the magic power of the sign of the cross increased; yet he did not formally renounce heathenism and did not receive baptism until in 337 he was laid upon the bed of death.

.   .   .   .

"He was far from being so pure and so venerable as Eusebius, blinded by his favor to the Church, depicts him in his bombastic and almost dishonestly eulogistic biography, with the evident intention of setting him up as a model for all future Christian princes. It must, with all regret, be conceded that his progress in the knowledge of Christianity was not a progress in the practice of its virtues. His love of display and his prodigality, his suspiciousness and his despotism, increased with his power.

The very brightest period of his reign is stained with gross crimes, which even the spirit of the age and the policy of an absolute monarch cannot excuse. After having reached upon the bloody path of war the goal of his ambition, the sole possession of the empire, yea, in the very year in which he summoned the great council Nicæa, he ordered the execution of his conquered rival and brother-in-law Licinius, in breach of a solemn promise of mercy (324). Not satisfied with this he caused soon afterwards, from political suspicion, the death of the young Licinius, his nephew, a boy of hardly eleven years. But the worst of all is the murder of his eldest son, Crispus, in 326, who had incurred suspicion of political conspiracy, and of adulterous and incestuous purposes towards his step-mother, Fausta, but is generally regarded as innocent. . . .

"At all events, Christianity did not produce in Constantine a thorough moral transformation. He was concerned more to advance the outward social position of the Christian religion than to further its inward mission. He was praised and censured in turn by the Christians and pagans, the orthodox and the Arians, as they successively experienced his favor or dislike. He bears some resemblance to Peter the Great both in his public acts and his private character, by combining great virtues and merits with monstrous crimes, and he probably died with the same consolation as Peter, whose last words were: 'I trust that in respect of the good I have striven to do my people (the Church), God will pardon my sins.' It is quite characteristic of his piety that he turned the sacred nails of the Saviour's cross, which Helena brought from Jerusalem, the one into the bit of his war horse, the other into an ornament of his helmet. Not a decided, pure, and consistent character, he stands on the line of transition between two ages and two religions; and his life bears plain marks of both. When at last on his deathbed he submitted to baptism with the remark: 'Now let us cast away all *duplicity*,' he honestly admitted the conflict of two antagonistic principles which swayed his private character and public life." [1]

After such an array of testimony, which might be extended much farther if space would permit, it seems unnecessary to say more than this: the personal character and the political attitude of Constantine make it impossible to think of him as a "Christian Emperor." He adopted and used the paganized Christianity of his time for personal ends, rather than because of true piety. The political aid which he gave it was overbalanced many times by the destruction of its best spiritual interests. Judged from the standpoint of the Bible and the facts of history, Constantine was the corrupter of Christianity, not its defender.

[1] *Church History*, vol. iii., pp. 14–18.

CHAPTER XI.

CONSTANTINE'S LEGISLATION CONCERNING THE PAGAN SUNDAY.

All his Tolerative Legislation Essentially Pagan—Christians did not Seek for Sunday Laws—The first Sunday Law, 321 A.D., Pagan in Every Particular—Essentially Identical with Existing Laws Concerning Other Days—Legislation against Heathen Religions Feeble and Unenforced—Constantine not a "Christian Prince."

THE representative legislation of Constantine, with reference to Christianity, was pagan both as to its genius and form. The various edicts in favor of Christians contained little or nothing of true liberty of conscience. They were the steps by which Christianity, already paganized, was recognized, and gradually raised to a dominant place among the legal religions. This accorded with the prevailing syncretism, and the policy which Rome had always exercised toward foreign religions. On the other hand, the Emperor, still acting as *Pontifex Maximus*, and long before he was baptized into the fellowship of the Church, became its dictator. He convened and controlled the famous council at Nice (325 A.D.)

while his hands were red with the blood of his kindred, whom he slew lest they might come between him and his ambition to be sole emperor.

The decisions of the Council of Nice mark the beginning of centuries in which imperial law determined what should be called Christianity, what orthodoxy, and what heterodoxy. The Bible was not the standard of faith, or practice. Traditions, imperial decrees, the decisions of councils called and dictated by the imperial power, determined the practice of the Church, and formulated her faith. This will be shown more in detail farther on. Meanwhile we pause to examine the character of one of Constantine's earliest laws, which has left a lasting influence on all Christian history—his " Sunday Edict " of 321 A.D. It is the more important to do this, since the question of Sunday laws and their enforcement is now at the front, and it is well that the reader understand the source from which Sunday legislation sprung. This edict of Constantine is the beginning of Sunday legislation, and it is not difficult to determine the influences which gave it birth. There is no evidence that such legislation was either sought or desired by Christians. They formed but a small fragment of the population of the empire, and in so far as the principles of New Testament Christianity remained, they forbade all such legislation.

The power to appoint holy days rested in the Emperor. His voice was supreme in all such matters. Although history has been carefully searched, there is no trace that any influence was brought to bear upon Constantine, by any person, any event, any custom which represented the Christians, or in which they were interested, to induce him to enact a Sunday law. There is every evidence that he acted in his proper capacity as *Pontifex Maximus*, and whatever notions may have entered into his determination to promulgate the edict, they could not have been Christian. On the other hand, there were abundant reasons why he should begin legislation in favor of Sunday. It was Apollo's day. Apollo was the patron deity of Constantine. He was the beautiful Sungod, and Constantine was proud of his own personal beauty, because of which his fawning courtiers were accustomed to liken him to Apollo. The sun-worship cult had been popular for a long time. Any favor shown to it would strengthen his influence with the "first families" of the empire. It was the settled policy of the emperors to overcome the discontent of the masses, under increasing taxation and burdens, by increasing holidays, games, and enjoyments. To exalt the day of the Sun at such a time was a stroke of policy wholly in keeping with the universal practice of Constantine. The general character of the man, his personal devotion to the Sun-god, and the surrounding demands, furnish all needful reasons for an act of legislation which was pagan, as we shall see, from centre to circumference. This famous edict runs as follows :

" Let all judges, and all city people, and all tradesmen, rest upon the Venerable Day of the Sun. But let those dwelling in the country freely and with full liberty attend to the culture of their fields ; since it frequently happens that no other day is so fit for the sowing of grain, or the planting of vines ; hence the favorable time should not be allowed to pass, lest the provisions of heaven be lost."[1]

This was issued on the seventh of March, A.D. 321. In June of the same year it was modified so as to allow the manumission of slaves on Sunday. The reader will notice that this edict makes no reference to the day as a Sabbath, as the Lord's day, or as in any way connected with Christianity. Neither is it an edict addressed to Christians. Nor is the idea of any moral obligation or Christian duty found in it. It is merely the edict of a heathen emperor, addressed to all his subjects, Christian and heathen, who dwelt in cities, and were tradesmen, or officers of justice, commanding them to refrain from their business on the " *venerable day*" of the god whom Constantine most

---

[1] *Cod. Justin.*, lib. iii., tit. xii., l. 3.

adored, and to whom he loved in his pride to be compared. There are several distinct lines of argument which prove that this edict was a pagan rather than a Christian document.

On the following day Constantine issued an edict with reference to consulting the pagan sooth-sayers in case of public misfortune, which, like the Sunday edict, is so purely heathen that no "Christian Emperor" could have conceived or issued it. It runs as follows :

Edict Concerning Aruspices.

" The August Emperor Constantine to Maximus :

" If any part of the palace or other public works shall be struck by lightning, let the sooth-sayers, following old usages, inquire into the meaning of the portent, and let their written words, very carefully collected, be reported to our knowledge ; and also let the liberty of making use of this custom be accorded to others, provided they abstain from private sacrifices, which are specially prohibited.

" Moreover, that declaration and exposition written in respect to the amphitheater being struck by lightning, concerning which you had written to Heraclianus, the tribune, and master of offices, you may know has been reported to us.

" Dated the 16th, before the calends of January, at Serdica (320) Acc. the 8th, before the Ides of March, in the consulship of Crispus II. and Constantine III., Cæsars Coss. (321)." [1]

---

[1] *Codex Theod.*, lib. xiv., tit. x., l. 1.

There is abundant evidence, beyond the above, that the Sunday-law was the product of paganism.

The language used speaks of the day only as the "*Venerable Day of the Sun*," a title purely heathen. There is not even a hint at any connection between the day and Christianity, or the practices of Christians.

Similar laws concerning many other heathen festivals were common. JOSEPH BINGHAM bears the following testimony, when speaking of the edict under consideration :

" This was the same respect as the old Roman laws had paid to their *feriæ*, or festivals, in times of idolatry and superstition. . . . Now, as the old Roman laws exempted the festivals of the heathen from all judicial business, and suspended all processes and pleadings, except in the fore-mentioned cases, so Constantine ordered that the same respect should be paid to the Lord's day, that it should be a day of perfect vacation from all prosecutions, and pleadings, and business of law, except where any case of great necessity or charity required a juridical process and public transaction."[1]

Bingham states correctly that such prohibitions were made by the Roman laws in favor of pagan festivals, but adds, incorrectly, that Constantine made the same in favor of the " Lord's day." It was not the Lord's day, but the " *Venerable Day of the Sun*," which the edict mentions ; and it is im-

[1] *Antiquities of the Christian Church*, book xx., chap. ii., sec. 2.

possible to suppose that a law, made by a *Christian* prince, in favor of a *Christian* institution, should not in any way mention that institution, or hint that the law was designed to apply to it.

MILLMAN corroborates this idea as follows :

" The earlier laws of Constantine, though in their effect favorable to Christianity, claimed some deference, as it were, to the ancient religion, in the ambiguity of their language, and the cautious terms in which they interfered with paganism. The rescript commanding the celebration of the Christian Sabbath, bears no allusion to its peculiar sanctity as a Christian institution. It is the day of the sun which is to be observed by the general veneration : the courts were to be closed, and the noise and tumult of public business and legal litigation were no longer to violate the repose of the sacred day. But the believer in the new paganism, of which the solar worship was the characteristic, might acquiesce without scruple in the sanctity of the first day of the week. . . .

" The rescript, indeed, for the religious observance of the Sunday, which enjoined the suspension of all public business and private labor, except that of agriculture, was enacted, according to the apparent terms of the decree, for the whole Roman Empire. Yet, unless we had direct proof that the decree set forth the Christian reason for the sanctity of the day, it may be doubted whether the act would not be received by the greater part of the empire as merely *adding one more festival* to the *fasti* of the empire, as proceeding entirely from the will of the emperor, or even grounded on his authority as supreme pontiff, by which he had the plenary power of appointing holy days. In fact, as we have before observed, the day of the sun would be willingly hallowed by almost all the pagan world, especially that part which had admitted any tendency toward the oriental theology.[1]"

Millman hints at some "direct proof." There is none; hence the correctness of his conclusion, that the people looked upon the new holiday, "as merely adding one more festival to the *fasti* of the empire." It was not only non-Christian but eminently unchristian.

Stronger still is the testimony of an English barrister, EDWARD V. NEALE. These are his words:

" That the division of days into *juridici et feriati*, judicial and non-judicial, did not arise out of the modes of thought peculiar to the Christian world must be known to every classical scholar. Before the age of Augustus, the number of days upon which out of reverence to the gods to whom they were consecrated, no trials could take place at Rome, had become a resource upon which a wealthy criminal could speculate as a means of evading justice; and Suetonius enumerates among the praiseworthy acts of that emperor, the cutting off from the number, thirty days, in order that crime might not go unpunished nor business be impeded."[2]

After enumerating certain kinds of business which were allowed under these general laws, Mr. Neale adds: " Such was the state of the laws with

[1] *History of Christianity*, book iii., chaps. i. and iv.
[2] *Feasts and Fasts*, p. 6.

respect to judicial proceedings, while the empire was still heathen." Concerning the suspension of labor, we learn from the same author that :

" The practice of abstaining from various sorts of labor upon days consecrated by religious observance, like that of suspending at such seasons judicial proceedings, was familiar to the Roman world before the introduction of Christian ideas. Virgil enumerates the rural labors, which might on festal days be carried on, without entrenching upon the prohibitions of religion and right ; and the enumeration shows that many works were considered as forbidden. Thus it appears that it was permitted to clean out the channels of an old water course, but not to make a new one ; to wash the herd or flock, if such washing was needful for their health, but not otherwise ; to guard the crop from injury by setting snares for birds, or fencing in the grain ; and to burn unproductive thorns." [1]

SIR HENRY SPELMAN, who is recognized as high authority, in discussing the origin of practices in the English courts, says that all ancient nations prohibited legal proceedings on sacred days. His words are :

" To be short, it was so common a thing in those days of old to exempt the times of exercise of religion from all worldly business, that the barbarous nations, even our *Angli*, while they were yet in Germany, the Suevians themselves, and others in those Northern parts would in no wise violate or interrupt it. Tacitus says of them

---

[1] *Feasts and Fasts*, p. 86, *et seq.*

15

that during this time of holy rites, *non bellum ineunt, non arma sumunt.   Clausum omne ferrum.   Pax et quies tunc tantum nota, tunc tantum amat.*"

Speaking of the origin of the English "court terms," Spelman says :

" I will therefore seek the original of our terms only from the Romans, as all other nations that have been subject to their civil and ecclesiastical monarch do, and must.

" The ancient Romans, while they were yet heathens, did not, as we at this day, use certain continual portions of the year for a legal decision of controversies, but out of superstitious conceit that some days were ominous and more unlucky than others (according to that of the Egyptians), they made one day to be *fastus* or term day and another (as an Egyptian day), to be vacation or *nefastus ;* seldom two fast days or law days together ; yea, they sometimes divided one and the same day in this manner:

" *Qui modo fastus erat, mune nefastus erat.*

" The afternoon was term, the morning holy day.

" Nor were all their *fasti* applied to judicature, but some of them to other meetings and consultations of the commonwealth ; so that being divided into three sorts, which they called *fastos proprie, fastos endotercisos,* and *fastos comitiales,* 'containing together one hundred and eighty-four days through all the months of the year, there remained not properly to the prætor, as judicial or triverbial days, above twenty-eight." [1]

[1] *English Works from Original MS. in Bodleian Library,* book ii., p. 75.

Nothing more is needed to show that the Sunday edict was the product of the heathen cult, as truly as that which was issued in connection with it, relative to the Aruspices. There is an evident connection between the two edicts. Apollo was the patron deity of the soothsayers, as well as of Constantine. At least nine years later than this, Constantine placed his new residence at Byzantium under the protection of the heathen goddess of Fortune; he never gave up the title of high-priest of the heathen religion; he did not formally embrace Christianity until sixteen years later.

Whatever he did to favor Christianity, and whatever claims he made to conversion, were the outgrowth of a shrewd policy, rather than of a converted heart. And when the conservative historian can say of him, "The very brightest period of his reign is stained with crimes, which even the spirit of the age, and the policy of an absolute monarch, cannot excuse," he cannot be called a *Christian* prince.

If he made any general laws against heathenism, they were little executed; for it was not suppressed in the empire until A.D. 390—seventy-nine years after his Sunday edict, and fifty-three years after his death. The few abuses against which he legislated were those which had been condemned before by the laws of the heathen rulers who had preceded him, such as the obscure midnight orgies, etc. Millman says on this point :

" If it be difficult to determine the extent to which Constantine proceeded in the establishment of Christianity. it is even more perplexing to estimate how far he exerted the imperial authority in the abolition of paganism. . . . The pagan writers, who are not scrupulous in their charges against the memory of Constantine and dwell with bitter resentment on all his overt acts of hostility to the ancient religion, do not accuse him of these direct encroachments on paganism. Neither Julian nor Zosimus lay this to his charge. Libanius distinctly asserts that the temples were left open and undisturbed during his reign, and that paganism remained unchanged. Though Constantine advanced many Christians to offices of trust, and no doubt many who were ambitious of such offices conformed to the religion of the emperor, probably most of the high dignities of the State were held by the pagans. . . . In the capitol there can be little doubt that sacrifices were offered in the name of the senate and the people of Rome till a much later period." [1]

The whole matter is tersely told by a late English writer, who, speaking of the time of the Sunday edict, says :

" At a *later period*, carried away by the current of opinion, he declared himself a convert to the church. Christianity then, or what he was pleased to call by that name, became the law of the land, and the edict of A.D. 321, being unrevoked, was enforced as a Christian ordinance." [2]

[1] *Historical Commentaries*, book iv., chap. iv.
[2] *Sunday and the Mosaic Sabbath* (Anonymous), p. 4.

The following words of the learned NIEBUHR, in his lectures on Roman history, are to the same effect :

" Many judge of Constantine by too severe a standard, because they regard him as a Christian ; but I cannot look at him in that light. The religion which he had in his head, must have been a strange jumble indeed. . . . He was a superstitious man, and mixed up his Christian religion with all kinds of absurd and superstitious opinions. When certain oriental writers call him equal to the apostles, they do not know what they are saying, and to speak of him as a saint is a profanation of the word." [1]

It is a curious and little known fact, that markets were expressly appointed by Constantine to be held on Sunday. This we learn from an inscription on a Slavonian bath rebuilt by him, published in Gruter's *Inscriptiones Antiquæ Totius Orbis Romani*, clxiv., 2. It is there recorded of the emperor, that "*provisione pietatis suæ nundinas dies solis perpeti anno constituit*" ; "by a pious provision he appointed markets to be held on Sunday throughout the year." His pious object doubtless was to promote the attendance of the country people at churches in towns. " Thus," says CHARLES JULIUS HARE, " Constantine was the author of the practice of holding markets on Sunday, which, in many parts of Europe, prevailed above a thousand

[1] Lect. V.

years after, though Charlemagne issued a special law (cap. cxl.) against it."[1]　In "Scotland, this practice was first forbidden on holy days by an Act of James IV., in 1503, and on Sundays in particular by one of James VI., in 1579."[2]

[1] *Philological Museum*, i., 30.

[2] *Cf*. Robert Cox, *Sabbath Literature*, vol. i., p. 359. For the Scotch laws mentioned by Cox, see *Critical History of Sunday Legislation*, by the writer, pp. 144–146.

CHAPTER XII.

OTHER FORMS OF PAGAN RESIDUUM IN CHRISTIANITY.

A Low Standard of Religious Life—Faith in Relics—The Cross an Ancient Pagan (Phallic) Symbol—A "Charm" Borrowed from Paganism—Constantine's use of the Composite Symbol as a Military Standard—Prevalence of Faith in "Charms"—Sign of the Cross in Baptism—Baptism and Holy Water as "Charms"—Stupendous Miracles, like Pagan Prodigies, through Baptism—Delayed Baptism—Orientation at Baptism, etc.

THOSE who have made a study of paganism as it appeared in Christianity during and after the third century know that many other forms of it were prominent besides those fundamental errors which have been discussed in the preceding pages. Some of these have attracted more attention than the fundamental ones, since they lie more plainly on the surface of history. We shall glance at several, that the reader may see the field yet more fully.

A Low Standard of Christian Life.

That the standard of individual character in the Church was brought far below that of the New Testament, and much below what would be accepted at the present day, appears in the history of morals and social life, and in many ways in the Church.

The degenerate character of his time is thus set forth by CHRYSOSTOM :

"Plagues too, teeming with untold mischiefs, have lighted upon the Churches. The chief offices have become saleable. Hence numberless evils are springing, and there is no one to redress, no one to reprove them. Nay the disorder has assumed a sort of method and consistency. Has a man done wrong and been arraigned for it? His effort is not to prove himself guiltless, but to find if possible accomplices in his crimes. What is to become of us? since hell is our threatened portion. Believe me, had not God stored up punishment for us there, ye would see every day tragedies deeper than the disasters of the Jews. What then? However, let no one take offence, for I mention no names; suppose some one were to come into this church to present you that are here at this moment, those that are now with me, and to make inquisition of them; or rather not now, but suppose on Easter day any one endued with such a spirit, as to have such a thorough knowledge of the things they had been doing, should narrowly examine all that came to Communion and were being washed [in baptism] after they had attended the mysteries; many things would be discovered more shocking than the Jewish horrors. He would find persons who practise augury, who make use of charms, and omens, and incantations, and who have committed fornication, adulterers, drunkards, and revilers,—covetous I am unwilling to add, lest I should hurt the feelings of any of those who are standing here. What more? Suppose any one should make scrutiny into all the communicants in the world, what kind of transgression is there which he would not detect? And what if he examined those in authority? Would he not find them eagerly bent upon gain? making traffic of high places? envious, malignant, vainglorious, gluttonous and slaves to money?" [1]

A similar vivid description, under the figure of a burning building, representing the Church as consumed with evil, is found in Homily 10, *On Ephesians.* Another description of the effect of heathenism upon those who professed to be Christians is sharply set forth in a *Treatise Attributed to Cyprian*, on the " Public Shows." [2] He says :

"Believers, and men who claim for themselves the authority of the Christian name, are not ashamed—are not, I repeat, ashamed to find a defence in the heavenly Scriptures for the vain superstitions associated with the public exhibitions of the heathens, and thus to attribute divine authority to idolatry. For how is it, that what is done by the heathens in honor of any idol is resorted to in a public show by faithful Christians, and the heathen idolatry is maintained and the true and divine religion is trampled upon in contempt of God? Shame binds me to relate their pretexts and defences in this behalf. 'Where,' say they, 'are there such Scriptures? where

---

[1] Homily 6, *On Ephesians.*

[2] ì go 222 of vol. ii. of *The Writings of Cyprian*, in Ante-Nicene Library.

are these things prohibited? On the contrary, both Elias is the charioteer of Israel, and David himself danced before the ark. We read of psaltries, horns, trumpets, drums, pipes, harps, and choral dances. Moreover, the apostle, in his struggle, puts before us the contest of the Cæstus, and of our wrestle against the spiritual things of wickedness. Again when he borrows his illustrations from the racecourse, he also proposes the prize of the crown. Why, then, may not a faithful Christian man gaze upon that which the divine pen might write about?' At this point I might not unreasonably say that it would have been far better for them not to know any writings at all, than thus to read the writings [of the Scriptures]. For words and illustrations which are recorded by way of exhortation to evangelical virtue, are translated by them into pleas for vice; because those things are written of, not that they should be gazed upon, but that a greater eagerness might be aroused in our minds in respect of things that will benefit us, seeing that among the heathens there is manifest so much eagerness in respect of things which will be of no advantage."

That these evils increased with the years, is shown by the words of AUGUSTINE, when he says:

" Accordingly you will have to witness many drunkards, covetous men, deceivers, gamesters, adulterers, fornicators, men who bind upon their persons sacrilegious charms, and others given up to sorcerers and astrologers, and diviners practised in all kinds of impious arts. You will also have to observe how those very crowds which fill the theaters on the festal days of the pagans, also fill the churches on the festal days of the Christians. And when you see these things you will be tempted to imitate them. Nay, why should I use the expression, *you will see*, in reference to what you assuredly are acquainted with even already. For you are not ignorant of the fact that many who are called Christians engage in all these evil things which I have briefly mentioned. Neither are you ignorant that at times, perchance, men whom you know to bear the name of Christians are guilty of even more grievous offenses than these." [1]

Such degradation of Christian life was the unavoidable fruitage of the various pagan influences which had substituted false standards of Church membership and of action for the true ones laid down in the Scriptures.

Faith in " Relics."

Faith in " Relics," bodies, bones, garments, places, etc., as retaining the virtues of the persons with whom they were associated, was a prominent characteristic of paganism, from the earliest time. Paganism brought this element into Christianity, where it took root and flourished, like a fast-growing, noxious weed. The whole system of relic worship, down to the " Holy Coat at Treves," in 1891, is a direct harvest from pagan planting. Relics were believed to be powerful agents for good, by direct influence, and by acting as charms

---

[1] *On the Catechising of the Uninstructed*, chap. xxv., ¶ 48.

to ward off evils of all kinds.　Take an example from one of the early Church historians, Sozomen, who gives the following with all the soberness of undoubted fact :

"While the Church everywhere was under the sway of these eminent men, the clergy and people were excited to the imitation of their virtue and zeal.　Nor was the Church of this era distinguished only by these illustrious examples of piety ; for the relics of the proto-prophets, Habakkuk, and a little while after, Micah, were brought to light about this time.　As I understand, God made known the place where both these bodies were deposited, by a divine vision in a dream to Zebennus, who was then acting as bishop of the Church of Eleutheropolis.　The relics of Habakkuk were found at Cela a city called Ceila. The tomb of Micah was discovered at a distance of ten stadia from Cela, at a place called Berathsatia. This tomb was ignorantly styled by the people of the country, 'the tomb of the faithful'; or, in their native language, Neph-sameemana.　These events, which occurred during the reign of Theodosius, were sufficient for the good repute of the Christian religion." [1]

The same author reports the discovery of the relics of Zechariah the prophet.　Calemerus, a serf, was directed in a dream to dig at a certain place in a garden, being assured that he would find two coffins, the inner one of wood, the other of lead; "beside the coffins you will see a glass

[1] *Ecc. Hist.*, book vii., chap. xxix.

vessel full of water, and two serpents of moderate size, but tame and perfectly innoxious, so that they seem to be used to being handled." Calemerus followed the directions, and found the body of Zechariah, "clad in a white stole," with a royal child lying at his feet; and "although the prophet had lain under the earth for so many generations, he appeared sound; his hair was closely shorn, his nose was straight; his beard moderately grown, his head quite short, his eyes rather sunken, and concealed by the eyebrows."[1] In a similar style,[2] Sozomen relates how the head of John the Baptist was discovered in the suburbs of Constantinople. That such ridiculous myths could be written down as a part of genuine Church history, shows how fully the pagan falsehoods corrupted the best currents of Christian life.

The Cross, its Sign, and other Charms.

Comparatively few readers realize that the cross was of heathen origin, and a religious symbol of the lowest order, and that it was not adopted as a symbol of Christianity until the Church was well paganized. Its origin lies in the shadows of the prehistoric period. It was a religious symbol in the Asiatic, Egyptian, Grecian, Roman, Druidic,

[1] *Ibid.*, book ix., chap. xvii.
[2] Book vii., chap. xxi.

and Central American heathenism. It originated in the lowest department of sun-worship *cultus.* Ishtar, the Assyrian Venus, was represented as holding a staff, the upper end of which was in the form of a Latin cross. The worship of Ishtar was one of the darkest features of the Babylonian religion. It was conducted with lascivious rites which may not be named. It corrupted the Hebrews on every side. We find it, with other forms of sun-worship, polluting the temple itself, and sharply condemned by the prophet of Jehovah. [1]

Tammuz was the young and beautiful sun-god, the bridegroom of Ishtar who bore the cross-crowned sceptre; and this mourning for him was associated with gross obscenity.

Another form of this same worship is condemned by Jeremiah, thus:

"Seest thou not what they do in the cities of Judah and in the streets of Jerusalem? The children gather wood, and the fathers kindle the fire, and the women knead *their* dough, to make cakes to the queen of heaven, and to pour out drink-offerings unto other gods, that they may provoke me to anger." [2]

There is evidence to show that these cakes were marked with one form of the cross, the Greek *tau* (*T*). In later times the Greeks offered cakes thus

[1] See Ezek. viii., 14–18.
[2] Jer. vii., 17–19.

marked to Bacchus, in connection with the vilest
orgies. Specimens of these are found at Hercu-
laneum. Similar ones have been found in the
catacombs. The "hot cross-bun" is the lineal
descendant of the *tau* (*T*)-marked cakes of the
obscene sun-worship *cultus*. Its association with
Friday—day of Ishtar, Venus, Frega—is a remnant
of paganism, although later efforts to Christianize
it have associated it with "Good Friday."

The cross appears in Assyrian history, worn as a
religious emblem by the priest-king, Samsi-Vul,
son of Shalamanezar, and also by Assur-Nazir-Pal.
These specimens may be seen in the British Museum. It is the Greek cross, and identical with
the "pectoral cross," worn by the Pope, and seen
on altar-cloths at the present day. Priority of
possession is several thousand years in favor of the
Assyrian. The same style of crosses are found in
the Etruscan department of the Vatican Museum
at Rome. They are on the breasts—painted—of certain large Etruscan male figures, and are taken from
mural decorations in ancient Etruscan burial-places.
Similar "pectoral" crosses may be seen also in the
British Museum on two figures from Thebes, in
the Egyptian Hall. They date from about 1100
B.C., and represent men of Asia bringing tribute.
In Wilkinson's *Ancient Egypt* the same cross may
be seen on the breast of two warriors.

There is a figure of the youthful Bacchus, taken from an ancient vase, with which antiquarians are familiar, holding a cup and fennel branch—a figure of much beauty. The head-dress is a band with crosses as of Horus. A portion of the band falls from the head, and with its fringe and single cross, if lengthened, would form a modern " stole."

The cross is also found on Greek pottery, dating from 700 to 500 B.C. It appears in relics of the Latin people of the same period. It was used as a symbol in Buddhism in India long before the time of Christ. It is also found in Thibet, Scandinavia, and other parts of northern Europe.

That the cross was extensively known and used before the Christian era is shown by an admirable article in the *Edinburgh Review* of October, 1870, on the pre-Christian Cross. The author of the article claims to have collected nearly two hundred varieties of the cross, in its heathen form. He speaks of it as follows :

" From the dawn of organized paganism in the Eastern world, to the final establishment of Christianity in the Western, the cross was undoubtedly the commonest and most sacred of symbolical monuments, and to a remarkable extent it is so still in almost every land where that of Calvary is unrecognized or unknown. Apart from any distinctions of social or intellectual superiority of caste, color, nationality, or location in either hemisphere it appears to have been the aboriginal possession of every people of antiquity—the elastic girdle, so to say, which embraced the most widely separated heathen communities, the most significant token of universal brotherhood, the principal point of contact in every system of pagan mythology, to which all the families of mankind were severally and irresistibly drawn, and by which their common descent was emphatically expressed. . . .

" Of the several varieties of the cross still in vogue as national or ecclesiastical emblems in this and other European states, and distinguished by the familiar appellations of St. George, St. Andrew, the Maltese, the Greek, the Latin, etc., there is not one amongst them the existence of which may not be traced to the remotest antiquity." [1]

It is also true that the cross does not appear as the symbol of Christianity until after its paganization under Constantine. He made a composite symbol, known as the *Chi-ro*, of which see below. It seems probable that he added these to the pagan cross. On this point BLAKE says :

"The Cross and the Crescent were combined in the Oriental standards (Fig. 29.) centuries before the time of Christ.

" Roman coins of the period of 269 B.C. show the cross of Saturn (Fig. 30.) with distinctness. According to Gaume, the illustrious writer, all the Roman standards bore this cross, and Constantine being unable to vary the banner of the empire, added ' XP ' the Greek sign for Christ, to the imperial flag, 312 A.D." [2]

[1] Pp. 224, 226.
[2] *The Cross, Ancient and Modern*, by Willson W. Blake, illustrated, pp. 18, 19, New York.

16

The similarity between the heathenism of Asia and Central America is a well-known fact of history.

" The religion of the Mexicans was purely Chaldean. They professed to believe in a Supreme God, but idol-worship was general. They had a regular priesthood, gorgeous temples and convents ; they had processions, in which crosses, and even red crosses, were carried ; and incense, flowers, and fruit-offerings were employed in their worship. They confessed to their priests, and generally confessed only once, receiving a written absolution which served for the remainder of their lives as an effectual safeguard against punishment, even for crimes committed after receiving the said absolution. They worshipped, and afterwards ate, a wafer-god, an idol made of flour and honey, which they called 'the god of penitence,' and they always ate him fasting. They also venerated the black calf, or bull, and adored a goddess-mother, with an infant son in her arms. They sacrificed human victims to the God of Hell, of whom they considered the cross to be a symbol, and to whom they were largely sacrificed, by laying them on a great black stone and tearing out their hearts.

" We are now prepared to see how easily the heathen, in adopting a nominal Christianity, as they did from the reign of Constantine, would have modified and Christian-ized their views of the heathen cross. Hitherto that em-blem had been associated with their worship of the gods. In their temples, in their houses, on their images, their clothes, their cattle, etc., the worshippers were accustomed to see the peculiar cross, or, crosses, dedicated to each. Bacchus had his, Serapis his, and so forth. Some of the new converts were themselves wearing on their own persons the emblem of their gods. This was the case with certain Asiatics and Etruscans, who wore the cross round their necks, but not, apparently, with the Egyptians as far as relating to a neck ornament. Wilkinson, chapter v., plate 342, gives the figures of four warriors from the monuments of Egypt, from Asiatic tribes, wearing crosses round their necks, or on their clothes. Their date is about 1400 B.C.

" In plate 47 of his *Peintures Antiques de Vases Grecs* (Rome, 1817, fol.), Milligen gives examples of the cross on the apron of the warrior, and within a circle on his horse.

" To enter then, into a heathen temple just rededicated to Christ, where the cross of the rejected pagan deity still existed, or where a new church cross had been substituted —to visit a temple so reconsecrated, or to enter a basilica (judgment hall) by the Emperor's order just handed over to the bishop for Christian use—all this would aid in making the change from the worship of the gods to the worship of the Emperor's God very easy to the convert.

" The old temples, and the old basilicas, the arrangements of the apse, etc., in the latter almost unchanged— the lustral, or holy water—the mural paintings sometimes left, sometimes altered to suit the persons of the new heroes, or saints—the incense, the pomp of worship, the long train of vested priests—all and much more, would make the transition from the old to the new faith, externally, a matter of little difficulty. As to the cross, there it was, and there it would continue, and has continued." '

In view of these and many similar facts, it is easy to understand how the cross became a permanent

---

' *The Cross, Heathen and Christian*, by Mourant Brock, M.A., pp. 18, 57-59, London.

and prominent feature in the symbolism of paganized Christianity. The famous vision of Constantine the Great, in which he is said to have seen a cross in the sky, in connection with the sun, is not supported by evidence which places it among facts. It was not unnatural, however, that he, a devout sun-worshipper, and familiar with the cross as the symbol of the lowest form of that worship, should associate the two, as he has been said to have done. The symbol which he adopted on his military standard was not the cross proper, but the two Greek initials of the name of Christ, the "*chi-ro.*" One of these letters, resembling the English X, gave the standard a similarity to the cross. Under Valens, Emperor of the East, who died in 378 A.D., the cross appears without the letters, and from that time the letters gradually disappear. The Empress Eudocia wore the heathen form of the cross on her head.[1] It was the exact counterpart of that which the moon-goddess, Diana, had worn before. The leading facts concerning the cross may be summed up as follows :

Up to the time of Constantine—early part of the fourth century—the cross remained what it had always been, a pagan symbol, type of its most revolting *cultus*. It is the same in India to-day. By the opening of the fifth century it had become

---

[1] Died 460 A.D.

the symbol of paganized Christianity.   The crucifix
—a figure of Christ nailed to the cross—appears
first about the middle of the fifth century.   The
following is the general order whereby the transition was accomplished :

1. Constantine adopts the initial letters, giving
the *chi-ro* standard, about 312 A.D.[1]

2. The *chi* (*X*) was gradually changed to the
form of a cross, while the *ro*, similar to the English
P, remained in its original position.

3. The *ro* was rejected, and the *chi* (*X*) was
changed to the Greek cross of Bacchus.

4. The heathen *tau* (*T*), as used in India and
Egypt, was brought in, probably because of its
supposed resemblance to the cross on which Christ
was (said to have been) put to death.

5. The *tau* appears, surmounted by a roundel,
evidently the sacred egg of the heathen.   This was
the emblem of the Goddess of Nature, the productive principle.   This brought the original
heathen symbol into still greater similarity to what
is now known as the Latin cross

[1] Boissier gives a minute account of the vision of Constantine and its
effects in leading him to favor Christianity.   He quotes from Lactantius,
tutor of Constantine's sons, who describes the vision of the Emperor in
his treatise, *The Death of the Persecutors*.   This summary, given by
Boissier, shows that the sign which Constantine saw in his vision, and
which he engraved upon his military standard, was not the cross proper,
but the monogram known as the Chi-Ro.   It is described by Lactantius in
these words : " The letter ' X ' crossed by a bar, the top of which was gently
recurved, forming thus the monogram of Christ "—(*cf. La Fin du Paganism*).

6. The *crux ansata,* or handled cross. This is the form usually seen in the hands of the gods of India and Egypt. It is the symbol of the sun-god, and is interpreted by modern Egyptologists as the symbol of life. It was primarily a phallic symbol of reproduction. An English writer (Rev. Mourant Brock) has pertinently said :

"And it is high time that Christians should understand a fact of which skeptics have been long talking and writing, that the cross was the central symbol of ancient paganism. What it represents, must remain untold; but it was probably made the medium of our Lord's death, through the crafty device of the wicked one, into whose hands he was for a while delivered, with a view to the future corruption of Christianity, and the carrying on, under its name, of all the abominations of the heathen."

The prominence and value which the "sign of the Cross" and its associate pagan symbols gained as "charms" in paganized Christianity can be readily understood in view of the foregoing facts. It is wholly unexplainable from the New Testament standpoint, and without these facts. A few examples must suffice, showing how this pagan conception was transferred to Christianity. Bingham, a learned and conservative writer, says :

"But there was one sort of enchantment, which many ignorant and superstitious Christians, out of the remains of heathen error, much affected; that was the use of charms and amulets and spells to cure diseases, or avert dangers or mischiefs, both from themselves and the fruits of the earth. For Constantine had allowed the heathen, in the beginning of his reformation, for some time, not only to consult their augurs in public, but also to use charms by way of remedy for bodily distempers, and to prevent storms of rain and hail from injuring the ripe fruits, as appears from that very law, where he condemns the other sort of magic, that tended to do mischief, to be punished with death. And probably from this indulgence granted to the heathen, many Christians who brought a tincture of heathenism with them into their religion, might take occasion to think there was no great harm in such charms or enchantments, when the design was only to do good, and not evil. However it was, this is certain in fact, that many Christians were much inclined to this practice, and therefore made use of charms and amulets, which they called *periammata* and *phylacteria*, pendants and preservatives to secure themselves from danger, and drive away bodily distempers. These phylacteries, as they called them, were a sort of amulets made of ribands, with a text of Scripture or some other charm of words written in them, which they imagined without any natural means to be effectual remedies or preservatives against diseases." [1]

The extent to which this evil existed in the Church is indicated by Chrysostom, as is also his belief in the sign of the cross as a superior "charm." He says :

" For these amulets, though they who make money by them are forever rationalizing about them, and saying,

[1] *Antiquities*, etc., book xvi., chap. v., sec. 6.

'We call upon God, and do nothing extraordinary,' and the like; and 'the old woman [who made the amulets] is a Christian,' says he, 'and one of the faithful'; the thing is idolatry. Art thou one of the faithful? sign the cross; say, this I have for my only weapon; this for my remedy; and other I know none. Tell me, if a physician should come to one, and, neglecting the remedies belonging to his art, should use incantations, should we call that man a physician? By no means: for we see not the medicines of the healing art; so neither, in this case, do we see those of Christianity.

"Other women, again, tie about them the names of rivers, and venture numberless things of like nature. Lo, I say, and forewarn you all, that if any be detected, I will not spare them again, whether they have made amulet, or incantation, or any other thing of such an art as this."[1]

"This sign [the cross], both in the days of our forefathers and now hath opened doors that were shut up; this hath quenched poisonous drugs; this hath taken away the power of hemlock; this hath healed bites of venomous beasts. For if it opened the gates of hell, and threw wide the archways of Heaven, and made a new entrance into Paradise, and cut away the nerves of the devil; what marvel if it prevailed over poisonous drugs, and venomous beasts, and all other such things?"[2]

TERTULLIAN shows his faith in the sign of the cross as a cure for disease,[3] in his discussion of the nature and cure of the scorpion's sting. He says:

[1] Hom. viii., *On Colossians.*
[2] Homily liv., ¶ 7, *On the Gospel of St. Matthew.*
[3] *Scorpiace*, xv.

"We have faith for a defense if we are not smitten with distrust, itself, also, in immediately making the sign [of the cross over the wounded part] and adjuring [that part in the name of Jesus] and besmearing the [poisoned] heel with [the gore of] the beast."

The Sign of the Cross in Baptism.

As one of the supreme charms, the sign of the cross was associated with baptism, which was also made a "charm" under the influence of pagan water-worship. It was associated with anointing, which was also a pure importation from paganism. Speaking of this sign Bingham says:

"The third use of it was in this unction before baptism. For so the author under the name of Dionysius, describing the ceremony of anointing the party, before the consecration of the water, says, The Bishop begins the unction by thrice signing him with the sign of the cross, and then commits him to the priest to be anointed all over the body, whilst he goes and consecrates the water in the font. St. Austin also may be understood of this when he says, The cross is always joined with baptism. And by this we may interpret several passages in Cyprian, as where he tells Demetrian, They, only, escape, who are born again, and signed with the sign of Christ. And what that sign is, and on what part of the body it is made, the Lord signified in another place, saying, 'Go through the midst of Jerusalem and set a mark upon their foreheads.' And so again in his book of the Unity of the Church, speaking of Uzziah's leprosy, he says, He was marked for his offense against the Lord in that part of his body, where those are signed who obtain his mercy. Which seems plainly to refer to the sign of the cross made in baptism. The author of the Apostolic Constitutions is very express in this matter. For explaining the meaning of the several parts and ceremonies used in baptism, he says, The water is to represent Christ's burial, the oil to represent the Holy Ghost, the sign of the cross to represent the cross, and the ointment or chrism, the confirmation of men's professions. And not improbably St. Jerome might refer to this, though his words be not so restrained to this time of unction, when he says, He was a Christian, born of Christian parents, and carried the banner of the cross in his forehead. Some add also those words of Cyprian. Let us guard our foreheads that we may preserve the sign of God without danger. And those of Pontius in his life, where speaking of the Christian confessors who were branded by the heathen in the forehead, and sent as slaves into the mines, he says, They were marked in the forehead a second time; alluding to the sign of the cross, which as Christians they had received before. But these passages do not necessarily relate to baptism, but are only general expressions that may refer to the use of the sign of the cross upon any other occasion; it being usual in those times to sign themselves upon the forehead in the commonest actions of their lives, upon every motion, as Tertullian expresses it, at their going out and coming in, at their going to bath, or to bed, or to meals, or whatever their employment or occasions called them to. Yet thus far it may be argued from them, that they who used it so commonly upon all other occasions, would hardly omit it in this solemn unction of baptism. And therefore these allegations may be allowed to be a sort of collateral evidence of the practice." [1]

Again he says :

" Secondly, I observe, that together with this prayer, it was usual to make the sign of the cross also, not, as before, upon the person to be baptised, but as a circumstance of the consecration. This we learn not only from Dionysius, but from St. Austin, who says, The water of baptism was signed with the Cross of Christ. And St. Chrysostom says, They used it in all their sacred mysteries ; when they were regenerated in baptism, when they were fed with the mystical food in the eucharist, when they were ordained, that symbol of victory was always represented in the action, whatever religious matter they were concerned in. To which we may add the author under the name of St. Austin, who runs over all the solemn consecrations of the Church and tells us, the symbol of the cross was used in every one, in catechising of new converts, in consecrating the waters of baptism, in giving imposition of hands in confirmation, in the dedication of Churches, and altars, in consecrating the eucharist, and in promoting priests and Levites to holy orders.

" Thirdly, I observe concerning the effects of this consecration, that the very same change was supposed to be wrought by it in the waters of baptism, as by the consecration of bread and wine in the eucharist. For they supposed not only the presence of the Spirit, but also the mystical presence of Christ's blood, to be here after consecration. Julius Firmicus, speaking of baptism, bids men

[1] *Antiquities*, book xi., chap. ix., sec. 5.

here seek for the pure waters, the undefiled fountain, where the blood of Christ, after many spots and defilements, would whiten them by the Holy Ghost." [1]

Superstitious regard for the sign of the cross grew as paganism ripened in the church ; witness the following words of Augustine :

" And lastly as every one knows, what else is the sign of Christ but the Cross of Christ? For unless that sign be applied, whether it be to the foreheads of believers, or to the very water out of which they are regenerated, or to the oil with which they receive the anointing chrism, or to the sacrifice that nourishes them, none of them is properly administered." [2]

Baptism and " Holy Water" as " Charms."

The pagan doctrine of baptismal regeneration involved the idea of water as a charm against disease and misfortune, in men, in animals, in growing crops, and fruits. These notions were brought into the Christian Church and soon became widely spread and firmly fixed. An excellent review of this subject is furnished by Canon FARRAR in his description of Cyprian's views relative to baptism. These are his words :

" Cyprian holds that in baptism the Priest commands the power of the Holy Ghost to forgive sin by means of sanctified and purified water, but only if he be a Catholic

---

[1] *Antiquities*, book xi., chap. x., secs. 3 and 4.
[2] Tractate 118, *On the Gospel of St. John.*

Priest, and free from every taint of what Cyprian or the Episcopate regards as Schism or heresy. When the grace of forgiveness for all past sins has been bestowed by this act it is not valid for future sins. They too require that satisfaction for them should be offered to God, and this satisfaction must be penitence, penance, and good works." [1]

" He might have adopted the language of Tertullian about baptism : ' in this way, without pomp, with no novelty of preparation, without cost, a man descends into the water, and being immersed, with the utterance of a few words, rises up out of it, scarcely, if at all, cleaner in body, but, incredible consequence, the possessor of eternal life.' " [2]

Miracles through Baptism.

SOCRATES, the Church historian, tells of miraculous cures through baptism as gravely as Sozomen does of the finding of " Relics." Hear him :

" This was one important improvement in the circumstances of the Church, which happened during the administration of Atticus. Nor were these times without the attestation of miracles and healing. For a certain Jew being a paralytic had been confined to his bed for many years ; and as every sort of medical skill, and the prayers of his Jewish brethren had been resorted to but had availed nothing, he had recourse at length to Christian baptism, trusting in it as the only true remedy to be used. When Atticus the bishop was informed of his wishes, he

[1] Epists. 64 and 69.
[2] *Lives of the Fathers*, by F. W. Farrar, D.D., F.R.S., vol. i., pp. 332, 333, Edinburgh, 1889.

instructed him in the first principles of Christian truth, and having preached to him to hope in Christ, directed that he should be brought in his bed to the font. The paralytic Jew receiving baptism with a sincere faith, as soon as he was taken out of the baptismal font found himself perfectly cured of his disease, and continued to enjoy sound health afterwards. This miraculous power Christ vouchsafed to be manifested even in our times; and the fame of it caused many heathens to believe and be baptised. But the Jews, although zealously 'seeking after signs,' not even the signs which actually took place induced to embrace the faith. Such blessings were thus conferred by Christ upon men." [1]

"A certain Jewish impostor, pretending to be a convert to Christianity, was in the habit of being baptized often, and by that artifice he amassed a good deal of money. After having deceived many of the Christian sects by this fraud—for he received baptism from the Arians and Macedonians—as there remained no others to practise his hypocrisy upon, he at length came to Paul bishop of the Novatians, and declaring that he earnestly desired baptism, requested that he might obtain it at his hand. Paul commended the determination of the Jew, but told him he could not perform that rite for him, until he had been instructed in the fundamental principles of the faith, and given himself to fasting and prayer for many days. The Jew compelled to fast against his will became the more importunate in his request for baptism; now as Paul did not wish to discourage him by longer delays, since he was so urgent, he consented to grant his request,

---

[1] Socrates, *Eccl. History*, book vii., chap. iv.

and made all the necessary preparations for the baptism. Having purchased a white vestment for him, he ordered the font to be filled with water, and then led the Jew to it in order to baptize him. But a certain invisible power of God caused the water suddenly to disappear. The bishop, of course, and those present, had not the least suspicion of the real cause, but imagined that water had escaped by the channels underneath, by means of which they are accustomed to empty the font ; these passages were therefore very carefully closed, and the font filled again. Again, however, as the Jew was taken there a second time, the water vanished as before. Then Paul, addressing the Jew, said : ' Either you are an evil-doer, wretched man, or an ignorant person who has already been baptized.' The people having crowded together to witness this miracle, one among them recognized the Jew, and identified him as having been baptized by Atticus, the bishop, a little while before. Such was the portent wrought by the hands of Paul bishop of the Novatians." [1]

That baptism was sought as a shield against bodily ills, without even the pagan notion of spiritual purity, is shown by the following from Bingham :

"Yet sometimes, as Euthymius relates in the same place, they would bring their children to the presbyters of the Church to be baptised after the Catholic way, because they had an opinion that both baptism and the cross were of some advantage to the body for the cure of diseases, but of no other efficacy, benefit, or virtue to purge

[1] *Ibid.*, chap. xvii.

the soul. And such an opinion possessed the minds of many others, who had no further regard for baptism, but only as it was of use to free the body of some distemper or uncleanliness." [1]

Delayed Baptism.

The pagan idea of " baptismal regeneration " took such hold of the Church as to become a grave evil, by inducing men to live in sin, under the belief that they could gain salvation at the last moment. The testimony of Bingham is presented again, which testimony is the more valuable, because coming from a conservative English Churchman.

" Others deferred it out of heathenish principles still remaining in them, because they were in love with the world and its pleasures, which they were unwilling to renounce, to take upon them the yoke of Christ, which they thought would lay greater restraints upon them, and deny them those liberties which they could now more freely indulge themselves in and securely enjoy. They could spend their life in pleasure, and be baptised at last, and then they should gain as much as those that were baptised before; for the laborers who came into the vineyard at the last hour, had the same reward as those that had borne the burden and heat of the day." [2]

[1] *Antiquities*, book ii., chap. ii.
[2] *Antiquities*, book ii., chap. vi., sec. 3.

Orientation at Baptism.

The corruption of baptism by the pagan sun-worship cult was especially shown in the practice of turning eastward and westward in connection with baptism.   This chapter has space for a single quotation on this point from Bingham :

" This custom of turning about to the East when they made their profession of obedience to Christ is also mentioned by St. Ambrose, Gregory Nazianzen, Cyril of Jerusalem, and the author under the name of Dionysius. For which they assign two reasons: 1, Cyril tells his disciples that as soon as they had renounced the devil, the paradise of God, which was planted in the East, and whence our first parent for his transgression was driven into banishment, was now laid open to them ; and their turning about from the West to the East, which is the region of light, was a symbol of this.   For the same reason, St. Basil and some others of the ancients tell us, they prayed toward the East, that they might have their faces toward paradise.   The other reason for turning to the East in baptism, was because the East or rising sun was an emblem of the Sun of Righteousness, to whom they now turned from Satan.   Thou art turned about to the East, says St. Ambrose, for he that renounces the devil, turns unto Christ. Where he plainly intimates with St. Jerome, that turning to the East was a symbol of their aversion from Satan, and conversion unto Christ,—that is, from darkness to light, from serving idols, to serve him who is the Sun of Righteousness and Fountain of Light." [1]

[1] *Antiquities,* book xi., chap. vii., sec. 7.

17

Faith in the magical effects of baptism increased, until its sway ruled the wisest and best of the leaders in the Church. The great Augustine recounts many cases which indicate, if possible, more than pagan credulity. Among them are the following. The chapter from which they are taken is entitled: "*Of Miracles which were wrought that the world might believe in Christ, and which have not ceased since the world believed.*"

"In the same city of Carthage lived Innocentia, a very devout woman of the highest rank in the state. She had a cancer in one of her breasts, a disease, which, as physicians say, is incurable. Ordinarily, therefore, they either amputated, and so separated from the body the member on which the disease has seized, or, that the patient's life may be prolonged a little, though death is inevitable, even if somewhat delayed, they abandon all remedies following, as they say, the advice of Hippocrates. This lady we speak of had been advised to by a skilful physician, who was intimate with her family; and she betook herself to God alone by prayer. On the approach of Easter she was instructed in a dream to wait for the first woman that came out from the baptistry after being baptised, and ask her to make the sign of Christ upon her sore. She did so and was immediately cured. . . .

"A gouty doctor of the same city, when he had given in his name for baptism, and had been prohibited the day before his baptism from being baptised that year, by black woolly-haired boys who appeared to him in his dream, and whom he understood to be devils, and when, though they trod on his feet, and inflicted the acutest pain he had ever yet experienced, he refused to obey them, but overcame them, and would not defer being washed in the laver of regeneration, was relieved in the very act of baptism, not only of the extraordinary pain he was tortured with, but also of the disease itself, so that, though he lived a long time afterwards, he never suffered from gout; and yet who knows of this miracle? We, however, do know it, and so, too, do the small number of brethren who were in the neighborhood, and to whose ears it might come.

"An old comedian of Curubis was cured at baptism not only of paralysis, but also of hernia, and being delivered from both afflictions, came up out of the font of regeneration as if he had nothing wrong with his body. Who outside of Curubis knows of this, or who but a very few who might hear it elsewhere? But we, when we heard of it, made the man come to Carthage, by order of the holy bishop Aurelius, although we had already ascertained the fact on the information of persons whose word we could not doubt.

"Hesperius, of a tribunitian family, and a neighbor of our own, has a farm called Zubedi in the Fussalian district; and finding that his family, his cattle, and his servants were suffering from the malice of evil spirits, he asked our presbyters, during my absence, that one of them would go with him and banish the spirits by his prayers. One went, offered there the sacrifice of the body of Christ, praying with all his might that vexation might cease. It did cease forthwith, through God's mercy. Now he had received from a friend of his own some holy earth brought from Jerusalem, where Christ, having been buried, rose again the third day. This earth he had hung up in his bedroom to preserve himself from harm. But when his house was purged of that demoniacal invasion, he began to consider what should be done with the earth; for his reverence for it made him unwilling to have it any longer in his bedroom. It so happened that I and Maximinus, Bishop of Synita, and then my colleague, were in the neighborhood. Hesperius asked us to visit him, and we did so. When he had related all the circumstances, he begged that the earth might be buried somewhere, and that the spot should be made a place of prayer where Christians might assemble for the worship of God. We made no objection; it was done as he desired. There was in that neighborhood a young countryman who was paralytic, who, when he heard of this, begged his parents to take him without delay to that holy place. When he had been brought there he prayed, and forthwith went away on his own feet perfectly cured.

" There is a country seat called Victoriana, less than thirty miles from Hippo-regius. At it there is a monument to the Milanese martyrs, Protasius and Gervasius. Thither a young man was carried, who, when he was watering his horse one summer day at noon, in a pool of a river, had been taken possession of by a devil. As he lay at the monument, near death, or even quiet like a dead person, the lady of the manor, with her maids and religious attendants, entered the place for evening prayer and praise, as her custom was, and they began to sing hymns. At this sound, the young man, as if electrified, was thoroughly aroused, and with frightful screaming seized the altar, and held it as if he did not dare or were not able to let it go, and as if he were fixed or tied to it; and the devil in him, with loud lamentation, besought that he might be spared, and confessed where and when and how he took possession of the youth. At last declaring that he would go out of him, he named one by one the parts of his body which he threatened to mutilate as he went out, and with these words he departed from the man. But his eye falling out on his cheek, hung by a slender vein as by a root, and the whole of the pupil which had been black became white. When this was witnessed by those present (others, too, had now gathered to his cries, and had all joined in prayer for him), although they were delighted that he had recovered his sanity of mind, yet, on the other hand, they were grieved about his eye, and said he should seek medical advice. But his sister's husband, who had brought him there, said, ' God who has banished the devil, is able to restore his eye at the prayers of his saints.' Therewith he replaced the eye that was fallen out and hanging, and bound it in its place with his handkerchief as well as he could, and advised him not to loose the bandage for seven days. When he did so, he found it quite healthy. Others also were cured there, but of them it were tedious to speak.

" I know that a young woman of Hippo was immediately dispossessed of a devil, on anointing herself with oil, mixed with the tears of the presbyter who had been praying for her. I know also that a bishop once prayed for a demoniac young man whom he never saw, and that he was cured on the spot." [1]

Many other similar miraculous occurrences are related by Augustine, in this same chapter, showing how fully paganism mingled with his belief.

[1] *The City of God*, book xxii., chap. viii.

He reports also many miracles performed by the power of a shrine which was situated near Carthage. The chapter sounds more like a record of heathen prodigies than like sober Christian history.

CHAPTER XIII.

SAME SUBJECT CONTINUED.

Lights in Worship—Worshipping " toward the East "—Easter Fires—Beltane or Baal Fires—Penance—Marioltry—The Mass—Purgatory and Prayers for the Dead—Peter's Keys—Christmas—Easter—Lent, etc.

SUN-WORSHIP, as the dominant cult in all pagan systems, furnished more elements of corruption than any other.

Lights in Worship.

The pagan origin of lights in worship is universally acknowledged. Their use was sharply condemned in the earlier times.[1] The Synod of Elviri (305 or 306 A.D.) condemned their use in cemeteries, where they already formed a part of the services for the dead. Canon 34 reads : " It is forbidden to light wax candles during the day in cemeteries for fear of disquieting the spirits of the saints."

Baronius explains this as follows : " Many Neophytes brought the custom from paganism of light-

---

[1] See Tertullian, *Apologeticus*, chap. xlvi., and *Ad Uxorum*, lib. ii., chap. vi.

ing wax candles upon tombs. The Synod forbids this, because, metaphysically, it troubles the souls of the dead ; that is to say, this superstition wounds them."

Abespine gives another explanation, which is, that the synod accepted the belief that was then general, that the souls of the dead hovered around their tombs. " The Synod consequently forbade that wax candles should be lighted by day, perhaps to abolish a remnant of paganism, but also to prevent the repose of the souls of the dead from being troubled." [1]

MAITLAND says :

" The burning of lights is specified among the idolatrous rites forbidden by the Theodosian Code : ' Let no one in any kind of place whatsoever in any city, burn lights, offer incense, or hang up garlands to senseless idols.' Vigilantius, in reference to the custom of using lights in divine service, exclaims : ' We almost see the ceremonial of the gentiles introduced into the Churches under pretence of religion ; piles of candles lighted while the sun is still shining ; and everywhere people kissing and worshipping, and I know not what ; a little dust in a small vessel wrapped up in a precious cloth. Great honor do such persons render to the blessed martyrs, thinking with miserable tapers to illumine those whom the Lamb, in the midst of the throne, shines upon with the splendor of his majesty.' This passage proves that Vigilantius,

[1] See Hefele, *History of the Councils*, etc., to 325 A.D., pp. 150, 151. Clark's edition, Edinburgh, 1872.

who must have known well the customs of paganism, was struck with the resemblance between them and the rites newly introduced into the Church." [1]

But love for paganism was too strong, and the custom soon became universal. Paulinus, Bishop of Nola (396 A.D.), gloried in the use of lights. *In Natalis* (3:100) he says:

"The bright altars are crowned with thickly clustered lamps, the fragrant lights smell of waxed papyri; day and night they burn; so that night glitters with the splendor of day; and day itself glories with heavenly honors, shines the more, its lustre being doubled by innumerable lamps." [2]

The persistency with which the use of lights yet holds a place in many branches of the Church shows how long and how vigorously paganism has continued to corrupt Christianity.

"*Orientation.*"

Another residuum from sun-worship led to building churches with the altar at the east, praying toward the east, burying the dead with reference to the east, etc. Of the pagan origin of the custom, GALE speaks as follows:

"Another piece of Pagan Demonolatry was their ceremony of bowing and worshipping towards the East. For the Pagans universally worshipped the sun as their su-

[1] *The Church in the Catacombs*, p. 225, London, 1846.
[2] See Maitland, p. 228.

preme God, even the more reformed of them, the new Platonists, Plotinus, Porphyry, and Julian the apostate, as it appears by his oration to the Sun. Whence it came to pass, that the sun rising in the east they usually worshipped in that way (as the Jews in Babylon usually worshipped west, because Jerusalem stood west thence). Hence also they built their temples and buried their dead towards the East. So Diogenes Laertius, in the life of Solon, says: that the Athenians buried their dead towards the East, the head of their graves being made that way. And do not Anti-Christ and his sons exactly follow this Pagan ceremony in building their temples and High Altars towards the East, and in bowing that way in their worship?"[1]

Various explanations were made concerning this practice, to cover up the prominence of this paganism. For instance, CLEMENT of Alexandria says:

" And since the dawn is an image of the day of birth, and from that point the light which has shone forth at first from the darkness, increases, there has also dawned on those involved in darkness a day of the knowledge of truth. In correspondence with the manner of the sun's rising, prayers are made looking towards the sunrise in the East. Whence also the most ancient temples looked towards the West, that people might be taught to turn to the East when facing the images. ' Let my prayer be directed before thee as incense, the uplifting of my hands as the evening sacrifice,' say the Psalms."[2]

[1] *Court of the Gentiles*, by Theophilus Gale, part iii., book ii., chap. ii., section 3, paragraph 4.

[2] *Stromata*, book vii., chap. vii.

TERTULLIAN seeks to avoid the charge of paganism, while defending this practice, as follows :

" Others, with greater regard to good manners, it must be confessed, suppose that the sun is the god of the Christians, because it is a well known fact that we pray toward the East, or because we make Sunday a day of festivity. What then? Do you do less than this? Do not many among you, with an affectation of sometimes worshipping the heavenly bodies, likewise, move your lips in the direction of the sunrise? It is you, at all events, who have even admitted the sun into the calendar of the week; and you have selected its day, in preference to the preceding day, as the most suitable in the week, for either an entire abstinence from the bath, or for its postponement until the evening, or for taking rest, and for banqueting." [1]

Easter Fires.

Another element of pagan sun-worship continues to the present time in the Easter fires, which abound especially in Northern Europe. Fire is regarded as a living thing, in Teutonic mythology. It is often spoken of as a bird, the " Red Cock." *Notfuer*, " Need-fire," is yet produced by friction, at certain times. Such fire is deemed sacred. On such occasions all fires in the neighborhood are extinguished, that they may be rekindled from the *Notfuer*. This fire is yet used to ward off evil,

[1] *Ad Nationes*, chap. xiii.

and to cure diseases in domestic animals. Traces of sex-worship appear in connection with the producing of this sacred fire; "two chaste boys" must pull the ropes which produce the friction necessary to generate the fire; and a "chaste youth" must strike the light for curing the disease known as "St. Anthony's fire." In Scotland such fire is held as a safeguard against the "bewitching of domestic animals."

GRIMM, who is the highest authority on the mythology of Northern Europe, has abundant material touching all forms of fire-worship in that region. Here is a single extract with reference to *Easter Fires*.

"At all the cities, towns and villages of the country, towards evening on the first (or third) day of Easter, there is lighted every year, on mountain and hill, a great fire of straw turf and wood, amidst a concourse and jubilation, not only of the young, but of many grown up people. On the Weser, especially in Schaumburg, they tie up a tar barrel on a fir tree wrapt around with straw, and set it on fire at night. Men and maids, and all who come dance, exulting and singing, hats are waved, handkerchiefs thrown into the fire. The mountains all around are lighted up, and it is an elevating spectacle, scarcely paralleled by any thing else, to survey the country for many miles around from one of the higher points, and in every direction at once to see a vast number of these bonfires, brighter or fainter, blazing up to heaven. In some places they marched up the hill in stately proces-

:sion, carrying white rods: by turns they sang Easter hymns, grasping each other's hands, and at the Hallelujah, clashed their rods together. They liked to carry some of the fire home with them.

" For these *ignes paschales* there is no authority reaching beyond the sixteenth century; but they must be a great deal older, if only for the contrast with Midsummer fires, which never could penetrate into North Germany, because the people there held fast by their Easter fires. Now seeing that the fires of St. John, as we shall presently show, are more immediately connected with the Christian Church than those of Easter, it is not unreasonable to trace these all the way back to the worship of the goddess Ostara, or Eastre, who seems to have been more a Saxon and Anglican divinity than one revered all over Germany. Her name and her fires, which are likely to have come at the beginning of May, would, after the conversion of the Saxons, be shifted back to the Christian feast. Those mountain fires of the people are scarcely derivable from the taper lighted in the Church the same day: it is true that Boniface calls it *ignis paschalis*, and such Easter lights are mentioned in the sixteenth century. Even now, in the Hildesheim country, they light the lamp on Maundy Thursday, and that on Easter day, at an Easter fire which has been *struck with a steel*. The people flock to this fire, carrying oaken crosses, or simply crossed sticks, which they set on fire and then preserve for a whole year. But the common folk distinguish between this fire and the wild fire produced by rubbing wood. Jager speaks of *a consecration fire of logs*." [1]

[1] *Teutonic Mythology*, by Jacob Grimm, four vols., London, 1883, vol ii., p. 115.

Midsummer Fires.

Midsummer was the central point of a great pagan festival in honor of the sun, who had then reached his greatest height, from which he must soon decline. Catholic Christianity continued these festivals, in St. John Baptist Day. Many of the peculiarities of these midsummer fires were similar to those of the Easter fires already noticed. The following description of the modern festival in Germany is taken from Grimm :

" We have a fuller description of a Midsummer fire, made in 1823 at Konz, a Lorrainian but still German village, on the Moselle, near Sierk and Thionville. Every house delivers a truss of straw on the top of the Stromberg, where men and youths assemble toward evening. Women and girls are stationed by the Burbach springs. Then a huge wheel is wrapt round with straw, so that none of the wood is left in sight, a strong pole is passed through the middle, which sticks out a yard on each side, and is grasped by the guiders of the wheel ; the remainder of the straw is tied up into a number of small torches. At a signal given by the Maire of Sierk (who according to the ancient custom, earns a basket of cherries by the service), the wheel is lighted with a torch, and set rapidly in motion ; a shout of joy is raised, all wave their torches on high, part of the men stay on the hill, part follow the rolling globe of fire, as it is guided down the hill to the Moselle. It often goes out first : but if alight when it touches the river, it prognosticates an abundant vintage, and the Konz people have a right to levy a tun of white wine from the adjacent vineyards. Whilst the wheel is rushing past the women and the girls, they break out into cries of joy, answered by the men on the hill, and inhabitants of neighboring villages, who have flocked to the river side, mingle their voices in the universal rejoicing." [1]

Beltane or Baal Fires.

The Beltane or Baal fires and the ancient sacrifices to the sun-god still continue in modified form in Scotland. Grimm speaks of them as follows :

" The present custom is thus described by Armstrong *sub v. bealtainn :* In some parts of the Highlands the young folks of a hamlet meet in the moors, on the first of May. They cut a table in the green sod, of a round figure, by cutting a trench in the ground, of such circumference as to hold the whole company. They then kindle a fire and dress a repast of eggs and milk, in the consistence of a custard. They knead a cake of oatmeal, which is toasted at the embers, against a stone. After the custard is eaten up, they divide the cake in so many portions, as similar as possible to one another in size and shape, as there are persons in the company. They daub one of these portions with charcoal, until it is perfectly black. They then put all the bits of the cake into a bonnet, and every one, blindfold, draws out a portion. The bonnet-holder is entitled to the last bit. Whoever draws the black bit is the devoted person who is *to be sacrificed to Baal, whose favor they mean to implore in rendering the year productive.* The devoted person is compelled *to leap three times over the*

[1] *Ibid.*, vol. ii., p. 619.

flames. Here the reference to the worship of a deity is too plain to be mistaken ; we see by the leaping over the flame, that the main point was, to select a human being to propitiate the god, and make him merciful ; that afterwards an animal sacrifice was substituted for him, and finally nothing remained of the bodily immolation but a leap through the fire, for man and beast. The holy rite of friction is not mentioned here, but as it was necessary for the ' needfire ' that purged pestilence, it must originally have been much more in requisition at the great yearly festival." [1]

Penance.

The pagan theory of baptismal regeneration created a necessity for the doctrine of penance. Under the idea that baptism removed all sins up to the time of the ceremony, something was necessary to atone for sins committed after baptism. Dr. SCHAFF describes the origin of penance as follows :

" The effect of baptism, however, was thought to extend only to sins committed before receiving it. Hence the frequent postponement of the sacrament, which Tertullian very earnestly recommends, though he censures it when accompanied with moral levity and presumption. Many, like Constantine the Great, put it off to the bed of sickness and of death. They preferred the risk of dying unbaptized to that of forfeiting forever the baptismal grace. Death-bed baptisms were then what death-bed repentances are now.

[1] *Ibid.*, vol. ii., p. 613.

" But then the question arose, how the forgiveness of sins committed after baptism could be obtained? This is the starting-point of the Roman doctrine of the sacrament of *penance*. Tertullian and Cyprian were the first to suggest that satisfaction must be made for such sins by self-imposed penitential exercises and good works, such as prayers and alms-giving. Tertullian held seven gross sins, which he denoted mortal sins, to be unpardonable after baptism, and to be left to the uncovenanted mercies of God; but the Catholic Church took a milder view, and even received back the adulterers and apostates on their public repentance." [1]

More need not be said. The reader will readily see the connection between these two elements of paganism; he will also see the deeply corrupting effect of them both.

Mariolatry.

The worship of a Mother Goddess and her son formed a distinct feature in the paganism of Babylon, India, Egypt, Assyria, Greece, and Rome. Though variant in conception, the core of Mariolatry runs through all these pagan systems. Those who desire to follow this theme in detail will do well to consult ALEXANDER HISLOP.[2] A single extract from page 82 of that work is all that space will permit:

---

[1] *Schaff*, vol. ii., p. 254.
[2] *The Two Babylons*, seventh edition, London, p. 21 ff.

18

" The worship of the Goddess-Mother with the child in her arms continued to be observed in Egypt till Christianity entered. If the gospel had come in power among the mass of the people, the worship of this goddess-queen would have been overthrown. With the generality, it came only in name. Instead, therefore, of the Babylonian goddess being cast out, in too many cases her name only was changed. She was called the Virgin Mary, and, with her child, was worshipped with the same idolatrous feeling by professing Christians, as formerly by open and avowed pagans."

The Mass.

The mass, which has been for centuries the central item in Roman Catholic worship, finds its origin in the "unbloody sacrifices" which were offered to the Paphian Venus, and to her counterpart in Babylonia and Assyria. It was this worship of the Queen of Heaven into which the apostate women of Judah were drawn, whom Jeremiah[1] condemns for " burning incense, pouring out drink offerings, and offering cakes to the Queen of Heaven." These cakes were marked with the phallic symbol of the cross. As before noted, they were the progenitors of the modern " hot cross-buns," which are associated with Friday—day of Venus.

The form of the cake-wafer adopted in paganized Christianity, its *roundness*, was borrowed from

[1] Jer. xliv., 19.

the Egyptians, to whom the form represented *the disk of the sun.* The mystic letters on the wafer form another link which connects it with Egyptian paganism. Christians explain these letters as meaning *Jesus Hominum Salvator ;* but when the worshippers of Isis, who were everywhere in the Roman empire in the early centuries, read them on the unbloody sacrifice, they understood by them *Isis, Horus, Seb, i. e.,* The Mother, the Child, and the Father of the Gods. The pagan character of this unbloody sacrifice was so patent at the first, that it was sharply condemned; but familiarity changed opposition to acceptance, and what was wholly pagan became the centre of worship in paganized Christianity.

Purgatory and Prayers for the Dead.

All the leading systems of pagan religions have some form of purgatory, with its associate prayers for the dead, for which large sums are paid by the surviving friends. The purgatory which was developed in the Christian cult is like its pagan prototype in almost every particular. An extract from Wilkinson describing the practical workings of the doctrine in pagan Egypt would need little changing to fit the facts connected with the purgatory of Christians. We quote from Hislop [1]:

[1] *Two Babylons*, p. 169. The references to Wilkinson's Egyptians are vol. ii., p. 94, and vol. v., pp. 383, 384.

" ' The Priest,' says Wilkinson, ' induced the people to expend large sums on the celebration of funeral rites; and *many who had barely sufficient to obtain the necessaries of life* were anxious to save something for the expenses of their death. For besides the embalming process, which sometimes cost a talent of silver, or about £250, English money, the tomb itself was purchased at an immense expense; and numerous demands were made upon the estate of the deceased, for the celebration of prayer and other services for the soul.' ' The ceremonies,' we find him elsewhere saying, ' consisted of a sacrifice similar to those offered in the temples, vowed for the deceased to one or more gods (as Osiris, Anubis, and others connected with Amenti); incense and libation were also presented; and a prayer was sometimes read, the relations and friends being present as mourners. They even joined their prayers to those of the priest. The priest who officiated at the burial service was selected from the grade of Pontiffs, who wore the leopard skin; but various other rites were performed by one of the minor priests, to the mummies, previous to their being lowered into the pit of the tomb after that ceremony. Indeed, they continued to be administered at intervals, *as long as the family paid for their performance.*' Such was the operation of the doctrine of purgatory and prayers for the dead among avowed and acknowledged pagans; and in what essential respect does it differ from the operation of the same doctrine in Papal Rome?"

Saint Peter's Keys.

Those who claim the primacy of St. Peter and his right to the keys of heaven, pretend to found that claim upon Christ's words to Peter. But an examination of the history and characteristics of the doctrine reveals its pagan origin too clearly to admit of question. Roman paganism had its college of pontiffs, headed by the emperor, as *Pontifex Maximus.* Babylonian and Assyrian paganism had a similar council of pontiffs. The especial primacy among the deities was associated with Janus and Cybele. Each of these bore a key. The Pope assumed them both in the fifth century, after Christianity had been paganized. The term cardinal is plainly derived from *cardo,* a hinge. Janus was God of the Hinges, and was called the " Opener, and Shutter."

The sovereign pontiff of the pagan cult was the representative of the divinity on earth, and was worshipped as a god. This continued in the Roman empire long after the emperors were called "Christian." After that the Pope became God's representative among men. A single quotation from OVID will close this glance at St. Peter and his keys. In it Janus is described, and he in turn describes his office :

" He, holding in his right hand a staff, and in his left a key, uttered these accents to me from the mouth of his front face. . . . ' Whatever thou beholdest around thee, the sky, the sea, the air, the earth, all these have been shut up and are opened by my hand. In my power alone is the guardianship of the vast universe, and the prerogative of turning the hinge is entirely my own. When it has been my pleasure to send forth Peace, from her tranquil habitation, then at liberty she treads her paths unobstructed *by the restraints of war.* The whole world would be thrown into confusion in deadly bloodshed, did not my rigid bolts confine imprisoned warfare. Together with the gentle seasons, I preside over the portals of Heaven ; through my agency Jupiter himself doth pass and repass.' " [1]

Representative Festivals.

Those who have given even a cursory examination of the subject, know that the swarm of festivals which came into Christianity, after the second century, were nearly, if not all, pagan days, with new or modified names, but with little or no change of character. A few of the representative ones will be noticed here.

Christmas.

The Scriptures are wholly silent as to the date of Christ's birth. The 25th of December, the winter solstice, was not fixed as Christmas until a long time after the New Testament period. But in spite of serious objections, historical and otherwise, that date triumphed. The winter solstice was the date of the birth of Osiris, son of Isis the

---

[1] Ovid, *Fasti*, bk. i.

Egyptian Queen of Heaven. The term "Yule," another name for Christmas, comes from the Chaldee, and signifies "child's day." This name for the festival was familiar to our Anglo-Saxon ancestors, long before they knew anything of Christianity. In Rome, this winter-solstice festival was Saturn's festival; the wild, drunken, licentious "Saturnalia." It was observed in Babylonia in a similar manner. When it came into Christianity its leading features were like those of the Saturnalia. These have been far too prevalent from that time. Lighted candles and ornamented trees were a part of the observance of the festival among the pagans. The "Christmas goose" and "Yule cakes" came, with the day, from paganism.

Easter.

The earliest Christians continued to observe the Jewish Passover on the 14th of the month *Nisan*. As the pagan element increased in the Church, and the anti-Jewish feeling accordingly, after a sharp struggle, the time was changed from the fourteenth of the month to the Sunday nearest the vernal equinox. This brought it in conjunction with the festival of the Goddess of Spring, an ancient pagan feast, which probably dates back to the time of Astarte-worship, in Babylonia. The name "Easter" is comparatively modern. It comes from Oestra, the Goddess of Spring, in the Northern European mythology. The forms of observance were almost wholly heathen. Easter eggs, dyed, and "hot cross-buns," figured in the Chaldean Easter, as they have done in the Christian. The Hindus, and Chinese, and Egyptians had a sacred egg, the history of which can be traced to the Euphrates and the worship of Astarte.

Lent.

Lent has been given some appearance of having a Christian origin by the assumption, for which there is not a shadow of scriptural, or even apostolic authority, that it is the counterpart of Christ's fast of forty days. But the history of Lent shows unmistakably its pagan origin. Its source is found in the fasting which the Babylonians associated with the Goddess of Reproduction, whose worship formed the starting-point of Easter. During that period of fasting, social joy and all expressions of sexual regard were forbidden, because the goddess then mourned the loss of her consort. From this came the germ of Lent, and especially the practice of abstaining from marriage at that season.

The pagan tribes of Koordistan still keep such a fast. Humboldt found the same in Mexico, and Landseer in Egypt. It came into Christianity comparatively slowly, and brought gross evils with it. Witness the following :

"This change of the calendar in regard to Easter was attended with momentous consequences. It brought into the Church the grossest corruption, and the rankest superstition in connection with the abstinence of Lent. Let any one only read the atrocities that were commemorated during the 'sacred fast' or pagan Lent, as described by Arnobius and Clemens Alexandrinus, and surely he must blush for the Christianity of those, who with the full knowledge of all these abominations 'went down to Egypt for help' to stir up the languid devotion of the degenerate Church, and who could find no more excellent way to 'revive' it than by borrowing from so polluted a source ; the absurdities and abominations connected with which the early Christian writers held up to scorn." [1]

Many devout Christians now observe Lent without taint of paganism ; but with the undevout, Lent is only a resting time from the fashionable dissipation of "society," which refreshes them for the excesses that follow Easter.

[1] Hislop, *Two Babylons*, p. 106.

CHAPTER XIV.

FIVE CONCLUSIONS.

THE FUNDAMENTAL PRINCIPLES OF PROTESTANTISM INVOLVED IN PRESENT ISSUES.

Protestants must Accept the Bible *in Fact*, as well as in Theory, or be Overthrown—The Bible must be Reinterpreted in the Light of " Higher Criticism " and Deeper Spiritual Life—The Present Tendencies in Bible Study Mark the Opening of the Second Stage of the Protestant Movement—Baptism must Cease to be the Foot-Ball of Denominational Polemics and be Raised to a Question of Obedience to the Example of Christ—Protestants must Return to the Sabbath, Christianized by Christ, and to True Sabbathism, Which is as Undenominational as Faith—Such Sabbathism, and God's Sabbath, must be Restored to the Place from Which Pagan No-Sabbathism and the Pagan Sunday Drove Them—" Sabbath " Legislation is Unchristian—All Union of Christianity with the State must Yield before the Normal Development of True Protestantism.

THE facts which have been set forth in the foregoing pages form the basis for certain important conclusions. Unconsciously perhaps, but not less certainly, the Protestant movement was the beginning of a definite reaction against paganism in Christianity. Since humanity must learn all higher truth through long and sometimes bitter experience, errors and evils must ripen before those who have once accepted them will let them go. All great upward movements illustrate this fact. Reformatory action begins when error reaches so low a point that the best interests involved are confronted with strangulation and destruction. When the slow-beating heart threatens the death of the sleeping patient, nature arouses all her forces in a final struggle for life. Thus truth, stifled and trodden under foot by the pagan elements in the Church, awoke for the final struggle as the morning began to dawn, after the ages of midnight.

(1) *Reinstatement of the Bible.*

As the first step in perverting Christianity was to set aside the authority of God's book, and to teach error for truth through false exegesis, so the first step toward reformation was the unchaining of that Word. Paganized Christianity had placed itself between men and God, and His Word. Faith, hedged and crippled, trusted in human traditions, forms, and ceremonies, and in priestly absolution from sin. Help could not come, neither could hope arise, until the pagan elements should be so far removed that men could stand face to face with the Bible, with Christ, and with God. Hence the central points in the first stage of the reformatory work were an open Bible, an accessible Christ, and a Father whose law was the ultimate appeal, and whose love was the ultimate source of hope and the foundation of faith. The upward movement started on the same plane of fundamental truth on which the downward movement began. Hence the first struggle, under Luther, centred around personal faith.

But it was in the nature of things that men whose inheritance had come from the centuries made dark and religiously corrupt through pagan residuum, could not rise above all these influences at once.

Though the leaders in such movements build better than they know, their work is always comparatively imperfect. The intensity with which they must pursue a single truth in order to make any progress, prevents them from seeing all truth. This the more, since the public mind, at such times, cannot grasp and hold more than one great truth at a time. The reformers could not wholly free themselves from the idea that " tradition and custom" have authority. They did not actually accept the Bible as the *only rule* of faith and practice. Protestantism has never done this. As between Protestantism and Romanism, from which it revolted, there can be no middle or common ground. The Roman Catholic claims that the Church made the Bible, and formulated authoritative traditions, and hence that the Church, as law-maker and interpreter of the Bible, is the supreme authority. The Protestant begins by denying the authority of the Church, and appealing to the Bible as the ultimate authority. Logic and history combine to declare that Protestantism must make its theory good, or fail. Hence we draw

Conclusion First.

Protestantism must fully accept the Bible as the ultimate and only standard of faith and practice, or it must be broken between the upper millstone of Roman Catholicism and the nether millstone of irreligious rationalism.

The years are ripe for decision. The backward drift toward Roman Catholicism and rationalism has well set in. The loss already sustained by Protestantism, though an incomplete movement, can be regained only by prompt and vigorous action.

These conclusions relative to the future of Protestantism, having been published in a magazine edited by the author of this book, *The Sabbath Outlook*, were commented upon by the *Catholic Mirror*, Baltimore, under date of March 19, 1892, as follows:

" Will 'Scriptural Simplicity' Save Protestantism?"

" This development of Christianity—assumed to be pagan and, therefore, corrupt—is naturally cause of much anxiety to Christian people who so regard it. We have said a few words to show how groundless is this concern. But the power and extent of the development gives most trouble. It is seen that the Catholic Church holds the key to the present position; and so Christians are warned that they must return to 'the simple truths of the New Testament,' if they would not yield to the development. One of these people, a clear-headed, consistent Protestant, commenting upon Harnack's researches, boldly proclaims: 'Protestantism must go back of these Gnostic speculations and rebuild Christian faith and practice on the New Testament records of the first century, or remain hopelessly weak in its efforts to overcome the tide of Roman Catholic influence and history.' He adds: 'This is a vital truth which Protestantism must recognize and act upon promptly, or the next century will witness its crushing defeat between the forces of Roman Catholicism, Irreligious Rationalism, and Worldliness.'

" There is a striking admission in this note of alarm. 'Roman Catholic influence and history' is the tide setting in with overwhelming power. The warning is clear and strong. There is no uncertain sound.

" It goes without saying that we can have no pleasure (God forbid!), but only sadness in imagining the 'crushing defeat' of our Christian brethren by 'irreligious rationalism' or 'worldliness.' We will not apply the term 'defeat' to their being brought to see the truth and submit themselves to the Catholic Church. We are wondering just now whether there is any practical good in the warning given them ; whether it is at all likely that Protestantism will ever go back to what are called 'the simple truths of the New Testament.' We don't believe it will, or can.

"When it is considered what the Protestantism of to-day is,—how much it has learned of the Church idea, —the Catholic idea,—it may be seen how useless it is to expect any such thing. To begin with, all or the immense majority of Protestants, in the simple matter of accepting the change from the Sabbath to the Sunday—from the last to the first day of the week,—quietly admit an extra-scriptural authority, the authority of the Church. Chillingworth's famous maxim, ' The Bible only, the religion of Protestants,' leaves this item at least out of the calculation. All unwittingly our separated brethren are here acting upon a Catholic principle, which does not deny or do away Scripture, but makes the Rule of Faith to consist of *Scripture and*—something else—even *Tradition ;* and by this principle the ever-living voice of the Church speaks with an authority always equal to that of the written revelation, and sometimes apparently transcending it."

The issue is not one of mere name, or of denominationalism, or of "Church" against "sects." It is, as said above, a question of the *reinstatement of the Bible* as the supreme rule of Protestant Christianity. The Protestant movement began in that issue. There can be no Protestantism outside of it. If it be not true, Protestantism is a failure. If it be true, Protestantism cannot remain where it is and survive. If it be not true, Romanism has the logical and historical right to the field. It is master of the situation, and its expectation that erring Protestants will return to "The Mother Church," or wander hopelessly away from Christianity, will be realized in less time than Protestantism has already existed. These facts challenge the attention of all parties. They sound the same key as do the words of Professor Harnack, spoken in July, 1889. I said to him : "Will the Protestantism of the next century be more spiritual than now, or less?" He answered, "It will be more spiritual, or it will die." I continued : "If it dies, what will be the next scene in church history?" He said : "Roman Catholicism will take possession of the world as a new form of paganism." These are not the words of an alarmist, nor a sectarian polemist ; they are the legitimate deductions made by a careful student of universal history. Will you ponder them ?

(2) *Biblical Interpretation ; Higher Criticism.*

Whoever has read the chapters on gnosticism, and the allegorical method of interpreting the Bible, and has traced the influence of these pagan elements upon the history of biblical interpretation, cannot fail to see God's guiding hand in the movements of the last half of this century. The revival of Bible study, the development of the "International Lessons," the call for something yet better, and the growth of exegetical literature form an epoch not less important, though less noisy, because less political, than the rise of Lutheranism, the development of Calvinism, or the birth of the English Reformation. The last half of this century has witnessed what no other century ever saw, the beginning of a systematic study of the Bible by the people. Such an epoch could not do less than create the "higher criticism." That phase of this Bible-study epoch is as legitimate a result as the "Diet at Worms" was of Luther's revolt, or as Puritanism was of the English Reformation. Therefore :

Conclusion Second.

Biblical study and biblical interpretation, including "Higher Criticism," are ushering in the second great feature of the Protestant movement.

Luther and his coadjutors unchained the Bible and opened its pages. They did not, could not, eliminate traditional authority and influence from its exegesis. Traditionalism was largely pagan. It had held sway for centuries, and is yet regnant in many ways. All past exegesis needs retrial in the fires of a devout criticism. That criticism must

19

introduce Christ's norm,—" By their fruits ye shall know them." Pour exegetical and theological traditionalism into that crucible. Heat it in the fires of the best and most devout scholarship. Let brave hearts and careful hands take away the dross, fearless as to consequences. The Bible and Protestantism are both on trial in the closing years of the nineteenth century. There need be no fear as to final results if Protestants are true and firm. If they are not, the closing years of the twentieth century will sit in sackcloth at the open grave of a Christianity which began the elimination of paganism well, but had not the bravery, and therefore the strength, to finish the work.

(3) *Concerning Baptism.*

The paramount question touching the residuum which came in from pagan water-worship does not lie primarily in the *mode* of baptism ; although historically, logically, and symbolically there were no *modes* of baptism until they were brought in by paganism. Paganism immersed, affused, sprinkled. It immersed once, or three times. In the use of holy water it sprinkled repeatedly and indefinitely. According to the New Testament, baptism is submersion, as the symbol of death to sin and resurrection to righteousness. All beyond that was pagan-born.

The central point of the evil which came from pagan water-worship is found in "baptismal regeneration"; *i. e.*, the idea that by virtue of the power and sacredness of water spiritual purity is produced, and the candidate is fitted for membership in the Church, and for heaven. In so far as this idea remains, paganism remains. The most prominent examples of this residuum which now survive are found in the use of "holy water," in the theory that an unconscious infant to which water has been applied as a religious ceremony, is thereby made a member of the organic church, and its future salvation thus assured; in the idea, still held by some, that "regeneration" takes place only in connection with immersion; and in the general idea that baptism is a "saving ordinance."

Conclusion Third.

The core of the question of baptism, as of salvation through faith, is obedience, conformity to the example of Christ; hence it does not follow that he who remains unbaptized, when thus remaining does not involve the spirit of disobedience and neglect, may not enter the kingdom of heaven.

(4) *Sabbathism.*

The Sabbath question is not merely "one of days." The fundamental conception centres around the fact that *God must come to men in sacred time.* Eternity is an attribute of God, and the measured portion we call "time" is the point where God and man come together as Creator and created. It is here that we "live in Him." Scriptural and extra-scriptural history show that man has always felt the need of communion with God, through sacred time, and that God has always sought to meet this want. Physical rest is not the primary idea of the Sabbath. It is only a means to higher ends, namely, communion with God, religious culture, and spiritual development. But since time is also the essence of human existence, so far as activities and duties are concerned, and since the use men make of time determines the character of each human life, specific sacred time which shall represent God, and draw men to Him, becomes an essential part of God's moral and religious government for man. The Sabbath finds its origin in God's desire and purpose to aid and culture men in holiness, and in man's need of God, and spiritual communion. Incidentally, and subordinately, the Sabbath is also a physical blessing to man. But its primal, central thought is religious, and the physical good depends largely on the motive for resting. The Fourth Commandment embodies these deeper principles, and is God's law concerning the Sabbath. The authority of the law is found in the reasons and necessities which lie back of it.

The Jews had never attained, or had lost sight of this higher law of the Sabbath, and had reduced its observance to unmeaning formalities and useless burdens. Christ brushed all these away, and glorified and established the Sabbath, enlarging and making it a blessing instead of a bondage. He taught His followers how to consider and observe it, by His example and His words.

Paganism, filled with anti-Jewish prejudices against the authority of the Old Testament, gave no heed to Christ's teachings concerning the Sabbath, but proclaimed that it was a " Jewish institution with which Christians had nothing to do." Borne on the waves of this false theory, Sunday, and its associate pagan days, gradually drove the Sabbath out. The Sunday of the Dark Ages, and the "Continental Sunday" of to-day, are the necessary results. So far as paganized Christianity could do it, sabbathism was slain and buried. A remnant, the denominational progenitors of the present Seventh-day Baptists, refused to accept the pagan theory, and remained true to the Sabbath through all the changes, from the Apostles to the English Reformation. They were not always organized, but they kept the light burning. In that Reformation the Seventh-day Baptists came to the front, demanding a recognition of the authority of the Fourth Commandment, and a return to the observance of the Sabbath. Opposed to them,

Roman Catholics and Episcopalians continued to assert that the customs and traditions of the Church formed the highest authority in the matter of Sabbath keeping. Between these two the Puritan party sought a compromise, and invented the theory (first propounded by Nicholas Bownde, in 1595 A.D.) that the commandment, being yet binding, might be transferred to the Sunday. This Puritan compromise has been tested, its fictitious sacredness has gone, and much in the present state of the Sunday question is the fruitage of that baseless compromise.

Sunday legislation, which, as we have seen in a former chapter, was pagan in conception and form, has continued, being made a prominent feature of the Puritan theory. At the present writing (1892) strenuous efforts are being made in the United States to save the failing fortunes of Sunday by a revival of Sunday laws. If, by any combination of efforts, this can be done, no permanent good will ensue. The verdict of history and the genius of Christ's kingdom combine to declare that men cannot be made good by act of Parliament, nor be induced to keep any day sacred by the civil law. If the " rest day " alone be exalted, the result is holidayism, rather than Sabbath keeping. If the enforcement of the Sunday laws is pressed it will result in their repeal.

Conclusion Fourth.

(a) *No day has ever been kept as a Sabbath except under the idea of divine authority.*

(b) *Everything less than this promotes holidayism.*

(c) *There is no scriptural and therefore no truly Protestant ground for Sunday observance.*

The only alternative is a return to the observance of the Sabbath, the Seventh day, under the law of obedient love, such love as Christ had for the will of His Father ; or to go down with the tide of No-Sabbathism, which, checked temporarily by the Puritan compromise, is now rushing on more wildly than before. The issue is at hand, *Christian Sabbathism and the Sabbath, or Pagan holidayism and the Sunday.* Culminating events demand that choice, and in the ultimate, *universal Sabbathism.*

(5) *Christianity and the State.*

Certain superficial investigators have claimed that the union of Christianity with the civil power was the outgrowth of the Hebrew theocratic idea. The claim is groundless. The theocracy was a State within the Church. The pagan theory, applied to Christianity under Constantine and his successors, gave a Church dominated by the State, and regulated, as to polity and faith, by civil law.

History has written some plain and pertinent

verdicts concerning the relations which ought to exist between Christianity and the civil power. Every verdict emphasizes the truth of Christ's words : " My kingdom is not of this world." The relations between Christianity and the civil power which began under Constantine have worked incalculable harm to Christianity as a spiritual religion. Its political triumph was a most disastrous defeat which became a large factor in producing the subsequent centuries of decline and darkness. Better conceptions of civil government, and increasing civilization have improved the status of State Churches since the Reformation ; but spiritual Christianity everywhere and always, is calling for " disestablishment." It is a singular fact that in the United States, where there has been the nearest approach to religious liberty, we are confronted with two phases of religio-civil legislation which are now coalescing, and which, however well meant, partake more of the spirit of the ninth century than of the nineteenth, or of the New Testament. These movements are " National Reform," which seeks to Christianize the nation by putting Christ's name into the National Constitution ; and the now popular Sunday-law movement. There are several points aimed at by the National Reform Association, such as divorce, gambling, etc., which are within the province of the civil law; but its primary aim, to secure legislation on all points covered by the Ten Commandments, is fundamentally pagan in concept and intent. The good men who are pressing the movement think that their theory of government is the true one, and that great good would come if it were adopted. But the verdict of every century since the pagan conception was introduced into Christianity, forbids belief in their scheme as a means of Christianizing the nation.

As to Sunday legislation we have seen that its origin was absolutely pagan, and that it has been destructive of true Sabbathism at all times. If the highest hopes of the present agitators could be realized; if the civil law should compel all citizens of the United States to rest on Sunday, every year of such a system would sink the people deeper into the slough of No-Sabbathism. The "Continental Sunday" is the product of a No-Sabbath theology, and civil Sunday-laws. The Sunday-law advocates seek the supremacy of an unscriptural Sabbathism, linked with Sunday by civil law. This has been fully tried, at a time when men had far more regard for Sunday as a sacred day than they have now. But with all things in its favor, the strength of youth, and the honest ignorance of the masses concerning its true character, the "Puritan Sunday" has returned to its original holidayism, in spite of Church and State combined. It could not do less, even if a fortuitous combination of influences should exalt it temporarily again. Religion and conscience are entitled to the protection of the civil law, without regard to creed or numbers. If immorality is practised in the name of religion, it may be suppressed as immorality. Beyond such protection the State may not go.

Conclusion Fifth.

All union of Church and State, or of Christianity and the State, is pagan-born, and opposed to the genius and purpose of Christ's kingdom.

Last Words.

Whatever prepossessions or conceptions the reader may have brought to the perusal of these pages, he cannot finish them without seeing that much which has come down to us as "Christianity" is so tinctured with paganism that it does not fairly represent what Christ taught. The purity of the earliest Christianity was the source of its wondrous conquering power. After it was paganized, and united with the State, it continued to conquer, but by the sword rather than by the spirit of God. It is clear proof of the divine char-

acter of Christianity, that it was not wholly destroyed by its contact with paganism. It is
surpassing proof of that same divine origin, that it
could rise from the grave of the Dark Ages, with
such vigor as produced the Reformation, and has
carried that work to the point already gained.
But in the crises that await it, in the solving of
the problems which confront it, Protestant Christianity must realize that its specific mission is to
complete the work of eliminating the pagan residuum, a work well begun by the Reformers, but
which must be carried on to higher victories, or
sink back to lower defeats. When the last stain
of paganism is removed, the world will see a Christianity which will be primarily a *life of purity*,
through love for God and truth and men, rather
than a *creed*, embodying speculations about the un-
knowable and abstractions concerning the un-
solvable. In such a Christianity, the Bible plainly
interpreted, without allegory or assumption, and
in the light of its own history, will hold the first
place. The Sabbath, as God's day, free from
burdensome formalism, and filled with good works
and spiritual culture, will be restored; and this
recognition of it as God's ever-recurring representative in human life will do much to bring in that universal Sabbathism towards which God is patiently
leading his truth-loving children. The pagan

Sunday, with its false claims, will be a thing of the past. Baptism as the symbol of entrance to Christ's kingdom, through spiritual life and faith in Him, will be no longer the foot-ball of polemic strife, nor the many-formed image of pagan water-worship, nor the creator of a false standard of Church membership through "baptismal regeneration." In that better day, the civil law will give all religion full protection and full freedom, without regard to majorities or creeds. It will neither oppose by persecution, nor control under the name of protection. The persecution of Jews in Russia, and useless efforts to make the world holy by act of Parliament, will pass away. To hasten that time, be it far or near, these pages go forth; and he who writes them will be thankful if they bear some part in freeing our holy religion from the poison of pagan residuum, and in giving that higher spiritual life, to the attainment of which all forms, ceremonies, times, and agencies ought to bring Christ-loving men.

INDEX.

A

Abespine, on use of " lights " at tombs, 264.

Achamoth, gnostic idea of, injected into N. T. exegesis, 45.

Alabaster, Henry, describes Brahmanic baptism, 93.

Allegorists, the " Fathers " as, 44.

Allegory, the mediator between philosophy and religion, 39; existed among the Greeks before the Christian era, 39; united paganism and Judaism, 39; corrupted the earliest methods of Scripture exegesis, 42; perverted the true doctrine of " inspiration," 43; great influence of, on " Christian exegesis, 46; destructive examples of, 49, 50; foolish application of, to clean and unclean food, 51, 52; unmeaning application of, to the " cross," 53; much used by Augustine, 64, 65; prevailing influence in Scripture interpretation, after the second century, 66; used by Barnabas in combining pagan and Christian ideas concerning baptism, 133 f.; destructive application of, to the Decalogue, 184 f.

Alzog, historian, describes the character of Constantine, 212.

Anointing, in baptism, borrowed from pagans, 123; use of, in baptism, as shown in apostolic constitutions, 138.

Antinomianism, wholly unscriptural, 166.

Anti-Sabbathism, appeared contemporaneously with Sunday observance, 159; wholly unscriptural, 166.

Apollo, the counterpart of Mithras and Baal, 156; the patron deity of Constantine, 219.

Apostolic Constitutions, teach pagan theories concerning baptism, 137 f.

Aringhus, on similarity between paganism and Roman Catholicism, 11.

Aruspices, Constantine's law concerning, associated with his Sunday edict, 222.

Astarte, worship of, reproduced in worship of the " Virgin Mary," 28; the worship of, at Rome, 199.

Augustine, influence of, on formation of Christian doctrines, 64; evil effect of allegorizing Scriptures by, 64, 65; describes corrupting influence of paganism on Christians, 224, 225; excessive superstition of, regarding miracles wrought by baptism, 258.

Aurelian, Emperor, " Triumph " of, 199; costly offerings to the Sun-god, 200.

Aztecs, baptism as practised by, 109 f.

B

Baal, the worship of, corrupted the Israelites, 156.

Baptism, character of, in the N. T., 71, 72; pagans sought spiritual purity by it, 77; mithraic and gnostic, 77; gnostics called it a " purifying fire," 79; pagans initiated candidates to their " mysteries " by it, 82; by blood, a feature of mithraicism, 82; administered at death as a means of salvation, 83; performed for the dead, 83; associated with serpent worship, 85; pagan, in Egypt, 87; of young children in Thibet and Mongolia, 93; pagan, of the dying, 93; modern Buddhistic, 94 f.; various forms of, in Oriental paganism, 97; an ancient Aryan rite, 103; pagan ideas and forms of, reproduced in the early

IMPORTANT RELIGIOUS WORKS.

Gospel-Criticism and Historical Christianity. A study of the Gospels and of the History of the Gospel Canon during the Second Century ; together with a consideration of the results of Modern Criticism. By Orello Cone, D.D. 8vo, cloth, gilt top $1 75

" The book is rich in material and is a good example of the proper study of Gospel literature."—*Public Opinion*, Washington, D. C.

The Religion of Humanity. By O. B. Frothingham. 4th edition, 12mo, pp. 338 . . . . $1 50

" A profoundly sincere book, the work of one who has read largely, studied thoroughly, reflected patiently."—*Boston Globe*.

Stories from the Lips of the Teacher. By O. B. Frothingham. Retold by a Disciple. Sixth edition, 16mo, pp. 193 . $1 00

" It is in style and thought a superior book, that will interest young and old."— *Zion Herald* (Methodist).

Stories of the Patriarchs. By O. B. Frothingham. Third edition, 16mo, pp. 232 . . . . $1 00

" The sublimest lessons of manhood in the simple language of a child."— *Springfield Republican*.

The Child's Book of Religion. By O. B. Frothingham. For Sunday-Schools and Homes. New edition, revised. 16mo, pp. xii. + 273 . . . . $1 00

Transcendentalism in New England. By O. B. Frothingham. A History. Second edition. 8vo, pp. iv. + 394 . . $1 75

" The book is masterly and satisfying."—*Appleton's Journal*.

The Cradle of the Christ. By O. B. Frothingham. A Study in Primitive Christianity. 8vo, pp. x. + 234 . . . $1 50

" Scholarly, acute, and vigorous."—*N. Y. Tribune*.

Theodore Parker. By O. B. Frothingham. A Biography. 8vo, pp. viii. + 588 . . . . $2 00

Gerrit Smith. By O. B. Frothingham. A Biography. 8vo, pp. 371 . . . . $2 00

" A good biography, it is faithful, sufficiently full, written with vigor, grace, and good taste." - *N. Y. Evening Post*.

Belief of the Unbelievers. By O. B. Frothingham. 12mo, sewed 25

Speaking of Mr. Frothingham's Sermons, the *Springfield Republican* says : " No one of serious intellectual character can fail to be interested and taught by these most thoughtful discourses."

Boston Unitarianism. By O. B. Frothingham. 1820–1840. A Study of the Life and Work of Nathaniel Langdon Frothingham. 8vo, pp. 272 . . . . $1 75

" The book, to a thoughtful reader, cannot fail to be elevating and suggestive of high ideals, high thinking, and noble living."—*Newark Advertiser*.

Recollections and Impressions. By O. B. Frothingham. 1822– 1890. 8vo $1 50

G. P. PUTNAM'S SONS, NEW YORK AND LONDON

Printed in the United States
67630LVS00006B/91